Following the Elephant

Ethnomusicologists Contemplate Their Discipline

A collection of articles from

ETHNOMUSICOLOGY

Edited by Bruno Nettl

COMMON THREADS

An anthology from the
University of Illinois Press

Library of Congress Control Number: 2016954187
ISBN 978-0-252-08255-9 (paperback)
ISBN 978-0-252-09960-5 (e-book)

Contents

PART II

PART III

Introduction

Bruno Nettl

Ethnomusicology is defined variously but, most frequently, as the study of music in or as culture and the study of all of the world's musical cultures from a broadly comparative perspective. Ethnomusicologists have devoted much space and energy to contemplating and writing about their own discipline, more than members of related fields such as historical musicology and anthropology. In articles and books, they have struggled with questions of definition and principal thrust, central methodology, and interdisciplinary associations. A large proportion of this literature has appeared in the journal *Ethnomusicology*, which set out, from its beginnings, to be a major force in establishing a place, and an appropriate niche, for its discipline in the American and the international academy. *Ethnomusicology* began as an informal "Ethno-Musicology Newsletter" (at first mimeographed) circulated to interested individuals between 1953 and 1955. In 1955 this newsletter—by then multilith printed by Wesleyan University Press—became the official organ of the Society for Ethnomusicology, which had been founded in that year. In 1958 it was turned into the journal that has been published by the University of Illinois Press since 1992.

The anthology of articles presented here includes a number of essays in which, in a variety of ways, ethnomusicologists wrote about their discipline in the half-century between 1963 and 2012. It illustrates both some of the abiding concerns of this field, as well as growth, development, and changes in orientation and rhetoric during those years. Among the authors are some of the founders of the Society and the journal (Mieczyslaw Kolinski, David McAllester, Alan P. Merriam, and Bruno Nettl—all early presidents of the Society for Ethnomusicology) and leading figures in more recent generations, including presidents Charlotte Frisbie, Kay Kaufman Shelemay, and Timothy Rice.

The anthology is divided into three sections, although the boundaries between these are sometimes indistinct and some article might be appropriate in more than one. Within each section, the order is chronological.

The first division provides articles in which scholars survey the field as a whole in a number of different ways. "Ethnomusicology, the Field and the Society," by David P. McAllester, comes from a special issue of ethnomusicology published to mark the tenth anniversary of the beginning of the newsletter. This issue contains several articles that assess the current state of the field, and McAllester contributed briefly to this effort. Providing a definition and principal conceptualization of their discipline was a significant strand of thought in the early days of this journal (and continues to be), and the article by Alan P. Merriam—one of the founders of the American branch of this field—surveys, quotes, and comments on over forty definitions, going back to 1885. As a sample of positions in this debate, George List's article, "Ethnomusicology, a Discipline Defined," makes a case for an unconventional definition of ethnomusicology—the study of music in oral (or aural) tradition.

Ethnomusicology 50, no. 2, celebrates fifty years of the Society and provides a series of articles that examine the field from the perspectives of authors in several academic generations. A sample of that issue is the essay by Charlotte Frisbie, "A View of Ethnomusicology from the 1960s," in which she gives an account of what struck her when she was a student and junior scholar. Ruskin and Rice's much later work, "The Individual in Musical Ethnography," is actually a history of ethnographic accounts in ethnomusicology, that is, descriptions of musical cultures based on fieldwork and closely tied to the other domains of culture. Such studies, which take a comprehensive view of musics, including the ideas that lead to them and the activities with which they are associated, constitute the central body of literature in ethnomusicology.

The second group of articles consists of milestones in the literature that make a case for a central activity or approach, in the context of the field's history (up to that point). Each asks what should be central to the investigators' concerns. Kolinski's "Recent Trends in Ethnomusicology" takes a critical look at a large number of important works from 1948 to 1964, which, he believes, have shifted the field's emphasis from the study of music itself to cultural contexts, and makes a case for greater emphasis on the musical text and on comparative study. Two decades after Kolinski, Timothy Rice ("Towards the Remodeling of Ethnomusicology"), again surveying the major works of the field from 1885 on, shows that each is built on a fundamental model, and concludes by defining the field as concerned with a single question: "How do people historically construct, socially maintain, and individually create and experience music?"

Witzleben's article, "Whose Ethnomusicology," concerns features of ethnomusicology that set it off from other kinds of music research—the personal relationship of the investigators to the culture they study, and the degree to which ethnomusicology itself is culture-specific. "What Do Ethnomusicologists Do?" by Adelaida Reyes does not make a case for a particular approach but, rather, encourages her colleagues to continue seeking a central focus. She provides, as a context, a broad overview of the history of ethnomusicology influenced by philosophical considerations and comments extensively on ethnomusicologists' concern for the explicit identity of their discipline.

The third section of this anthology consists of articles that contemplate ethnomusicology from the perspective of specific, but abiding, strands of thought. Describing his relationship to four "teachers" in his fieldwork, Nettl, in "In Honor of Our Principal Teachers," calls attention to the central contributions of informants or consultants in fieldwork to the success of the ethomusicological endeavor. Jeff Todd Titon's "Music, the Public Interest, and the Practice of Ethnomusicology" is the introductory article in an issue of the journal devoted to "music and the public interest" and views the field from the perspective of a fundamental question: "Are we doing anyone any good?" Though brief, the article lays out the principles of the subfield known as "applied ethnomusicology" that has become prominent in the twenty-first century.

Kay Kaufman Shelemay's article, "Towards an Ethnomusicology of the Early Music Movement," engages another very significant trend that began in the late 1980s, the ethnomusicological study of Western "art" or "classical" music, surveying the earlier literature and making a case study of the performance and study of Medieval and Renaissance music, particularly in late twentieth-century Boston. Here the study of "one's own" culture as an insider or outsider—in a field thus far devoted almost explicitly to the outsider's contribution—is the principal issue. In "Ethnomusicology and Difference," Deborah Wong discusses a number of trends of the period from 1990 to 2003, showing ways in which ethnomusicology responded to social and academic change—and itself changed—in its embrace of new approaches such as "cultural studies," and the increased inclusiveness in its population, its subject matter, and its relationship to various components of the academy.

Gabriel Solis, in "Thoughts on an Interdiscipline," studies the relationship of ethnomusicology to the framework of ideas and methodology in music theory (including transcription and analysis), and in social theory (the "anthropology" component of ethnomusicology), using a historical framework and surveying a large body of literature going back to 1885 but concentrated in the period since 1990. It takes as its point of departure Rice's articles on "remodeling" ethnomusicology, also included in this anthology.

The articles presented here are, we hope, a broad sampling of the ways in which ethnomusicologists—aside from carrying out their various specialized researches—contemplate the character, history, and contributions of their discipline; and the importance of the journal *Ethnomusicology* in this endeavor.

PART I

Ethnomusicology, the Field and the Society[1]

DAVID P. MCALLESTER / Wesleyan University,
Middletown, Connecticut

The roots of the Society for Ethnomusicology in the work of Stumpf, Ellis, Hornbostel and others and in the *Zeitschrift für Vergleichende Musikwissenschaft* have been delineated ably and in detail in earlier issues of ETHNOMUSICOLOGY and elsewhere (Seeger 1956; Rhodes 1956; Kolinski 1957; Nettl 1956: 26–44).

My pleasant task is to recount the developments that have taken place in our Society, and in the field of ethnomusicology in the United States, since 1953. The description of events at such close range cannot be termed history but should be considered as an interpretation, or what one person *thinks* has been happening. I hope the thoughts set down here will elicit from other interested persons the corrections and amplifications that will help round out the picture.

This particular decade has been more eventful for ethnomusicology than has all the history of our field before the founding of the Society in 1953. The formation of the Society was only one indication of the ground swell of a very large international movement with many manifestations indeed. Musically this ten-year era is very much akin to the Age of Discovery with Prince Henrys suddenly appearing on the horizons of a dozen new continents at once.

If any gauge is needed for the strength of the work it can be seen with sociological perspective in the rise of institutions. Where once was an archive in Berlin and two or three beginnings in the United States, are now innumerable sophisticated collections both special and general. Where once was a single perishing publication are now at least a dozen journals of all sorts, national and international, including one devoted to archiving. Most of them represent organizations or societies and this means regular meetings of scholars. Very importantly, where once were wax cylinders is now magnatic tape, affording a convenience and fidelity undreamed of a few years ago. In addition to all this

From *Ethnomusicology*, Vol. 7, No. 3 (September 1963), pp. 182–86 there is the popular enthusiasm for folk music which is beginning to extend to world music. In ways perhaps too subtle to assess this awakening of general interest means support for the scholar.

A recent survey lists thirty educational institutions in the United States offering anywhere from one course, in or related to ethnomusicology, to as many as fourteen (Winkelman 1963). In addition there are institutions and have been special meetings that are hard to classify, such as the Institute for Ethnomusicology at UCLA and the Symposium on Ethnomusicological Field Method at the University of Washington held in March 1963. Large scale projects involving a number of researchers focussed on a single problem are another new manifestation in the field.

I shall discuss certain of these indications of the impressive vitality of ethnomusicology in my effort to describe what I think are major trends in our field and in our Society. Since the borderline between suggesting trends and coming right out and making predictions is a fine one, I shall not hesitate to assume a prophetic mien.

The emphasis in our work alternates between studying music to find out more about culture and vice versa. Which it is, of course, is simply a function of the interest and background of the particular investigator. The marriage between music and the social sciences is celebrated anew with each issue of our journal. It is a sometimes uneasy union but it is evident that since each partner has so much to learn from the other, neither can afford a divorce.

Most of the Jobs Are in Music

It is interesting that at the beginning of our decade the academic jobs in ethnomusicology seemed to be in a few anthropology departments and that now they are much more plentiful and seem to be largely in music departments. It is in the latter that ethnomusicology majors are beginning to appear. The plain fact is that music departments are beginning to shake themselves awake to the fact that music, real music, is a world phenomenon. There are more and larger music departments than there are anthropology and sociology departments in American universities. It is to be expected therefore that greater academic muscle will be brought into play by musicians than by social scientists. More degrees in ethnomusicology will go to Calliope than to Caliban.

This may be seen at UCLA where the largest graduate program in the field is to be found (Hood 1957). The extent of the training offered at Los Angeles does not appear in the Winkelman survey. This is especially true with regard to the many "study groups" in the theory and performance of different musics such as Mexican mariachi, Javanese gamelan, African drumming, and Chinese orchestra. The excellent argument is made that the actual performance of an exotic music is essential to the full understanding of its structure and purpose. A strong aspect of the UCLA program is the presence of native musicians from the many cultures represented. Equally important is the practice of sending the advanced student to the country whose music he is studying for one or two years of research and apprenticeship. When he returns such a student is likely to be in a position to write the first definitive book in English on the music of his area of study (Maim 1959) and typically carries the study group idea with him as he begins his teaching career: Robert E. Brown, South India, Wesleyan University; Robert Garfias, Japan, University of Washington; William P. Maim, Japan, University of Michigan.

The anthropology in the UCLA program is "home grown." The students who undergo a musical apprenticeship overseas in India, Africa, etc. develop what anthropological perspective they may from the necessities of first hand experience. This method has its disadvantages but at present the program at Los Angeles is moving towards intensive musical analysis in terms of computer theory and melograph techniques rather than a deepening exploration of the insights of the social sciences.

More Money in Connection with Anthropology

To look at the other side of our equation, the group research projects are finding their impetus in anthropology. For better or worse, the sciences at present are receiving greater support from national foundations than are the arts. Two current programs rising out of anthropology may be cited to illustrate this trend. Alan Lomax is investigating a system of musical analysis which involves linguistic, psychological, physiological and social factors as well as musical ones. The National Institute of Mental Health is supporting this two year study which involves Victor Grauer and Conrad Arensberg and has benefited from the advice of Margaret Mead, Edith Trager and others. The publications of the project have appeared in anthropological journals (Lomax 1959, 1962). It is significant that the scope of the project permits secretarial help—a commonplace in the sciences but an unheard-of luxury in ethnomusicological research. Wesleyan University has received a grant from the National Science Foundation for a three-year study of Navaho ceremonialism. Here again the emphasis is to be on the interrelatedness of various aspects of culture. The study is linguistic and sociological as well as musicological. Charlotte Johnson, Katchen Coley, and Gerry Johnson, all graduate students, are assisting in the project and here again secretarial help is available.

Due to the availability of large funds, "task force" projects are on the increase in anthropology. The Columbia University project in culture and linguistics under George Herzog included the study of Comanche music (McAllester 1949)

and the Harvard University studies in comparative values included ethnomusicology as an avenue to the understanding of deep-seated attitudes (McAllester
1954). Nicholas England's studies of Bushman music in the Kalahari Desert
have been in cooperation with an extensive joint project, the Marshall-Peabody
Museum Expeditions, involving many people, mostly anthropologists.

More Success in Interrelating the Two Disciplines

How well music and social science may be blended in a single institution is more
likely to be a matter of atmosphere and personalities than of disciplinary ideologies. The University of Hawaii may be cited for the happy interrelation between
the music department and anthropology, as represented by the Department of
Anthropology at the University and the Bernice P. Bishop Museum of Honolulu.
The East-West Center at the University of Hawaii profits by this cooperation and
its combination of students from Asia, Oceania, and the United States. Hawaii
also demonstrated its aloha spirit last year by its invitation to an anthropologist
to be a visiting professor of music. Indiana University shows excellent promise
of cooperation between music and the social sciences with Walter Kaufmann
in music, Alan Merriam newly appointed in anthropology, and the superb
Archive of Folk and Primitive Music under the direction of George List. The
recent appointment of Nicholas England to the Music Department at Columbia and the purchase of the Laura Boulton Collection gives this department
unusual strength. Willard Rhodes's extensive training in anthropology and
England's anthropological research in connection with his Bushman studies
gives this team an impressive breadth of perspective. Richard Waterman and
Bruno Nettl teach in the anthropology and music departments, respectively, of
Wayne State University. The projected Theater-Art-Music Center at Wesleyan
University will include ethnomusicology under its aegis. This reflects a mutual-
ity of interest in these departments that suggests an interesting variation on the
music-anthropology axis. A similar trend can be discerned at the University
of Washington where music and the Center for Asian Arts (including theater)
are in active cooperation. It was the Center, at Washington, that sponsored an
unusual and imaginative symposium on ethnological field method this spring.
A glance at the many offerings at the University of Hawaii shows a similar
awareness of the mutual dependency of the arts, particularly dance and music.

The examples given here were chosen to exemplify the trends that have
developed in our decade. Their effects on the Society as such are represented
in various ways in the Journal. The intimate relationship of music to dance has
been acknowledged from the first by the inclusion of dance articles, bibliography,
and news, and a dance editor on the staff of the Journal. One can feel sure that a
similar hospitality will be extended to the graphic arts and literature as research

finds the way to significant relationships between them and music. What will become then of our already difficult name is hard to imagine: "Ethno-Arts"? "Ethnohumanities"? In any case inter relatedness is clearly a permanent part of the ethos of the Society.

The Journal, the principal enterprise of the Society, is finding increasing support in the scholarly world at large. More subsidies of various kinds from universities, foundations, and other institutions, a steady growth in size as finances permit, are all indications of good health and gratifying recognition.

The Society serves as a clearing house for information in ethnomusicology and related fields. Inquiries of many kinds come to the officers and editors and the existence of the Society enables them to find the right person to answer these inquiries. As this function develops it seems entirely likely that the Society as such will come to act as referee in a variety of scholarly contexts. Hopefully it may find itself in a financial position to offer grants-in-aid for research. Here the possibility would arise of a Board sponsored by the Society which could use our resources to suggest fruitful or crucial areas of research and introduce an element of planning into the activity of the field as a whole.

Our initial purpose when the *Newsletter* was begun, ten years ago, was to encourage communication between ethnomusicologists and foster scholarship in the field. The pages of our Journal and the forum of our meetings have contributed considerably toward these goals. It is plain that there are still other ways, dreamed of and as yet undreamed of.

Note

1. This paper is based, in part, on remarks made by the author at the 1962 annual meeting of the Society for Ethnomusicology in Bloomington, Indiana.

References Cited

Hood, Mantle
    1957   "Training and research methods in ethnomusicology," *Ethnomusicology Newsletter* no. 11, 2–8.
Kolinski, Mieczyslaw
    1957   "Ethnomusicology, its problems and methods," *Ethnomusicology Newsletter* no. 10, 1–7.
Lomax, Alan
    1959   "Folk song style," *American Anthropologist* 61:927–54.
    1962   "Song structure and social structure," *Ethnology* 1:425–51.
McAllester, David P.
    1954   *Enemy Way music*. Cambridge, Mass.: Peabody Museum Publications in Anthropology 61, no. 3.
McAllester, David P.
    1949   *Peyote music*. New York: Viking Fund Publications in Anthropology no. 13.

Maim, William P.
  1959 *Japanese music and musical instruments*. Rutland and Tokyo: Tuttle.
Nettl, Bruno
  1956 *Music in primitive culture*. Cambridge: Harvard University Press.
Rhodes, Willard
  1956 "On the subject of ethnomusicology," *Ethnomusicology Newsletter* no. 7, 1–9.
Seeger, Charles
  1956 "Past organization," *Ethnomusicology Newsletter* no. 6, 1–3.
Winkelman, Donald M.
  1963 "Ethnomusicology at American universities: a curricular survey," *ETHNOMUSICOLOGY* 7:113–23.

Definitions of "Comparative Musicology" and "Ethnomusicology": An Historical-Theoretical Perspective[1]

ALAN P. MERRIAM

Readers of this, and other, journals hardly need be reminded of my persistent interest over the years in definitions of what ethnomusicology is and what it ought to be (e.g., Merriam 1960; 1969; 1975). It is now more than 25 years since, according to common belief, Jaap Kunst first put "ethno-musicology" into print (Kunst 1950), and we thus ought to be able now to look back with some objectivity at what has since happened to that word, and what happened to its predecessor—"comparative musicology"—before it. In other words, the points are now historic, though the end result is far from settled, and it is in this spirit that I wish to treat the materials to be discussed herein. While I have not gone through the literature with a fine-toothed comb in an attempt to find *all* definitions, I have located a substantial number of them, enough, I trust, to indicate fairly the overall trends and changes. Neither have I gone outside the United States for the most part, though some such definitions are included where they seemed especially pertinent. My major purpose, then, is to discuss what happened over time to these two terms in the United States, and what consequences occurred because of the changes that took place.

Problems of definition can, of course, be extremely sticky. When we define a concept, are we attempting to deal with what it is or with what it ought to be? The former, of course, is based upon the premise that a definition—in this case of ethnomusicology—can be based upon what it is that ethnomusicologists do; in other words, it is essentially descriptive and is drawn from observation of normative activity. The difficulty with this approach is that it is essentially uninformative, both because it is only descriptive, and because it is circular. That is, in order to know what ethnomusicology is, we must be able to identify the ethnomusicologist, but the latter is only definable in terms of the former.

From *Ethnomusicology*, Vol. 21, No. 2 (May 1977), pp. 189–204

On the other hand, if we are concerned with a definition which tells us what ethnomusicology ought to be, we enter into the debatable realm of advocacy. My own bias, however, is toward the latter type of definition since it attempts to set the standard for the field.

Another difficulty centers on the problem of whether the item to be defined is, in fact, definable. The answer of the strict positivist, of course, is that it is, and that any phenomenon is susceptible of definition "by means of symbolic logic in empirical terms" (Ladd 1973:418). The answer of the Ordinary Language philosopher is different, however, in that his approach "gives full recognition to the fact that there are some valid, rational concepts that are not strictly definable in scientific terms . . . ," these being "inexact, fuzzy concepts that are quite different from scientific concepts. . . ." Thus, for example:

> Aesthetic and ethical concepts are distinct from purely descriptive, empirical concepts in that they a) are open-textured, b) are multi-functional, c) involve criteria, d) are essentially contestable, and e) employ persuasive definitions. (*loc. cit.*)

While examination of some definitions of ethnomusicology might well persuade the reader that they meet these criteria, and that, indeed, the term is not definable, I do not believe this to be true. By the very nature of the word itself, ethnomusicology is linked to science: "logy" as a root is a combining form which names sciences or bodies of knowledge. If our definitions frequently seem primarily persuasive, it is not the fault of the word form, but that of the definers!

We can also, in definition, find ourselves struggling with the very words we use. Thus, for example, Hood, in the Introduction to *The Ethnomusicologist,* writes that "One point is clear: The *subject* of study in the field of ethnomusicology is music" (1971:3). While surely almost all of us would agree that this is so, we have only to stop to wonder how to define "music" to discover ourselves in difficulty again. That is, if ethnomusicology is crosscultural in its approach, which it certainly is, the problem of identifying the phenomenon "music" becomes crucial. Ethnomusicologists need hardly be told that people in some societies simply have no concept "music," and that others who do, view it in a sharply different light from what is implied in Hood's statement. The point here is not that the statement is incorrect, in the conventional sense of the word, but rather, that it is not cross-cultural, and that the difficulties inherent in making it cross-cultural are almost overwhelming in their magnitude. Perhaps in this case, we *are* dealing with a concept which does not lend itself to definition in the scientific sense, but this, in turn, leads us still further afield and is not of central concern to the present discussion.

Despite these, and other, problems, ethnomusicologists have defined their field of study over and over again, and rightly so, since definition is of primary importance, and for a number of reasons. In the first place, because we are professionals in a field of study, we wish to understand all we can about ethnomusicology; this is at the root both of intellectual curiosity and professional responsibility. Second, the most cursory examination of the content of our publications reveals an extraordinarily mixed bag of interests, and this becomes a puzzle in itself, for what kind of field is it that can encompass such variety, and how can it possibly be defined?

More important are two further reasons for seeking definition of the field. The first is that theory, method, and data are inextricably intertwined: one simply does not exist without the others, and all three constantly interact in any intellectual enterprise. Without theory we can hardly have significant method, not only in the sense that no method *can* be theory-free, but also that no method *should* be theory-free. And without method, no significant gathering of data can occur, for the results will inevitably be random. Finally, both in inductive and deductive procedures, theory is based upon data. The point is not only that the three are interrelated, but that if one cannot define his field of study, he can have no theory in respect to it, for he is dealing with it as an amorphous area of concern which he can only treat in the most general terms.

Thus definition is of vital concern because we can face no other questions until this one has been faced; and once it has been faced, then we arrive at the absolutely necessary position of having to face all questions. In short, all disciplines must question all assumptions; all assumptions derive in one way or another from what its practitioners claim their field, or discipline, to be. Definition is crucial because it forces us to face the bases of our intellectual activities; lacking such honest confrontation, we can have little hope of changing ethnomusicology from the status of a variegated field of study to that of a real discipline. Such status in no way implies uniformity of view, study, or approach, but it does imply commonality of purposes and goals.

I

The earliest definition of "comparative musicology" *per se* was that proposed by Guido Adler in 1885 (see Appendix for definitional quotations), and his emphasis was laid upon "folksongs . . . of the various people of the earth," both for "ethnographical" and classificatory purposes. Hornbostel seems never to have put forward a definition as such, and perhaps the earlier days of the field were less marked by definitional concerns than the later, as, for example, those of Lachmann in 1935, and Roberts a year later. However, the summary definition of comparative musicology in the United States was made by Glen Haydon in 1941 in his *Introduction to Musicology.* Thus:

> Non-European musical systems and folk music constitute the chief subjects of study; the songs of birds and phylogenetic-ontogenetic parallels are subordinate topics. (p. 218)

If *comparative musicology* means the study of extra-European musical systems, it is natural that the study of Chinese, Indian, Arabian, and other musical systems should fall to the lot of comparative musicology. (p. 235)

Comparative musicology has its characteristic subject matter chiefly in extra-European and folk music. . . . (p. 237)

Most, if not all, of the music studied in comparative musicology is transmitted by oral tradition. . . . (p. 219)

These statements carry two important messages, the first of which is advanced more forcefully than the second. They are that comparative musicology is the study of "extra-European and folk music," and that comparative musicology studies music which is "transmitted by oral tradition." Both themes had been foreshadowed, of course, and both were repeated over and over by subsequent authors, but it was the "non-European" aspect of the definition that received the greatest play; it is echoed by Sachs (1943), Apel (1946), Herzog (1946), Koole (1955: "exotic" is the term used), Bukofzer (1956), Nettl (1956), Rhodes (1956), Schaeffner (1956: but note the disclaimer as to whether comparative musicology should study these musics), Schneider (1957), Kunst (1959), and Seeger (1961), among many others.

By 1961, the use of "comparative musicology" as a label had disappeared except in historic references; while it reappeared later (Kolinski 1967), it was no longer applied to the field in general but rather, to a portion of it. Indeed, both Kunst and Seeger, in the citations immediately above, were already using the term historically, and from Nettl, in 1956, forward, the two terms "comparative musicology," and "ethnomusicology" were used together as synonyms. This period of overlap occurred roughly during the latter half of the decade of the 1950's.

Three major points can be made concerning these definitions. First, they are virtually identical and unanimous in what they stress. Second, they define comparative musicology unanimously in terms of certain musics to be studied, namely, either "non-Western" (or an equivalent term such as "exotic"), or "orally transmitted" musics. Third, they do not deal with what is meant by "comparative method" or what the aim of comparison is; indeed, they seldom stress anything comparative at all.

It was the question of the "comparative" in comparative musicology, however, which led ultimately to the abandonment of the term. While it has sometimes been suggested that the question of comparativism arose at the same time as, and as a consequence of, the introduction of the new term, "ethnomusicology," the evidence does not support the case. Two main arguments have been advanced for the inadequacy of the term.

The first can be expressed roughly in the statement: "Because we don't compare any more than anyone else does," and this kind of objection appeared almost as soon as the term itself (Hornbostel 1905). Haydon again provides us with a clear statement:

> The term [comparative musicology] is not entirely satisfactory, however, for the comparative method is frequently used in the other fields of musicology, and studies in this field are often not directly comparative. (p. 216)

This point of view was expressed over and over again in essentially the same form, by, for example, Sachs (1943:29), Herzog (1946:11), Kunst (1950:7), Koole (1955:228), Rhodes (1956:459), List (1962:20), and others. The unanimity of the argument is notable in the following passage by Sachs, written twenty years after Haydon's statement:

> But today 'comparative musicology' has lost its usefulness. For at the bottom every branch of knowledge is comparative; all our descriptions, in the humanities no less than in the sciences, state similarities and divergences. . . . Walter Wiora is certainly right when he emphasizes that comparison can denote only a method, not a branch of learning. (1961:15)

The second objection came at a much later time, and was probably an outgrowth of factors other than those which motivated the scholars noted above. This is the view that comparison itself is not central to ethnomusicology's concern, and it has been expressed in two ways. The first is that comparison in ethnomusicology has been undertaken prematurely, and this has been emphasized by Hood, for example, who wrote in 1963:

> . . . it seems a bit foolish in retrospection that the pioneers of our field became engrossed in the comparison of different musics before any real understanding of the musics being compared had been achieved. (p. 233)

Hood later expressed the point of view somewhat more strongly when he wrote in 1969:

> An early concern with comparative method, before the subjects under comparison could be understood, led to some imaginative theories but provided very little accurate information. . . . A vast number of musical cultures . . . are yet to be studied systematically . . . before comparative methods can "give musicology a truly world-wide perspective." (p. 299)

The second anti-comparative view was expressed earlier in time; it hinges on the idea that since meanings may differ from one culture to another, comparison of musics may be comparison of unlike things. One of the early statements of this objection is Meyer's opinion written in 1960.

> Appearances are often deceptive. For instance, two cultures may appear to employ the same scale structure, but this structure might be interpreted differently by the members of each culture. Conversely, the music of two cultures may employ very different materials, but the underlying mechanism governing the organization of these materials might be the same for both. (pp. 49–50)

John Blacking was expressing the same point of view when he wrote:

> Statistical analyses of intervals, . . . are all very well, provided that we know that the same intervals have the same meanings in all the cultures whose music we are comparing. If this is not certain, we may be comparing incomparable phenomena. In other words, if we accept the view that patterns of music sound in any culture are the product of concepts and behaviours peculiar to that culture, we cannot compare them with similar patterns in another culture unless we know that the latter are derived from similar concepts and behaviour. Conversely, statistical analyses may show that the music of 2 cultures is very different, but an analysis of the cultural 'origins' of the sound patterns may reveal that they have essentially the same meaning, which has been translated into the different 'languages' of the 2 cultures. (1966: 218)

Other objections to comparison have been made, but they are not central to the present discussion. What is important is that the reaction against the term, "comparative musicology," was first expressed, in print, at least, in terms of the suppositions that its practitioners did not compare any more than anyone else, and that comparison was both premature and dangerous.

II

These objections bracket in time one of the most significant periods of development in the history of our field of study. This period occurred in the first half of the decade of the 1950's, and it was marked by the appearance for the first time in the United States of a small group of specially trained students who were disciples of older men in the field: I am thinking here of such persons as Mantle Hood, David McAllester, Bruno Nettl, myself, and others. It was also marked by the organization of a successor to the American Society for Comparative Musicology which had existed briefly in the 1930's. This effort was begun in 1953, and the formal organization of the Society for Ethnomusicology took place in 1955. And finally, the increase in activity in the field was marked by the introduction of the new term, "ethnomusicology."

It is unanimously agreed, so far as I know, that the first use of the term in print occurred in Jaap Kunst's little booklet, *Musicologica* (1950); it is interesting to note that Kunst was reacting against "comparative musicology" on precisely the grounds cited previously herein. He wrote: "The name of our science is, in fact, not quite characteristic; it does not 'compare' any more than any other science. A better name, therefore, is that appearing on the title page of this book: *ethno-musicology*" (p. 7). I do not know whether, in fact, this *was* the first printed appearance of the word, and it is quite possible that an industrious search would reveal an earlier citation, for certainly the word was in currency before 1950. Regardless of this possibility, the Kunst usage is the significant emotional one for students of the field, and will quite possibly always remain so.

Two important points must be made concerning the introduction of this new term. The first is that it was accepted virtually immediately, and undoubtedly the establishment of the Society for Ethnomusicology (without the hyphen) had a very substantial impact upon the new public convention. By the second half of the decade of the 1950's the two terms were being used simultaneously as synonyms, and by the end of the same decade, "comparative musicology" had been reduced almost exclusively to the status of an historic term which only referred to something in the past. Thus within five years a significant change had occurred, and within ten, the earlier term had been almost completely replaced as a working symbol.

The second point is that the very speed of acceptance must have indicated a significant desire for change, and the assumption is strengthened when we recall that the first objections to the prior term had been raised at least as early as 1905! This in itself has certain implications:

1) something must have been lacking in the old term, i.e., it did not adequately express what the practitioners of comparative musicology felt they were doing, or ought to be doing;
2) something fresh must have been visualized in the new term, which better expressed the sense of the field and the ideas or ideals of its practitioners;
3) something must have changed in the minds of the persons involved in the field that required a change in its appellation.

The fact that these assumptions did not, for the most part, turn out to be true, does not affect them as reasonable hypotheses. A change of name of an entire field of study, coupled with its eager and virtually immediate acceptance, is not an event to be dismissed lightly.

A considerable amount of similarity was noted in the definitions of "comparative musicology"—in fact, they tended to be as alike as peas in a pod. The definitions of "ethnomusicology," however, do not follow quite the same pattern. Two major types can be distinguished in the twenty-odd years after Kunst's publication, of which the first can be subdivided into three related, but slightly different, approaches.

The first type consists of definitions which closely parallel, or are identical to, those which had been used for comparative musicology, and the first subtype includes those based upon the named kind of music being studied. Thus in 1950, Kunst included as the object of study, "mainly the music and the musical instruments of all non-European peoples, including both the so-called primitive peoples and the civilized Eastern nations" (1950:7), and in Third Edition of the same work, he spoke of "*traditional* music and musical instruments of all cultural strata of mankind," but specifically named "tribal and folk music," and "every kind of non-Western art music," while specifically excluding "Western art- and popular (entertainment-)" music (1959:1). This lead was followed by others, such as Nettl, who wrote "Ethnomusicology . . . [is] . . . the study of non-Western music and, to an extent, . . . folk music . . ." (1961:2) and others, including, for example, Greenway (1962), Hood (1963), and Nettl again (1965).

The second subtype takes the second stressed aspect of the old comparative musicology definitions and makes it the central focus of the new definition; this concerns music as oral tradition, which Lachmann had emphasized as early as 1935, and which had been a part of Haydon's (1941) and Kunst's (1959) discussions. Characteristic here is List's statement that "ethnomusicology is to a great extent concerned with music transmitted by unwritten tradition" (1962), a position he has reiterated since (1963; 1969), and one which has also been suggested by others (Gillis 1969). More recently, Nettl has discussed the same matter, but from a rather different standpoint, noting that *all* music traditions employ a strong oral component. He writes:

> I feel therefore that I should not devote myself simply to what we call orally transmitted music, or what we were once permitted to call folk music, but instead to the study of all music from the point of view of its oral tradition; and this, for me, is one of a number of acceptable definitions of the field of ethnomusicology. (1975:69)

The third subtype defines the field as showing primary concern with music "outside one's own society." Statements of this type are less frequent than the others, but they have been made by Nettl (1964:11; 1965), and perhaps most specifically in print by Wachsmann, who wrote: ". . . ethnomusicology is concerned with the music of other peoples" (1969).

These definitions of ethnomusicology are all of one essential type, for they approach the problem from the standpoint of what the supposed sphere of interest is, conceptualized in terms of things. Of the three subtypes, the first two represent essentially different emphases on the same point, and both are used today, though with decreasing frequency. The third has dropped almost completely out of the picture, under the criticism of Kolinski (1957) and Seeger (1961), among others, both of whom pointed out that such a statement is basically ethnocentric and that by its tenet, the definition of what ethnomusicology is depends at any given point on who is studying what.

In sum, the definitions discussed to this point parallel the prior definitions of "comparative musicology," for they are statements of what particular kinds of music should be studied. Further, they represent by far the largest proportion of definitions suggested for the new term, and, contrary to expectations, they do not represent a change in position or in thought. Instead, these majority definitions seem to indicate that for their proponents, ethnomusicology represented no significant break with comparative musicology.

The second kind of definition does indicate the beginnings of a sharp rupture with the past, for in this case, process is stressed over form: the kind of music to be studied is no longer central, and instead, the focus of attention is placed upon the way it is to be studied. While these definitions are relatively rare, they become more common through time; and while the early examples are groping, and perhaps even accidental, they do represent a new feeling about the field of study.

Early in the field was McAllester's report of the organizational meeting of the Society for Ethnomusicology, in which he spoke of the "general concensus" as favoring the idea that ethnomusicology "is by no means limited to so-called 'primitive music,' and is defined more by the orientation of the student than by any rigid boundaries of discourse" (1956). A year later, Hood borrowed a definition of ethnomusicology from musicology which mentioned no types of music to be studied, but instead emphasized "the investigation of the art of music . . ." (1957). In 1960, I suggested a flatly processual definition of ethnomusicology as ". . . the study of music in culture" (1960), and two years later Nketia wrote that "the study of music as a universal aspect of human behavior is becoming increasingly recognized as the focus of ethnomusicology" (1962). Hood's well-known definition in the *Harvard Dictionary* spoke of ethnomusicology as "an approach" (1969), and others have followed with variations on the same general theme, including Seeger (1970), List (1971), Chase (1972), and Merriam (ca. 1973).

These definitions represent a qualitative difference from others in that they stress process rather than form. By defining ethnomusicology in terms of "things," the scholar is constantly forced into making taxonomies, into cutting and splitting, drawing boundaries, differentiating between one thing and another: the conclusion must always be that a significant difference exists, as Hood (1969) and others (Seeger 1961, for example) insist, between music sound and the context of music sound, and that both for practical and analytic purposes, never the twain shall meet.

On the other hand, definitions which stress process force the investigator to focus on a totality rather than a set of component parts, to view description as a beginning in the course of study, and to conceptualize music sound not as separate from, but as a part of the totality of society and culture. The debate between the two views is a continuing, and healthy one which represents a hoary division of intellectual domains in Western thought: it is sharply reflected in the definitions put forward for the word, "ethnomusicology."

III

In the 1970's, definitions of the field have declined in number, presumably either because ethnomusicologists tired of the subject or because they felt that definitional problems had been solved and that they could operate comfortably with one or another of the formulations previously suggested. Further, most of the more recent definitions have been very broad and general, almost as if whatever battles had been fought were no longer appropriate, or as if the problem did not require further sharp and precise thinking. Thus Chenoweth says only that "ethnomusicology is the study of the musical practices of a particular people" (1972), and Blacking writes that "Ethnomusicology is a comparatively new word which is widely used to refer to the study of the different musical systems of the world" (1973; see also Blacking 1974). Nettl has recently suggested a broadly encompassing working definition which he regards as descriptive of most study currently being done in the field.

> Ethnomusicology is the comparative study of musical cultures, particularly as total systems including sound and behavior with the use of field research. (1974)

At the same time, a few definitions have recently appeared which represent either idiosyncratic ideas of what ethnomusicology is, or new directions in which it may be going. Thus it has been suggested that the primary task of ethnomusicology may be to seek correlations between music sound structure, on the one hand, and society and culture, on the other. I have recently commented that if we do "define" ethnomusicology in terms of "what ethnomusicologists do," and given the significant expansion of "world music performance groups," ethnomusicology might well be forced into such a definition as "the performance and dissemination of ethnic music" (1975: 56). This suggestion goes against my own strong conviction that no field of study can be defined on such a basis. Most recently, the growing concern manifested by students and professors around the world with the problems of logical positivism and the scientific method, have been reflected in yet another definition, one which stresses, perhaps, things to come: "Ethnomusicology is the hermeneutic science of human musical behavior" (Elizabeth Helser 1976).

The definitions of comparative musicology and ethnomusicology cited here reflect their eras and the thinking of their proponents, as is to be expected. But by looking at them in historic perspective, we learn something not only of the history of our field of study *per se,* but of its intellectual development as well. I have no doubt that new definitions of ethnomusicology will continue to be proposed and that they, too, will reflect the growing maturity of the field and its practitioners.

Note

1. I wish to express my deep appreciation to Frank Gillis, Elizabeth Helser, and Bruno Nettl, each of whom has given me permission to quote his or her unpublished definition of ethnomusicology. I trust I have not distorted any of these friends' views in so doing.

References Not Cited in Appendix

Blacking, John
    1966   Review of *The Anthropology of Music. Current Anthropology* 7:218.
Hood, Mantle
    1971   *The ethnomusicologist.* New York: McGraw-Hill.
Hornbostel, Erich M von
    1905   Die Probleme der vergleichenden Musikwissenschaft. *Zeitschrift der Internationalen Musikgeselschaft* 7:85–9 7.
Kolinski, Mieczyslaw
    1957   Ethnomusicology, its problems and methods. *Ethnomusicology Newsletter* No. 11:2–8.
Ladd, John
    1973   Conceptual problems relating to the comparative study of art. *In* Warren L. d'Azevedo (Ed). *The traditional artist in African societies.* Bloomington: Indiana University Press, pp. 417–24.
Merriam, Alan P.
    1969   Ethnomusicology revisited. *ETHNOMUSICOLOGY* 13:213–29.
    1975   Ethnomusicology today. *Current Musicology* No. 20:50–66.
Meyer, Leonard B.
    1960   Universalism and relativism in the study of ethnic music. *ETHNOMUSICOLOGY* 4:49–54.
Sachs, Curt (Edited by Jaap Kunst)
    1962   *The wellsprings of music.* The Hague: Martinus Nijhoff.

Appendix

References are cited in chronological, rather than alphabetical, order.

Adler, Guido
    1885   Umfang, Methode und Zeil der Musikwissenschaft. *Vierteljahrsschrift fur Musikwissenschaft* 1:5–20.
            p. 14: ". . . die vergleichende Musikwissenschaft, die sich zur Aufgabe macht, die Tonproducte, insbesondere die Volksgesange verschiedner Vtilker, Lander und Territorien behufs ethnographischer Zwecke zu vergleichen und nach der Verschiedenheit ihrer Beschaffenheit zu gruppiren und sondern." (". . . comparative musicology has as its task the comparison of the musical works—especially the folksongs—of the various peoples of the earth for ethnographical purposes, and the classification of them according to their various forms.")
Lachmann, Robert
    1935   Musiksysteme und Musikauffassung. *Zeitschrift fur Vergleichende Musikwissenschaft* 3:1–23.
            p. 1: By implication "non-European music," as in the following: "Aussereuropaische Musik wird ohne das Mittel der Schrift uberliefert; ihre Untersuchung erfordert daher andere Methoden als die der abendlandischen Kunstmusik." ("Non-European music is handed down without the means of writing; its investigation demands, therefore, other methods than those for Western art music.")
Roberts, Helen H.
    1937   The viewpoint of comparative musicology. Proceedings of the Music Teachers National Association for 1936, pp. 23 3–38.
            p. 233: ". . . the kind of studies that are now coming to be classified under the term 'comparative musicology' deal with exotic musics as compared with one another and with that classical European system under which most of us were brought up."

Haydon, Glen
    1941   *Introduction to musicology*. New York: Prentice-Hall.
        p. 218: "Non-European musical systems and folk music constitute the chief subjects of study; the songs of birds and phylogenetic-ontogenetic parallels are subordinate topics."
        p. 235: "If *comparative musicology* means the study of extra-European musical systems, it is natural that the study of Chinese, Indian, Arabian, and other musical systems should fall to the lot of comparative musicology."
        p. 237: "Comparative musicology has its characteristic subject matter chiefly in extra-European and folk music. . . ."
        p. 219: "Most, if not all, of the music studied in comparative musicology is transmitted by oral tradition. . . ."
Sachs, Curt
    1943   *The rise of music in the ancient world east and west*. New York: W. W. Norton.
        p. 29: "comparative Musicology . . . [is] . . . the primitive and Oriental branch of music history."
Apel, Willi
    1946   *Harvard dictionary of music*. Cambridge: Harvard University Press.
        p. 167: "Comparative musicology . . . [is] . . . the study of exotic music."
        p. 250: "Exotic music . . . [is comprised of] . . . the musical cultures outside the European tradition."
Herzog, George
    1946   Comparative musicology. *The Music Journal* 4 (Nov.–Dec.): 11 et seq.
        p. 11: "There are many other musical languages, employed by Oriental and primitive—preliterate—peoples. The study of these bodies of music is Comparative Musicology, which aims to discover all the variety of musical expression and construction that is to be found within the wide array of types of cultural development all over the world. Comparative Musicology embraces also folk music. . . ."
Kunst, Jaap
    1950   *Musicologica*. Amsterdam: Koninklijke Vereeniging Indisch Institut.
        p. 7: "To the question: what is the study-object of comparative musicology, the answer must be: mainly the music and the musical instruments of all non-European peoples, including both the so-called primitive peoples and the civilized Eastern nations. Although this science naturally makes repeated excursions into the field of European music, the latter is, in itself, only an indirect object of its study."
Koole, A. J. C.
    1955   The history, study, aims and problems of comparative musicology. *South African Journal of Science* 51:227–30.
        p. 227: "The Englishman Alexander John Ellis . . . is rightly considered to be the founder of this branch of science [comparative musicology], for although a few studies of exotic music had been published. . . ."
Bukofzer, Manfred F.
    1956   Observations on the study of non-Western music. *In* Paul Collaer (Ed). *Les colloques de Wegimont*. Bruxelles: Elsevier, pp. 33–36.
        p. 33: "From the beginning [musicology] has included also the study of oriental and primitive music or what can best be summarized as non-western music. This special branch is known by the somewhat clumsy name 'comparative musicology' or 'ethno-musicology.' . . . The study is supposed to include also the musical folklore of western nations." (See remarks in opposition by Constantin Brailoiu, pp. 35–36.)
[McAllester, David P.]
    1956   The organizational meeting in Boston: *Ethno-musicology Newsletter* No. 6:3–5.
        p. 5: "The proper subject matter for the society was discussed at length. The general consensus favored the view that 'ethno-musicology' is by no means limited to so-called

'primitive music,' and is defined more by the orientation of the student than by any rigid boundaries of discourse. . . . It was further felt that the term, 'ethno-musicology' is more accurate and descriptive of this discipline and its field of investigation than the older term, 'comparative musicology.' "

Nettl, Bruno

  1956   *Music in primitive culture*. Cambridge: Harvard University Press.

  p. 1: "The study of primitive music falls within the scope of comparative musicology, or, as it is often termed, ethnomusicology, the science that deals with the music of peoples outside of Western civilization."

Rhodes, Willard

  1956   Toward a definition of ethnomusicology. *American Anthropologist* 58:457–63.

  p. 460–61: "Here, under the imprint of comparative musicology, are bound together studies of the music of the Near East, the Far East, Indonesia, Africa, the North American Indians, and European folk music. Of those ethnomusicologists whose interests are confined solely to primitive music I ask, 'Can we refuse our inheritance?' Let us not be provincial in the pursuit of our discipline. Oriental art music, the folk music of the world, and primitive music, all await our serious study."

Schaeffner, Andre

  1956   Ethnologie musicale ou musicologie comparee? *In* Paul Collaer (Ed). *Les colloques de Wegimont*. Bruxelles: Elsevier, pp. 18–32.

  p. 24: "J'ai dit . . . que rien dans son nom ne spécifiait que la musicology comparée étudierait plutôt les musiques non-européennes. Or elle s'est intéressée essentiellement à celles-ci." ("I said that nothing in its name specified that comparative musicology must study non-European musics. But it is interested essentially in these.")

Hood, Mantle

  1957   Training and research methods in ethnomusicology. *Ethnomusicology Newsletter* No. 11:2–8.

  p. 2: "[Ethno]musicology is a field of knowledge, having as its object the investigation of the art of music as a physical, psychological, aesthetic, and cultural phenomenon. The [ethno]musicologist is a research scholar, and he aims primarily at knowledge about music."

Schneider, Marius

  1957   Primitive music. *In* Egon Wellesz (Ed). *Ancient and Oriental music*. London: Oxford University Press, pp. 1–82.

  p. 1: "This new discipline was called 'comparative musicology', its primary aim being the comparative study of all the characteristics, normal or otherwise, of non-European art."

Kunst, Jaap

  1959   *Ethnomusicology*. The Hague: Martinus Nijhoff, Third Edition.

  p. 1: "The study-object of ethnomusicology, or, as it originally was called: comparative musicology, is the *traditional* music and musical instruments of all cultural strata of mankind, from the so-called primitive peoples to the civilized nations. Our science, therefore, investigates all tribal and folk music and every kind of non-Western art music. Besides, it studies as well the sociological aspects of music, as the phenomena of musical acculturation, i.e., the hybridizing influence of alien musical elements. Western art- and popular (entertainment-) music does not belong to its field."

Merriam, Alan P.

  1960   Ethnomusicology: discussion and definition of the field. *ETHNOMUSICOLOGY* 4:107–14.

  p. 109: ". . . the study of music in culture."

Nettl, Bruno

  1961   *Reference materials in ethnomusicology*. Detroit: Information Service, Inc., Detroit Studies in Music Bibliography Number 1.

p. 2: "Ethnomusicology . . . [is] . . . the study of non-Western music and, to an extent, . . . folk music. . . ."

Seeger, Charles

 1961   Semantic, logical and political considerations bearing upon research in ethnomusicology. *ETHNOMUSICOLOGY* 5:77–80.

 p. 79: "The study of non-European musics was launched in 1900 . . . and was eventually given the name 'comparative musicology.'"

Greenway, John

 1962   *Primitive music.* Boulder: University of Colorado.

 p. 1: ". . . the systematic study of music as it is manifested among the more primitive and unfamiliar peoples of the world. . . ."

List, George

 1962   Ethnomusicology in higher education. *Music Journal* 20:20 *et seq.*

 p. 24: "Ethnomusicology is to a great extent concerned with music transmitted by unwritten tradition."

Nketia, J. H. Kwabena

 1962   The problem of meaning in African music. *ETHNOMUSICOLOGY* 6:1–7.

 p. 1: "The study of music as a universal aspect of human behavior is becoming increasingly recognized as the focus of Ethnomusicology."

Hood, Mantle

 1963   Music, the unknown. *In* Frank Ll. Harrison, Mantle Hood, and Claude V. Palisca. *Musicology.* Englewood Cliffs: Prentice-Hall, pp. 215–326.

 p. 217: "The discipline is directed toward an understanding of music studied in terms of itself and also toward the comprehension of music within the context of its society. Ethnomusicology is concerned with the music of all non-European peoples . . . and includes within its purview the tribal, folk, and popular music of the Western world, as well as hybridizations of these forms. It frequently crosses into the field of European art music, although such material is only an indirect object of concern. In other words, ethnomusicology embraces all kinds of music not included by studies in historical musicology, i.e., the study of cultivated music in the western European tradition."

List, George

 1963   Ethnomusicology and the phonograph. *In* Kurt Reinhard and George List. *The demonstration collection of E. M. von Hornbostel and the Berlin Phonogramm-Archiv.* New York: Ethnic Folkways Library, album notes for FE 4175, pp. 2–5.

 p. 2: by implication: "[Ethnomusicology is] the study of aurally transmitted music. . . ."

Nettl, Bruno

 1964   *Theory and method in ethnomusicology.* Glencoe: Free Press.

 p. 1: ". . . ethnomusicologists in the past have been students of the music outside Western civilization and, to a smaller extent, of European folk music."

 p. 11: "We can summarize the consensus in stating that ethnomusicology is, in fact as well as theory, the field which pursues knowledge of the world's music, with emphasis on that music outside the researcher's own culture, from a descriptive and comparative viewpoint."

Nettl, Bruno

 1965   *Folk and traditional music of the western continents.* Englewood Cliffs: Prentice-Hall.

p. 26: "The field that provides research in . . . [folk and non-Western music] . . . is now known as ethnomusicology. Before about 1950 it was commonly called comparative musicology, and it is a sort of borderline area between musicology (the study of all aspects of music in a scholarly fashion) and anthropology (the study of man, his culture, and especially the cultures outside the investigator's own background)."

Kolinski, Mieczyslaw
1967   Recent trends in ethnomusicology. *ETHNOMUSICOLOGY* 11:1–24.
p. 5: "One of the most ambitious objectives of musicological research is the comparative analysis of the known musical styles of the world's peoples designed to establish their distinguishing features and, ultimately, to search for universals providing a common basis for the immense variety of musical creations. The most appropriate term for this field of study appears to be *comparative musicology*."

Gillis, Frank
1969   Personal communication.
"[Ethnomusicology is] the study of those world musics which are aurally transmitted."

Hood, Mantle
1969   Ethnomusicology. *In* Willi Apel (Ed). *Harvard dictionary of music.* Cambridge: Harvard University Press, Second Edition, pp. 298–300.
p. 298: "Ethnomusicology is an approach to the study of *any* music, not only in terms of itself but also in relation to its cultural context."

Wachsmann, K. P.
1969   Music. *Journal of the Folklore Institute* 6:164–91.
p. 165: ". . . ethnomusicology is concerned with the music of other peoples. . . . The prefix 'ethno' draws attention to the fact that this musicology operates essentially across cultural boundaries of one sort or another, and that, generally, the observer does not share directly the musical tradition that he studies. . . . Thus it cannot surprise us that in the early stages the emphasis was on comparison, and the field was known as comparative musicology until, in the 1960's, it was renamed."

List, George
1969   Discussion of K. P. Wachsmann's paper. *Journal of the Folklore Institute* 6:192–99.
p. 195: "A third definition (and one to which I subscribe) defines ethnomusicology in the broadest sense as the study of traditional music. What does the term 'traditional music' mean? It refers to music which has two specific characteristics: it is transmitted and diffused by memory rather than through the use of writing, and it is music which is always in flux, in which a second performance of the same item differs from the first."

Seeger, Charles
1970   Toward a unitary field theory for musicology. *Selected Reports* 1(3):172–210.
In reading the following, one should recall that Seeger holds "ethnomusicology" to be the proper term for what is now called "musicology."
p. 179: ". . . musicology is (1) *a speech study*, systematic as well as historical, critical as well as scientific or scientistic; whose field is (2) *the total music* of man, both in itself and in its relationships to what is not itself; whose cultivation is (3) *by individual students* who can view its field as musicians as well as in the terms devised by nonmusical specialists of whose fields some aspects of music are data; whose aim is to contribute to *the understanding of man,* in terms both (4) of human *culture* and (5) of his relationships with the *physical universe.*"

List, George
1971   *Inter-American program in ethnomusicology.* Bloomington: Indiana University Publications.
n.p.: "Ethnomusicology is conceived as an interdisciplinary study in which approaches derived from many disciplines can be usefully applied."

Chenoweth, Vida
1972   *Melodic perception and analysis.* Ukarumpa, Papua New Guinea: Summer Institute of Linguistics.
p. 9: "Ethnomusicology is the study of the musical practices of a particular people."
Repeated in Second Edition, 1974.

Chase, Gilbert
   1972   American musicology and the social sciences. *In* Barry S. Brook, Edward O. D. Downes, and Sherman Van Solkema (Eds). *Perspectives in Musicology.* New York: W. W. Norton, pp. 202–26.
           p. 220: "I favor the *idea* of an 'ethnomusicology' . . . but I do not favor the terminology. . . . What we need is a term of larger scope. . . . For this I propose the term 'cultural musicology' [the task of which is] 'to study the similarities and differences in musical behavior among human groups, to depict the character of the various musical cultures of the world and the processes of stability, change, and development that are characteristic to them.'"
Blacking, John
   1973   *How musical is man?* Seattle: University of Washington Press.
           p. 3: "Ethnomusicology is a comparatively new word which is widely used to refer to the study of the different musical systems of the world."
Merriam, Alan P.
  ca 1973   Unpublished thoughts.
           "Ethnomusicology is the study of music as culture."
Blacking, John
   1974   In memoriam Antonio Jorge Dias. *Lisboa*, Vol. III, pp. 71–93.
           p. 74: "The discipline is concerned chiefly with 'ethnic' or 'folk' music and thus tends to be an area study. The methods used are generally anthropological and sociological, or musicological: thus scholars are concerned with either the rules of a particular society or culture, of which music-making is a feature, or the rules of a particular society's musical system."
Nettl, Bruno
   1974   Personal communication.
           "Ethnomusicology is the comparative study of musical cultures, particularly as total systems including sound and behavior with the use of field research."
Nettl, Bruno
   1975   The state of research in ethnomusicology, and recent developments. *Current Musicology* No. 20:67–78.
           p. 69: "[Ethnomusicology is] the study of all music from the point of view of its oral tradition; . . ."
Helser, Elizabeth
   1976   Personal communication.
           "Ethnomusicology is the hermeneutic science of human musical behavior."

Ethnomusicology: A Discipline Defined

George List

A quarter of a century ago Jaap Kunst, dissatisfied with the term "comparative musicology," invented the new term "ethno-musicology." In so doing he placed the prefix or combining term "ethno" in front of the word "musicology" to indicate that the study was of the music of the races of man (1950:7). However, his definition was restrictive in that the study of Western art and popular music was excluded. In a later redefinition of the term, he indicated that the study also included the sociological aspects of music (1959:1).

Since that time that field of study known as ethnomusicology has expanded so rapidly that it now encompasses almost any type of human activity that conceivably can be related in some manner to what may be termed music. The data and methods used are derived from many disciplines found in the arts, the humanities, the social sciences, and the physical sciences. The variety of philosophies, approaches, and methods utilized is enormous. It is impossible to encompass them all within one definition. In my opinion, ethnomusicology cannot be adequately defined as an interdisciplinary activity. It is too diffuse, too amorphous. Ethnomusicology can only be defined when we consider what the ethnomusicologist is better equipped to accomplish than the anthropologist, the folklorist, the historian, the linguist, the so-called historical musicologist, the psychologist, or the sociologist. If we focus upon this, that activity which is uniquely ethnomusicological, we are then in a position to define ethnomusicology. However, in this process ethnomusicology becomes a discipline in its own right and, like other disciplines, has not only its own focus, its own subject matter or particular type of activity, but shows some limitations in its fields of interest.

How then would one define ethnomusicology as a discipline, a *Wissenschaft*, a *scientia* in its own right? It is the study of humanly produced patterns of sound, sound patterns that the members of the culture who produce them or the scholar

From *Ethnomusicology*, Vol. 23, No. 1 (January 1979), pp. 1–5 who studies them conceive to be music. Since the definition includes the words "humanly produced," bird song lies without the province of ethnomusicology. Since the definition includes the term "patterns of sound" the written or printed score that forms the guide to a performance is not the focus of our discipline. In this we differ from the so-called historical musicologist. He focuses upon the written or printed score, we focus upon the performance of music whether or not a written prescription for its performance exists.

All humanly produced music shares to some extent a particular characteristic: two performances of what is considered to be the same item always differ in some manner. This is as true of a performance of a Mozart symphony as it is of a song sung by the Vedda. Not only do we deal with diverse cultures located in differing geographic areas but we also study a human product that is always in flux: this leads us to the social sciences as well as the humanities for the tools of our research.

The study of concomitant activities is necessary to our full understanding of the style and structure of music. Thus we study the texts of the songs sung, the making and playing of musical instruments, the kinetic activities that occur simultaneously with the music. Of particular interest are the concepts held by the members of the culture concerning the music they produce. These non-musical activities are of course of interest in themselves but the ethnomusicologist studies them in order to gain a greater understanding of various aspects of music. For example, a knowledge of what aspects of music are important to those who make it assists us in transcribing this music. The musical concepts held by the informants, however, are not always consonant with those of the ethnomusicologist. An informant, for example, may believe that he performs two items at the same tempo. When the recordings of both performances are checked with a metronome or a watch it may be seen that considerable change in tempo has occurred. Custom and psychological factors are operative here. A study based entirely upon the concepts held by the members of the culture, the results of which are not compared with the more objective conclusions within the capability of the ethnomusicologist is not, according to the definition offered, ethnomusicology. It lies within the scope of another discipline—psychology or perhaps one of those omnivorous disciplines, anthropology or sociology, which profess that they encompass all studies dealing with man and his works. For a study to be ethnomusicological the scholar must transcribe the music by one means or another, analyze its style and its structure, and compare his results with the concepts concerning the music held by the members of the culture in question if such concepts are available.

Music can obviously be studied as a means of solving a nonmusical problem. For example, Clark Wissler in his book concerning the American Indian (1922:155) suggested that music is a very stable cultural trait and therefore provides a useful means for determining the diffusion of other cultural traits. Such studies are of course feasible but they lie outside ethnomusicology as a discipline. For the study to be ethnomusicological the reverse purpose would have to be served. Other cultural traits would be studied in order to arrive at conclusions concerning the diffusion of music. It is a matter of focus. Thus Alan P. Merriam's *The Anthropology of Music* (1964), as its name indicates, is an anthropological rather than an ethnomusicological work. It is concerned primarily with human behavior in making and reacting to music rather than in the musical product itself. Were the work ethnomusicological in character a reversed title would be required, *The Musicology of Anthropos,* the study of the music of man.

A detailed example may clarify this problem of focus. A number of years ago I published in *Ethnomusicology* an article concerning song melody and speech melody in central Thailand (1960). The article was recently republished in a collection of essays entitled *Intonation,* edited by a linguist (Bolinger 1972). Five tones are utilized in the dialect of central Thailand. The purpose of my study was to determine how the tones of the language affect the melody of song. In other words, I was utilizing linguistic data in order to arrive at a better understanding of the melodies of the songs. The editor of *Intonation* apparently believed that the linguist could derive from my study information concerning the modification tones undergo when sung rather than spoken. In other words, musical data would be used to arrive at a better understanding of linguistic phenomena. Possibly the article is useful for this purpose. However, what I would consider basic linguistic data is missing. I do not offer the texts of the songs in either Thai characters or in phonetic or phonemic symbols. I secured from my informants merely the tones they would have utilized if they had spoken the text of the song. However, without listening to the text of the song the informants could not have distinguished the tones as such. Thus, in my opinion, my study better serves an ethnomusicological than a linguistic purpose.

I am not arguing against interdisciplinary studies. Such studies have been carried on, are being carried on, and should be carried on. Insofar as they focus on the study of humanly produced sound patterns they can be described as partially ethnomusicological in character. No work can be said to be fully ethnomusicological, however, unless its primary focus is on such study.

This leads us to methods or lines of inquiry. Ethnomusicology shares with other disciplines certain underlying points of view or methods. These are the securing of an adequate sample of the material to be studied, care and accuracy in all operations and procedures performed, and objectivity. The latter, objectivity, requires that one approach the problem—whether it be fieldwork, transcription, analysis, or comparison—with an open mind. The scholar should not be limited by one methodology or by one theoretical framework. Rather, he should apply the approach that seems most efficacious in solving the particular problem. Should no useful procedures be available he must invent those needed. One method in common use is for the scholar himself to learn to perform the music of the culture being studied. This method was suggested by von Hornbostel in the early part of this century (Abraham and von Hornbostel 1909–10:15). It is a useful method as long as the performance itself does not become the goal. Then the activity becomes applied music rather than forming an aspect of ethnomusicological research.

Our field methods are those of the anthropologist, the folklorist, and the sociologist modified to meet our particular needs. New developments derived from physics—acoustics, electronics, optics—are probably more useful to us than to most other field workers. We take advantage of every new tool of this type.

Any approach, theoretical framework, or method can be utilized if it proves efficacious: models, paradigms, ethnoscience, cognitive process, semiotics. A knowledge of these is certainly useful in securing grants. All should be viewed with a critical eye, however, before any are applied to a particular problem. Does the emphasis lie so strongly upon process that the process is rarely completed? Are the results produced by such a lengthy process such that one could arrive at equally valid conclusions through the use of a traditional procedure in much less time? Does the model bring together two events that do occur simultaneously in time but that in reality have no significant relationship one to the other? One of course wishes to be *au courant* but one should be cautious in dealing with fashions that change from time to time. Nevertheless, any method or data derived from any discipline or source can be used if it is helpful in developing a better understanding of humanly produced sound patterns. This is the interdisciplinary character of ethnomusicology as a discipline.[1]

Note

1. This article is a revised version of a statement made at a colloquium, "Future Directions in Ethnomusicology," at Indiana University, November 28, 1977.

References Cited

Abraham, Otto and Erich M. von Hornbostel
    1909–   "Vorschläge für die Transkription exotischer Melodien," *Sammelbände der*
    1910   *Internationalen Musikgesellschaft* 11:1–25.
Bolinger, Dwight, ed.
    1972   *Intonation.* New York: Penguin.
Kunst, Jaap
    1950   *Musicologica.* Amsterdam: Uitgave van het Indisch Institut.
    1959   *Ethnomusicology.* The Hague: Nijhoff.
List, George
    1960   "Speech Melody and Song Melody in Central Thailand," *Ethnomusicology* 5:16–32.
Merriam, Alan P.
    1964   *The Anthropology of Music.* Evanston: Northwestern Univ. Press.
Wissler, Clark
    1922   *The American Indian.* 2nd ed. New York: Oxford Univ. Press.

A View of Ethnomusicology from the 1960s[1]

CHARLOTTE J. FRISBIE / Southern Illinois University, Edwardsville

It seems almost unbelievable now that the same year Rosa Parks did this nation a great favor by refusing to give up her seat on the bus, a group of people were in Boston at the 54th American Anthropological Association annual meeting, formally organizing SEM.[2] And now, here we are at our 50th, a highly complex historic meeting which hopefully will allow participants time for reflection, taking stock, and wondering about our future. We come together to celebrate our individual and collective survival, while also mourning the loss of numerous colleagues this year.[3]

Unlike Bruno Nettl, who can reflect on SEM in 1955, my own introduction to ethnomusicology as a term and field happened in the spring of 1962, during the last semester of my senior year at Smith College, where I was in the music honors program. When the fall semester began, I was focused on finishing course work, writing the required thesis, preparing for the required senior recital, while teaching piano to children from town, singing with the Chamber Singers, doing volunteer work in music therapy at a nearby nursing home, and playing piano in a local bar on weekends to have some pocket change. When looking at what I needed to take during the spring, my last semester there, I discovered I had two free hours in my structured course program. Having always been interested in Native Americans, I spotted a seminar under Sociology (there was no Anthropology department there at that time) on this topic offered by a Canadian anthropologist, Richard Slobodin, who was there as a visiting professor. I added that seminar to my program and soon became excited about new worlds opening through it. Professor Slobodin[4] had friends come occasionally to do special things for his class; one happened to be David McAllester from nearby Wesleyan University, who came to talk about the different musics to be

From *Ethnomusicology*, Vol. 50, No. 2 (Spring/Summer 2006), pp. 204–13

found among American Indians. Through his lecture and discussions with him afterwards, I learned about ethnomusicology as an option for graduate training.

Alas, my music department advisor was *not* any more supportive of this new idea than she had been earlier of my suggestion of music therapy, which would have combined my music major and psychology minor. According to her, ethnomusicology was "a fad that would go nowhere and soon fade away," and "definitely not something worthy of graduate work and career planning." On my own, I researched programs that offered ethnomusicology as well as what I had been told to do: prepare to teach college level music history courses or work as a music librarian forever. In the end, I applied to three of the programs that McAllester had told me about, having received literature from a number of them. After visiting two during the summer after graduation, I enrolled at Wesleyan in the fall of 1962 to work on an M.A. in ethnomusicology. David McAllester and Bob Brown were the major instructors; performance options included the Javanese gamelan and various opportunities in South Indian music, once Ranganathan, Ramanatham, Balasaraswati, and the rest of that family arrived. McAllester was teaching several anthropology courses in the Psychology Department, so I added those to the core ethnomusicology courses, tutorials in American Indian studies and Navajo linguistics, work-study jobs in the library and ethnomusicology lab, and an organist job in a nearby town. Women were new at Wesleyan in 1962, and most of those on campus were in the M.A.T. (Master of Arts in Teaching) program. The Ethnomusicology program was small; students included Peter Pease, Gerald Johnson, Martin Hatch, and Jon Higgins, as well as myself, and I was the only one focused on American Indian musics.[5] I was not the first McAllester student, however, since David had already worked with Victor Grauer before I came, and Victor had already graduated with his M.A. and gone to New York to work with Alan Lomax.

The program required fieldwork, and since McAllester had a grant at the time for a study of Blessingway music, I was given a chance to start working with Navajo singers on one piece of Blessingway hitherto unstudied, at least from ethnomusicological perspective: the girls' puberty ceremony. In the course of that first summer of hard knocks, I was invited to the Pecos Conference where I met other friends of McAllester's, including Leland C. Wyman, W. W. Hill, Evon Z. Vogt, Florence H. Ellis, and Odd Halseth, as well as other graduate students, such as Oswald (Ossie) Werner, Bob Black, and others associated with either the Ramah project or the Museum of Northern Arizona. I was already very aware of the fact that Navajo music was *one small piece* of Navajo culture and if I ever wanted to understand it and where it fit, I needed to have much more training in anthropology. Thus, my second and final year at Wesleyan, which included writing the thesis, was spent trying to decide whether I should apply to Anthropology doctoral programs, take a year off to do something different (such as pursue another dream, that of teaching in Alaska), or stay after graduation, and "hang out at Wesleyan" and wait for the Ph.D. program in Ethnomusicology, then under discussion, to pass through all of the hurdles. I ended up applying to three Anthropology Ph.D. programs as well as to government teaching opportunities, and when it all came out in the wash, I had four options to choose from, besides that of just hanging out. Leland C. Wyman, whom I had gotten to know better during my second year at Wesleyan, had already hired me to do some Navajo fieldwork for him after graduation. With that and further work under the auspices of McAllester's grant, I decided to bite the bullet, switch into Anthropology, and go to the University of New Mexico where I could work with the only other Navajo specialist known at the time, W.W. or "Nibs" Hill. Ethnomusicology continued for me at UNM through a job in the lab of the music library headed by Don Roberts, who became a good friend and colleague. There I worked on various collections, especially the Dean Robb one, and also facilitated the donation of that assembled by Odd Halseth and his wife, Ruth.

My story exemplifies the importance of both a mentor and serendipity. While I was at Wesleyan, McAllester encouraged me to submit an article to *Ethnomusicology* based on a tiny part of my fieldwork, namely, corn grinding songs. It emerged in 1964 as my first publication. He also encouraged Wesleyan University Press to consider publishing a revised version of my M.A. thesis, a study of the Navajo Girl's Puberty Ceremony. That, too, was published while I was at UNM, in 1967. Not only did he give me my first opportunity to do fieldwork; he modeled active involvement in SEM and instilled a commitment among his students to help the Society by participating in its work. We all learned a lot about the Society's inner workings by listening to McAllester talk in and outside of classes. The other students and I saw him involved with the journal, the board, the annual meetings, the council, and various other doings. I joined SEM in 1962 because it was expected of ethnomusicology students at Wesleyan. That fall, McAllester drove a group of us to the 7th annual meeting, my first, at Indiana University in his famous VW bus. He was Program Chair for that meeting, and we learned much about that job during the trip. The next year, in 1963, the 8th annual meeting was at Wesleyan; David was Local Arrangements Chair, and you better believe that *all of us* were pressed into service. While the 1962 meeting was a wonderful introduction to the field, its scholars, and students, the Wesleyan meeting was a godsend, despite its unending gofer work. Maybe because I was among the gofers, I was able to spend time in one-on-one discussions with some of my heroines and heroes, as well as to meet others. The group included: Gertrude Kurath, Barbara Smith, Barbara Krader, Laura Boulton, Mantle Hood, Willard Rhodes, Alan Merriam, and lots of other people I had learned about. By the time I left Wesleyan with my M.A. in ethnomusicology in 1964, I already had a network established with people who shared my interests, and I was committed to reading the journal and going to SEM meetings. Thus, despite living barely above the poverty line as an anthropology graduate student, I did travel from Albuquerque in 1964 to go to the 9th one in Detroit. The 10th one was held at UNM in 1965, and since I was there as a Ph.D. student in Anthropology, again I got to be a gofer and work an annual meeting. Robert Black was the Program chair, and Don Roberts chaired local arrangements.

While I was focused on completing my Ph.D. work, my dissertation research continued the examination of subceremonies of Blessingway, this time the House Blessing ceremony. I wrote another article, this time for *El Palacio*, and continued expanding my Southwestern research network. A group of us interested in American Indian matters had already identified ourselves within SEM and started making it a point to gather and share research efforts, questions, and ideas at annual meetings. Many in that group also started to get involved in the 1970s, or to say "Yes" when asked to do things for SEM. For me, without going into extensive details, the requests included chairing sessions at annual meetings, giving papers, and starting service work. First the latter included being editor of the Newsletter from 1972 until 1976, in the days of producing camera-ready copy, *before* computers. That service work proved enormously important to me, giving me a strong link both to the discipline and the Society at a time when it was becoming clear that I would never win the battle at Southern Illinois where, as a new Ph.D., I had started teaching anthropology in 1970. While my department was interested and willing, the Music Department refused to cross-list courses with anthropology, or to include ethnomusicology in their list of "approved-for-credit courses" for majors, even though they eventually did add a jazz course. Thus, my efforts remained in the Anthropology Department, in the Anthropology and the Arts course, seminars for small groups of students, and tutorials for individuals. When possible, I also facilitated attendance of interested students at SEM chapter and annual meetings. The Newsletter editorship was followed by service on the Council in the 1970s and 1980s, reviewing books and records for the Journal, regular participation in annual meetings, and giving priority to correspondence with colleagues in my network (via snail-mail!). Whenever possible, I agreed to serve on national SEM committees (such as officer and council nominations, program, and finance). When the meeting came to St. Louis, jointly with CMS in 1978, I of course ended up as Program Chair. That unforgettable experience was followed by a decade of intermittent service on the Board of Directors, first as Secretary, then 2nd Vice President, then President-Elect, President, and Past President. Since leaving the Board in 1990, I have continued to serve on various committees as time permits.

When I found ethnomusicology in the spring of 1962, it was a welcome relief from total immersion in the Western art canon, or Western European music first, last, always. It was wonderful to discover that my musical training could be put to good use in another discipline. SEM was a place to find new friends and colleagues, people interested in similar questions, and to gradually band together to form "interest groups."[6] In the beginning, SEM was a small group, especially when compared to entities like the AAA or AMS. If you were interested in service, the Society offered many opportunities for contributing individual skills.

So, who else was joining in the 1960s and what was happening then in ethnomusicology? When I researched our membership lists to learn who had joined SEM in the decade of the 1960s I learned several things besides the fact that there were many of us. First, the Society's membership list has not yet been tracked back earlier than 1961 in the database at Indiana University[7]; one can, however, reconstruct it through earlier newsletters and journals.

After carefully removing those on the earlier "Joined by 1955" and "Joined by 1959" lists, *among* those who had joined by 1963, or actually between 1959 and 1963, were: Lois Anderson, Louis Ballard, John Blacking, Donald Brown, Robert Brown, Gilbert Chase, Dieter Christensen, Catherine Ellis, Stephen Erdely, Hormoz Farhat, Bob Garfias, Pekka Gronow, Ida Halpern, Judith Hanna, Jon Higgins, Pandora Hopkins, Charlotte Johnson, Gerald Johnson, Adrienne Kaeppler, Maud Karpeles, Joann Kealiinohomoku, Charles Keil, Boris Kremenliev, Samuel Marti, Judith McCulloh, Kwabena Nketia, S. Ramanathan, Don Roberts, Gertrude Robinson, Naomi Ware, and Henrietta Yurchenco. *Among* those who joined between 1963 and the next list, in 1966, were: Judith Becker, Laura Boulton, Vida Chenoweth, Charlotte J. Frisbie (name change only, from Johnson), Alan Kagan, Jonathan Kamin, James Koetting, Fred Lieberman, Lorraine Sakata, and Mark Slobin.

The journals and the newsletters from the 1960s provide glimpses of some of the issues important in ethnomusicology at that time.[8] For example, the 10th Anniversary Issue of *Ethnomusicology* 7(3), Sept. 1963, revisited the first decade of 1953–63 as one of progress in the discipline, society, and the field according to the views of Willard Rhodes and David McAllester. Other essays included Merriam's on the purposes of ethnomusicology from an anthropological view and Seeger's on the "Tasks of Musicology." The May 1963 issue (*Ethnomusicology* 7[2]:113–23) included the results of the second program survey wherein twenty-eight schools were reportedly offering ethnomusicology courses, a far cry from the first survey reported in *Newsletter* 3 (Dec. 1954) wherein only a few schools had any courses and only one had more than two. Essays in other issues during the 1960s discussed the significance of music; the whys, hows, for what purposes, and when issues of transcription; research on specific musical instruments through time and space; analyses of intervals, tempi, melodies, ornamentation, structure, and rhythm; and a variety of other subjects, including the Noh drums, Ponca dance, Maori chant analysis, origin of the Oklahoma 49er, and fiddling. Essays were also devoted to such topics as: composition techniques, problems of musical meaning, specific musical styles and genres, relativism, and music and dance, language and music, boundaries of speech and song, and dance ethnology. Journals included bibliographies, memorials, and special bibliographies. In the 1960s, debates concerned a number of matters, some of which have re-emerged for further discussion in the twenty-first century, including the "right name" for the Society, and the "little man" logo. There were healthy examinations of definitions of terms and styles, and how best to do our work and with what equipment, both in the field and at home, in the lab. Among the big bugaboos of the decade were: the role of performance in one's training, or the value of what Mantle Hood called "bimusicality." Another was, of course, transcription. The 1960s brought more textbooks, including, in 1964, both Merriam's *Anthropology of Music* and Nettl's *Theory and Method in Ethnomusicology*. Developments in the Journal were many during the decade; among them were the inclusion of a record in 1964, and a special, single-focus issue, the Latin American one in 1966, with Gilbert Chase as editor. In the 1960s, we were *not* yet worrying about emic *vs.* etic, insider *vs.* outsider, self *vs.* other, or colonialism in our own work

Reflecting in 2005 on what SEM meant to me in my beginning years in the discipline, I realized that by finishing or getting my Ph.D. in anthropology and subsequently teaching that, I essentially moved to the outside and thus became somewhat of an outsider.[9] Another view, however, is that in so doing, I had acquired from ethnomusicology and SEM another hat, another home full of like-minded colleagues, as well as another profession. For me, equally trained in music, ethnomusicology, and anthropology, it was wonderful to have a discipline which focused on all musics to be found in cultures all over the world, and which did its work through fieldwork, in addition to text-based or library work. Here was another discipline to which I could apply the questions being raised in anthropology as these came along, first with the civil/human rights, and women's rights wake-up calls, and later, through literary criticism, the postmodern critiques, self-reflexivity, and deconstruction of founders and intellectual roots.

Most important to me initially were the questions that came on board in the early 1970s, when many women woke up. As I fought feminist battles in my own department, to change the way we talked about human evolution (so women evolved as well as men), and to add new courses to be cross-listed with the Women's Studies program, it became obvious to me that SEM, like all other academic organizations and disciplines, was in need of similar critique, and yes, some house-cleaning. Becoming interested in re-examining our history all over again, I began to research, speak, and publish on our early women, their roles,

and the numerous contributions they were "quietly making" while the founding fathers were being publicly acclaimed (Frisbie 1988a, 1988b, 1989, 1991).[10]
That led rapidly to other questions about equality and SEM. Because I was on
the Board at that point, sometimes my queries were framed structurally. For
starters, how many women had served as President of SEM by 1989 when Mark
Slobin succeeded me and became our eighteenth president? The answer? Three.
Barbara Krader was the first in 1971–73. She was followed by Carol Robertson
in 1983–85, and then myself, in 1987–89. Where was the evidence of inclusiveness in SEM, of various ethnic groups being involved on the Council or on the
Board? Besides women, where were African-Americans, Hawaiians, American
Indians, and other minorities? While we mouthed interest in and support of
musics from all cultures and all times, what did our membership data and our
scholarship show?

As the years passed, I continued to watch things unfold and discuss issues
with colleagues. SEM has certainly changed on gender issues, as most of its long
time members recognize.[11] Yes, it took years for women within the discipline to
start meeting, first for late-night discussions in hotel bedrooms at the annual
meeting. Eventually, interest groups were formed and approved; witness now
the Section on the Status of Women, and the Gender and Sexualities Taskforce.
Now these have regularly scheduled meeting times to discuss common concerns
at annual meetings, and among other things, often develop and submit sessions
for the program.

But are we through doing what needs to be done on these issues and others
related to them, such as inclusiveness, specially challenged individuals, or a truly
diverse professional society? I would say *no*, and I think others would agree; see,
for example, Koskoff (2005) and Rice (2004b). Witness the standing committee
that was organized after our 2003 meeting known as the Crossroads Project
on Diversity, Difference, and Under-representation, and the special session on
Ethnomusicology and Diversity at last year's meeting in Tucson. While our latest
2002 membership survey shows sensitivity to many issues of identification, we
still lag behind in championing diversity. As our current President, Tim Rice
(2004b) recently noted, we still need to increase African American and Hispanic/
Latino memberships, and the number of women in tenure-track academic jobs.
We need to recognize and listen to ethnomusicologists working in the public
sector (applied ethnomusicology) as well as in K–12 environments. And we
need to welcome the viewpoints and participation of our foreign members.

I am proud of SEM for having survived the onslaught of various institutional
and other foes. We have continued to adopt concerns important first in other
disciplines, such as folklore, anthropology, or even literary criticism, be these
gender, identity, ethnicity, or others. We seem to have survived the self-reflexivity
of postmodernism, and to have started to identify areas of under-representation.

We have deconstructed orchestras, music schools, and conservatories, and here in Atlanta, this list is being expanded by examinations of university marching bands. On this program, some are revisiting what was earlier known as music and healing, or music therapy by addressing music and AIDS, or music and autism. Why can't there be a medical ethnomusicology, or ethnomusicology of violence or traumatic experience?[12] I remember earlier spurts of interest in music and healing. But then there were also other blips on earlier horizons, such as interests in children's music, music and cognition, and musical aesthetics. And, one could ponder the years spent arguing about whether or not to include music education and educators, and/or popular music!

We recognize that the world is ever changing and that yes, we need to get involved, even through political advocacy (addressed in the first President's roundtable in 2003 during Ellen Koskoff's Presidency; see Koskoff 2004, and Rice 2004a). There will always be new buzzwords and concepts, usually borrowed from sister disciplines. The Atlanta program is, of course, full of them: hybridity and hybrids; identity and its construction and negotiation; mimesis; universalizing systems; globalization of music through mass media; alterity; commodification; how to re-image and reimagine communities, and reinvent histories and national identities; how to perform nostalgia. Yes, we are in a global, digital world wherein at least some people live in cyberspace, and hold up banks while talking on cell phones![13] Starting in the 1990s, at least in anthropology, it became clear that our earlier ideas about fixed places, boundaries, geographic entities, and even maps were obsolete, given the widespread fluidity of people, universalizing of economic and political systems, transnationalism, and the rapid social, technological, economic transformations, most often in the direction of Western capitalism. The commercialism is overwhelming, and the issues of ownership, labels, local/national/global/cultural politics, and all the rest, daunting.

While we struggle to use process-oriented paradigms to deal with all of the hybrids, fusions, unending transformations, shifting boundaries, and renegotiations, I would urge us to remember that underneath all of the chaos are *real people*, living real lives that include music and often, music-making. There is more to individuals than their constructed and reconstructed identities, reinvented histories, and nostalgia for homelands. Without real people continuing to be important parts of our work, the "ethno-" is gone, and we cease to be ethnomusicologists!

Notes

1. It should be understood that this paper does *not* speak for others who joined SEM in the 1960s. In Atlanta, many interesting things were discussed as spin-offs after this panel. Among them was the idea of doing fieldwork among those who joined SEM by each decade to see what, if any,

experiences and expectations were shared by the decade. I regret to say that I did no such fieldwork for this paper.

2. The early Newsletters document the history of SEM and the efforts of the four founding fathers, (McAllester, Merriam, Rhodes, and Seeger) which began in December, 1952 with the first discussions and were followed in 1953 by sending out a letter to seventy-five individuals asking for an exchange of news and information, and support for the newsletter. This letter was signed by Manfred Bukofzer, Frances Densmore, Miecyzslaw Kolinski, David McAllester, Alan Merriam, Willard Rhodes, Curt Sachs, Charles Seeger, Harold Spivacke, and Richard Waterman (*Ethno-Musicology Newsletter* 1:1, December 1953). Those present at the Nov. 18, 1955 meeting (once again, during an annual AAA meeting, the 54th) in Boston, wherein SEM was formally founded, included: Moses Asch, Elizabeth Bacon, John Blaut, Edwin Burrows, Donald Cantor, Helen Codere, John Fisher, Linton Freeman, Merrill Gillespie, Thomas Hazard, Melville Herskovits, Richard Hirshberg, Barbara Krader, Gertrude Kurath, Mieczyslaw Kolinski, David McAllester, Roxanne McCollester, W. J. Mayer, Bruno Nettl, Carol Rachlin, Willard Rhodes, Hugh Thurston, John Ward, and Gene Weltfish (*Ethno-Musicology Newsletter* 6:3, January, 1956).

3. These included two past presidents of SEM, Gerard Béhague and Mantle Hood, as well as Joyce Aschenbrenner, Janice Kleeman, Dorothy Sara Lee, Tullia Magrini, Kishibe Shigeo, Robert Brown, and others identified during the Necrology section of the Business Meeting in Atlanta.

4. Dick Slobodin and I ended up becoming friends and eventually, colleagues. He specialized in northern Athapaskan ethnology, working in the Northwest Territories, Yukon, and Alaska with the Metis, Gwich'in, and other peoples. He founded and developed the anthropology program at McMaster University, and spent much of his professional teaching career there, after short-term jobs at Cornell University, Smith College, and the Canadian Indian and Northern Affairs research center. Dick died on Jan. 22, 2005 (*Anthropology News* 2005).

5. Most of the students on this list were undergraduates, when I came to Wesleyan. Jon Higgins and I were the only graduate students in the M.A. Ethnomusicology program during my second and final year, 1963–64, and we both had assistantships in the ethnomusicology lab, rotating our working hours because of space and availability of equipment. I had come to know Jon earlier when singing groups I was in at Smith sang with comparable ones he was in at Wesleyan, and when he started dating one of my very good friends at Smith, Rhea Padis (who became his wife). Thus, when Jon was tragically killed by a drunk driver while walking their dog at night in the fall of 1984, many, many people were devasted, including me.

6. This, of course, was without Board recognition. Now such groups apply for recognition as SIGS, Special Interest Groups; see, for example, the current Archiving and Sexualities Committees. After three years of continuing commitment and Board approval again, SIGS can now become SECTIONS.

7. At present, those listed in the database as belonging in 1961 may or may not have joined before then. One needs to consult earlier membership lists to determine that information. Specifically, see *Ethno-Musicology Newsletter* 4, April 1955 and *Ethnomusicology* 3(3), September 1959. Slightly later journals, specifically 7(2), May 1963; and 10(2), May 1966 include the next lists. In 1970, for the first time, the Society published the membership list as a separate booklet, available from the Ann Arbor Business Office for $1.

8. Remember that our Newsletter had eleven issues, all of which were later considered as Vol. 1 of the Journal; the Journal itself started with 2(1), January 1958.

9. Among the questions stimulated by this session in Atlanta were several that emerged among the anthropological members of SEM. At present, I am in the process of identifying who is in this group so that round-robin discussions of some of the issues can begin.

10. This project, "Women and the Society for Ethnomusicology, 1952–1961," is still ongoing. The initial archival fieldwork was supported in the summer of 1988 by a research grant from SIUE for which I am grateful. I hope to finish the fieldwork and publish the results in the next decade!

11. But, as Koskoff (2005) noted, feminist and genderist work in ethnomusicology now seems to have slowed down. Her important observations deserve further examination and discussion.

12. A meeting for all of those interested in medical ethnomusicology was held Friday evening, Nov. 18, from 6 to 7 pm during the 50th annual SEM meeting in Atlanta. Other demands made it impossible for me to attend what may have been the initial gathering of what will become another SIG.

13. This incredible event had happened the week before the Atlanta meeting and the suspect was apprehended as our conference began.

References

Anthropology News 2005. "Obituary of Richard Slobodin" (submitted by Harvey Feit). *AN* 46(6):52. September.

Frisbie, Charlotte J. 1988a. "Women and the Society for Ethnomusicology, 1952–1961." Paper presented by invitation at the conference, "Ideas, Concepts, and Personalities in the History of Ethnomusicology" held at the University of Illinois at Urbana-Champaign, April 14–17.

———. 1988b. "Frances Theresa Densmore (1867–1957)." In *Women Anthropologists, a Biographical Dictionary*, edited by Ute Gacs, Aisha Khan, Jerrie McIntyre, and Ruth Weinberg, 51–58. Westport, CT: Greenwood Press.

———. 1989. "Helen Heffron Roberts (1888–1985): A Tribute." *Ethnomusicology* 33(1):97–111.

———. 1991. "Women and the Society for Ethnomusicology: Roles and Contributions from Formation through Incorporation (1952/3–1961)." In *Comparative Musicology and Anthropology of Music*, edited by Bruno Nettl and Philip V. Bohlman, 244–65. Chicago: University of Chicago Press.

Koskoff, Ellen. 2004. "SEM and Political Advocacy: Report on the President's Roundtable." *SEM Newsletter* 38(3):6–7.

———. 2005. "(Left *Out in*) *Left* (the *Field)*: The Effects of Post-Postmodern Scholarship on Feminist and Gender Studies in Musicology and Ethnomusicology, 1990–2000." Keynote address, SEM Midwest Chapter meeting, April 1–3, Bowling Green State University, Bowling Green, Ohio.

Rice, Timothy. 2004a. "SEM Soundbyte: SEM and Political Advocacy." *SEM Newsletter* 38(2):1,3, 4.

———. 2004b. "SEM Soundbyte: How is SEM Doing on Diversity?" *SEM Newsletter* 38(4):1, 3.

Society for Ethnomusicology. 1970. "Society for Ethnomusicology Membership List for 1970." Ann Arbor: SEM. Business Office.

The Individual in Musical Ethnography

Jesse D. Ruskin / University of California, Los Angeles
Timothy Rice / University of California, Los Angeles

The individual musician occupies a seemingly paradoxical position in ethnomusicology. On one hand, the name of the discipline, whose roots include
the Greek word for nation, race, or tribe (*ethnos*), suggests that it will focus on the
study of groups of people, not on individuals. In fact, ethnomusicologists have
tended to follow the path implied by the discipline's name by studying the role,
meaning, and practice of music within social groups and communities defined
by geography (the music of Japan), ethnic or kinship group (African American music), institutions (music in the national conservatory of Uzbekistan), or
genre-affinity groups (performers and fans of flamenco). These communities
are assumed to share social behaviors and cultural concepts with respect to
music, and the object is to understand how musical performance, composition,
creativity, and musical works themselves are expressions of and contribute to
these shared behaviors and concepts; music, in other words, is viewed as part
of a social and cultural system.

On the other hand, at least four factors pull ethnomusicologists toward the
study of individual musicians. First, when conducting fieldwork, they work with
and rely on individual musicians who are sometimes—but not always—among
the most exceptional individuals in a given musical community. Second, as
communities under the pressures of globalization and political instability frag-
ment and "deterritorialize," as Arjun Appardurai (1990, 1991) put it, ethnomusicologists have been drawn to the study of individual musicians who are trying
to make sense of collapsing worlds, create new individual identities, and knit
themselves into emerging or newly encountered social formations. Third, ethnomusicologists belong to a subculture that values the exceptional and valorizes
individual achievement. Fourth, interventions in theory and method over the
last quarter century have led ethnomusicologists to highlight individual agency

From *Ethnomusicology*, Vol. 56, No. 2 (Spring/Summer 2012), pp. 299–322

and difference, and acknowledge their own roles in the musical communities they study.

Given these paradoxical forces—long-standing notions of the coherence of social life and culturally shared experience versus dynamic, unstable political realities, the practical exigencies of fieldwork, and new developments in social theory—we were curious about how ethnomusicologists have tried to reconcile the competing poles of the social and the individual in their musical ethnographic work and in their assessments of the field.

One of the seminal interventions in this respect was Kenneth Gourlay's 1978 devastating critique of the pretense of objectivity and scientific omniscience that had characterized ethnomusicological reports up to that point, and his suggestion that the "research process" involved a dialogue between historically and socially positioned individuals (1978:22). In the same year, Charlotte Frisbie and David McAllester brought a single musician and his voice to the foreground of their narrative and shifted authorial credit away from themselves to their primary subject Frank Mitchell (Mitchell 1978). In 1984, the *Worlds of Music* textbook featured an individual in each of its chapters about a particular region of the world (Titon et al. 1984). In 1987, Rice suggested that ethnomusicologists had a long history of foregrounding individual musical creativity as well as the historical construction and the social maintenance of music, which he claimed were the principal "formative processes" of human music making.

In 2001, Jonathan Stock, responding to Gourlay, Frisbie and McAllester, and Rice, among others, proposed an "ethnomusicology of the individual" in the wake of what he saw as a recent rise in biographical and historical writing in ethnomusicology (see, for example, Rees 2009). He argued that this "literary trend" was motivated by three factors: the recognition of individuality and exceptionality within the musical communities ethnomusicologists study, the reflexive turn and critique of representation in the social sciences, and reconceptualizations of culture that account for individual variation and agency.

For some ethnomusicologists, however, the developments of late modernity drove their interest in the theoretical and methodological significance of individual musicians. Mark Slobin, in *Subcultural Sounds: Micromusics of the West* (1993), followed anthropologist Arjun Appadurai (1990, 1991) in imagining an ethnomusicology that accounts for the deterritorialization of culture and the fragmentation of experience in late modernity. He suggested that individuals might profitably become the new locus of ethnomusicological research, since, as he put it, "we are all individual music cultures" (1993:ix). Following Slobin, Rice (2003) proposed a model for a "subject-centered musical ethnography."

These and other calls for an ethnomusicology of the individual appear to have the quality of an oxymoron. But despite a focus on communities suggested by the discipline's name, ethnomusicologists have a long tradition of placing individuals prominently in their conception of the field. This article examines how they do this in practice, in their writing of particular case studies. While such scholarly reporting occurs in many forms and genres, we focus on the book-length musical ethnography.

For this study we define a musical ethnography as a book that (1) asks and answers questions about the meaning and function of music in culture and society, and (2) is based on fieldwork as an indispensable research method. (Of course, such books may also include other methods such as extensive musical analysis and the use of historical sources.) In the last thirty-five years, book-length musical ethnographies have come to rival journal articles as the most important form for reporting the results of ethnomusicological research. Bruno Nettl (2005:234) described the musical ethnography as the "meat-and-potatoes book of our field." In our view, the large and fast-growing corpus of book-length musical ethnographies is the fruit of the successful marriage of ethnomusicology's parent disciplines, anthropology and musicology. This rapprochement began to appear in books written during the second half of the 1970s by a new generation of ethnomusicologists trained in schools and departments of music but strongly influenced by the first generation of anthropologically trained ethnomusicologists and in particular by Alan Merriam's *The Anthropology of Music* (1964).

To understand the position of the individual in musical ethnography, we examined a large sample of the musical ethnographies published between 1976 and 2002. We chose 1976 as the start of the period because we believe that Mark Slobin's *Music in the Culture of Northern Afghanistan*, published in that year, was the first musical ethnography written by a person trained primarily as an ethnomusicologist and not as an anthropologist. We ended the survey period when our sample reached more than 100 books and we saw that certain patterns had been well established. We believe that a review of work published in the ten years between 2003 and 2012 would not significantly alter our conclusions. (The books in our sample are listed in the Appendix.)

In order to be included in our sample, books had to be based in some measure on fieldwork methods; deal with problems suggested by an anthropological approach to music study; and be written by scholars who self-identify as ethnomusicologists, or who engaged in conversations with ethnomusicologists as evidenced by their citations and references. If there was any doubt about whether a book should be included in the sample, we privileged the author's characterization of the work. So, for example, Virginia Danielson's (1997) study of the popular Egyptian singer Umm Kulthūm, while at one level a biography of a deceased individual, was included because the author foregrounded fieldwork and cultural analysis. The vast majority of the books in our sample were published in the United States and other Anglophone countries, but we did include a few English-language works published elsewhere that came to our attention (e.g., Moisala 1991; Weisethaunet 1998; Pejcheva and Dimov 2002). While we do not view ethnomusicology as exclusively an English-language enterprise, it was not practical for us to include a fair sampling of the important work being published in dozens of other languages (e.g., Coppet and Zemp 1978; Allgayer-Kaufmann 1987).

In this article we use the word "individual" in as neutral a sense as possible—that is, as a single human being as opposed to a group of human beings. In doing so, we avoid taking a position on any of the many philosophical debates about the nature of the individual and its relationship to a world, although the authors of some of the studies we cite may do so either implicitly or explicitly. For the same reason, we prefer "individual" to some other possible words we might have used such as "person," which seems to be tied to legal discourse, and "subject," which seems to imply something about individual experience, ideation, and agency that may not be true of all the works in our corpus, though it is certainly true of some of them.

In order to locate and define the study of the individual in our sample of musical ethnographies, we address five themes: (1) the importance of individuals in musical ethnographies; (2) the types of individuals discussed and analyzed; (3) the theoretical purposes served by these treatments of individuals; (4) the nature of ethnomusicologists' encounters with individuals; and (5) the narrative strategies employed when individuals are included in musical ethnographies.

The Importance of Individuals in Musical Ethnographies

To understand how important individuals are to the narrative structures of musical ethnographies, we placed each book into one of four categories: (1) individuals largely absent from the narrative; (2) individuals present in the narrative to a limited extent; (3) individuals central to the narrative; and (4) single individual as sole subject (biography). We considered individuals largely absent when the author seemed primarily concerned with normative description over individual experience and where individuals were not named or, if they were named, were secondary to generalization about the group (e.g., Chenoweth 1979; Besmer 1983). Only fourteen books in our sample fell into this category. By contrast, individuals were present to a limited extent in just under half of the sample. We placed books in the "present" category when individuals were named and described briefly in passing, often to provide specificity to a broader cultural treatment or to support or complicate a larger argument (Neuman [1980] 1990); when individuals were named and quoted as sources of information but were neither the primary anchors of the narrative, nor the primary objects of analysis (Schechter 1992); when individuals drove the narrative in places, but were not the main point of the narrative as a whole (Reily 2002); or when characters were drawn through brief biographies in sectional or chapter-length profiles (Berliner 1978). Most of the remainder of the sample (that is, nearly half) occupied the "central" category, in which individuals anchored the narrative throughout the book. In such cases, they were treated as the primary objects of analysis, or the primary lenses through which to look at broader topics (Keyes 2002); there was extensive use of attributed quotation (Vander 1988); the book contained detailed biographies or profiles integral to the work as a whole (Bakan 1999); or the researcher's interaction with particular individuals was featured prominently (Hagedorn 2001). Finally, only ten books were placed in the "biography" category, indicating a narrative centered on the life and work of a particular musician, musical family, or ensemble. Six of them named an individual in the title (Mitchell 1978; Porter 1995; Stock 1996; Danielson 1997; Loza 1999; Vélez 2000), one named a band (Hayward 1998), and three did not name their subjects in the title (Rice 1994; Quigley 1995; Groemer 1999). Of these ten, three are about the stars of popular music (Danielson 1997; Hayward 1998; Loza 1999) and the remaining seven focus on individuals who would qualify as "traditional" musicians.

Using this method, we reached three principal conclusions. First, ethno-musicologists attended significantly to individuals throughout the period from 1976 to 2002. Second, the small number of books devoted in the main to a single named individual supports our earlier claim that ethnomusicologists treat individuals more often as members of communities than as autonomous actors. Third, books that focus solely on communities without considering individuals represent a very small portion of the sample.

Viewing the sample temporally yielded two slightly contradictory trends. On one hand, individuals have been centrally important to the musical ethnographies in our sample from its beginnings in the late 1970s (Berliner 1978; Mitchell 1978). On the other hand, books that ignore individuals completely occupy a prominent part of our corpus only during the early years up to about 1990. Such studies disappear after 1995. Since then, individuals play at least a peripheral role in every musical ethnography. Also, in the mid-1990s publications focused on a single individual begin to appear. In short, the survey shows that individual-centered studies have increased over the past two decades. This trend occurred early, however, and the place of individuals in musical ethnographies remains a mostly invariant characteristic of books published from the mid-1980s onward.

What Kinds of Individuals do Ethnomusicologists Study?

Having established that ethnomusicologists frequently feature individuals in their musical ethnographies while rarely making them the exclusive focus, we then asked ourselves about the types of individuals ethnomusicologists study. Are they the compositional titans and stylistic innovators constructed in studies of the history of Western art music, the stars of popular music studies, average musicians who represent a widespread cultural practice, or nonmusicians of various types (listeners, fans, producers, and the like)?

Ethnomusicologists have claimed, for example, that since music is a communicative art, audiences and the act of listening should be legitimate objects of study for a social science interested in music. In conversations, they once debated whether it was more valuable to study (or study under) the most exceptional musicians in a given community or its most typical practitioners. Some felt that the focus should be on learning the best music from the greatest artists, whereas others, such as the anthropologist John Blacking, felt it more important to form a picture of the "average" musician (see, for example, Baily 2001:88). Regardless of whom they worked with, all acknowledged that close involvement with individual musicians is an essential part of ethnomusicological method and integral to its theoretical insights as well (Nettl 1984:173).

The debate over what type of individual to work with seems to have faded with the increasing recognition that the two categories are not exclusive, but exist in a dialectical relationship. The exceptional individual does not necessarily stand outside or against the consensus of culture; rather, "the personal, the idiosyncratic, and the exceptional . . . [are] very much part of the collective, the typical, and the ordinary" (Stock 1996:2). Just as shared tradition thrives on individual innovation, as Colin Quigley's (1995) study of Canadian fiddler Émile Benoit suggests, so too does individual innovation often find its greatest expressive potential in shared tradition, as Virginia Danielson's (1997) study of the popular Egyptian singer Umm Kulthūm vividly illustrates. Furthermore, the question of exceptionality may also be a question of scale. From a distance, an individual such as Émile Benoit may appear as typical, but a deeper understanding of his musical style and role in the community reveals his exceptionality. With these complexities in mind, our analysis shifts toward the types of individuals treated in our sample of musical ethnographies.

Broadly speaking, we suggest that ethnomusicologists write about four types of individual in their musical ethnographies: (1) innovators in a tradition; (2) key figures who occupy important roles in a musical culture; (3) ordinary or typical individuals; and (4) normally anonymous audience members and others who play a role in music production, dissemination, and reception. Although ethnomusicologists have pointed out that, theoretically and as a matter of principle, they could study average musicians and even non-musicians, the vast majority of musical ethnographies in our survey focus on innovators and other key figures who play some important role in their musical culture.

Innovators

The authors of about a quarter of these musical ethnographies examine the contributions of innovators within a musical tradition. Innovators tend to play prominent roles in musical ethnographies that take a historical approach, focus on popular music, or feature the encounter between tradition and modernity. As in historical musicology, ethnomusicologists tend to view innovators as agents who move the history of a style down the temporal road. In studies of popular music, where the fame of named individuals and stars and their contributions to the history of a genre are some of the hallmarks of this research domain, innovators often are featured in the narrative. Furthermore, the encounter of a tradition with modernity is frequently personified in these musical ethnographies by an individual who articulates and acts on this key moment in the history of a tradition.

An early example of all three tendencies is Manuel Peña's *The Texas-Mexican Conjunto: History of a Working-class Music* (1985). Peña's basic purpose was to mount a Marxist analysis of the economic and social conditions that cause a musical genre to emerge and develop. Using historical and ethnographic methods, he documented the individual innovators (such as Narciso Martínez, Valerio Longoria, and Tony de la Rosa) of *conjunto* music within the contexts of twentieth-century Mexican-American migration, urbanization, class differentiation, and identity formation. Peña's study is fairly typical of the approach to innovative individuals in ethnomusicology. Ethnomusicologists are not allergic to the innovators so lionized by historical musicology, but they figure prominently in only about a quarter of this corpus. When ethnomusicologists do treat innovators, they tend to look not at lives and works, but rather at the unusually effective or creative ways in which these musicians responded to their changing social and historical circumstances.

Key Figures

The second category of individual in musical ethnography is what we call the "key figure." Over half of the books in our corpus focus on such individuals, who are considered to be "key" in two senses: they play some crucial musical role in the culture—such as being extremely popular, occupying an important position, or being an outstanding representative of the style—and they play an important role in the narrative as a particular example of a general point the author wishes to make. Rice's *May It Fill Your Soul: Experiencing Bulgarian Music* (1994), for example, chronicles the history of Bulgarian traditional music from the 1920s to 1989 by focusing on the musical experience of two key figures: Kostadin Varimezov and his wife Todora. Kostadin occupied an important position in the official musical culture of Bulgaria during its communist period (1944–89) as the solo bagpipe player in the orchestra of traditional Bulgarian instruments at the national radio station. His wife Todora was a key figure in the sense that she possessed an exceptionally large repertoire of traditional songs learned in the pre-communist period. By focusing on Kostadin's transformation from a musically illiterate village player to a literate professional musician, Rice was able to humanize the more general story he wished to tell about Bulgarian musical culture in two distinct historical periods. Neither Kostadin nor Todora was an innovator in the tradition, but Rice shows how their deep knowledge of tradition made possible the innovations of others at the moment Bulgarian tradition encountered modernity.

Average Musicians

The third category of individual, used in only a small number of musical ethnographies, consists of average or ordinary musicians who must, we suppose, be an important part of every musical tradition. They are chosen not because of their special mastery of—or position in—a tradition but to help the author tell an interesting story. One example of such a study is Harris Berger's *Metal, Rock, and Jazz: Perception and the Phenomenology of Musical Experience* (1999). This book examines how musicians performing in these three genres attend cognitively to music during performance in order to create a powerful musical groove. In this book, understanding individual musical experience is the point. So, any individual will do, including local and regional journeyman musicians crucial to the vitality of these styles but with little or no apparent artistic or historical significance in the wider world.

Nonmusicians

The fourth category of individual comprises non-musicians, in effect the audience for music. Ethnomusicologists have long argued that, in principle, listeners should be considered musicians, and that they deserve to be studied as seriously as performers and composers are. For example, Danish anthropologist Marc Schade-Poulsen's *Men and Popular Music in Algeria: The Social Significance of Raï* (1999) examines this Algerian urban popular music through its audience. He elicited the biographies of seven "young men in the city" (ibid.:75–96) who listened to but did not perform raï. He wanted to make the point that there is not a single, unified view of raï, a controversial genre for both traditionalists and Islamic fundamentalists because of its association with discos, parties, and "obscene" cabarets. These individual stories served as particular instances of "the generalizations [the author was] making about social life among youth in Algeria" (ibid.:76). Since we found only two books in the sample featuring this type of individual (see also Muller 1999), we conclude that it is safe to say that ethnomusicologists rarely follow this principle.

What Theoretical Purpose does the Study of Individuals Serve?

How individuals are treated in musical ethnographies depends to a large extent, we believe, on the author's view of culture. In one view, evident in roughly one-third of the books in the corpus, the author tends toward a "classic" concept of culture in which individuals' ideas and actions are seen as molded by a larger whole (Ortner 2006:12). From this perspective, culture is constituted of shared ideas and behaviors and the point of the narrative is to explicate the general principles at work in a musical culture. The second view, true of about two-thirds of the books, draws on a host of more recent critical interventions in the social sciences in which the differences between and among individual actors and agents in a society or community are seen as crucial to the reproduction and transformation of its musical culture.[1]

Studies based on the Theory that Cultures are Constituted of Shared Ideas

In the category of works that rest on the theory of shared culture, only a small number either marginalize or ignore individuals altogether in order to tell a general story. The majority of books focus on general cultural principles, but use individuals in the narrative in one of two ways: (1) as specific examples to illustrate and give a human face to the social and cultural principles at stake in the book; or (2) to acknowledge individuals as the primary sources of the ethnomusicologist's knowledge, in many cases without giving them life through extensive biographies or anecdotes about their life in the musical culture. Daniel Neuman's *The Life of Music in North India: the Organization of an Artistic Tradition* ([1980] 1990), for example, provides a brief account of a competent but otherwise unremarkable *tabla* player named Yusuf Ali, who concertized in the West with distinguished melodic-solo artists. Western audiences' enthusiastic reception of Ali as a musical equal of the melodic artists helped to transform tabla players' musical, economic, and social status in India. They began to demand more money and more performance time to display their creativity. Neuman tells us about Yusuf Ali not because he is in any sense exceptional but because he illustrates and humanizes the larger point Neuman wishes to make about the homology between musical and social organization in India.

In ethnomusicological field work, individuals are the principal sources of cultural understanding and teachers of musical knowledge and, in some sense, are equivalent to historical musicologists' manuscript sources. One example is Finnish ethnomusicologist Pirkko Moisala's *Cultural Cognition in Music: Continuity and Change in the Gurung Music of Nepal* (1991). Her main goal was to understand music cognition, and so she spent a lot of time with the two most prominent musical specialists in the village, from whom she elicited verbalizations about music. Although she introduces them briefly as characters with lives (ibid.:87–90), they are mainly useful to her narrative when she is describing their performances and documenting what they told her about their thought processes. Ethnomusicologists' naming of individuals as sources of information and reporting on the particular musicians who teach them typically flow from their research methodology rather than from their research goals. Such naming and reporting is sometimes the only reason that individuals appear in these musical ethnographies (compare, however, Browner [2002], who has other reasons for naming individuals).

Studies Concerned with Difference in Culture

The second category is based on a different theoretical foundation. The view of culture as shared among people living in well-defined social groups has been challenged by critical theorists in the social sciences who have argued that societies are not happily homogenous but fragmented along lines of gender, social class, and ethnicity, and that, as a result, cultural ideas and expressions will be similarly fragmented. According to this theoretical perspective, the contestation of musical meaning by individuals and cultural subgroups must be as true as any claims about common, shared meanings and understandings. This is not to say that the shared aspects of culture cease to matter, only that they are refracted through individual personality, social differentiation, and relations of power. In ethnomusicology, this relatively recent development in social theory has taken at least four forms: (1) valorizing individuality, individual skill differences, individual identity, and individual experience among musicians in a culture; (2) reporting on the differences and tensions that exist between and among individuals operating from different social and historical positions within a society; (3) viewing individuals as agents who operationalize, put into motion, give meaning to, and change social, cultural, and musical systems; and (4) foregrounding the experiences of ethnomusicologists and their encounters with individuals during fieldwork.

The valorization of individual difference and individual identity comes rather easily to ethnomusicologists, trained as most of them are in Western traditions that value individuality in general and various forms of musical distinction in particular. In this category are books that focus on differences in knowledge and skill levels, individual musical experience, differences of interpretation, and questions of individual identity. Benjamin Brinner's *Knowing Music, Making Music: Javanese Gamelan and the Theory of Musical Competence and Interaction* (1995) provides a rich example of individual difference in musical competence. In it he develops a general theory of musical competence and a particular theory of Javanese musical competence. One of the more interesting features of his theory concerns the "individualized" nature of musical knowledge. This individualized knowledge is then deployed within communities of individuals interacting in particular musical contexts (see also Monson 1996; Vélez 2000).

A second approach to registering fragmentation in musical cultures is to claim that culture is defined as much by contestation between and among people operating from different social positions such as age, class, occupation, education, and urban-versus-rural residence as it is by shared understandings and practices. Ethnomusicologists are increasingly addressing the differences of musical interpretation and experience that result from such social stratification. For example, in one part of Raúl Romero's *Debating the Past: Music, Memory, and Identity in the Andes* (2001), he takes individuals as tokens for three competing social positions—traditionalist, modernist, and radical—within the world of contemporary *orquesta típica*, an ensemble of *quena* flute, violin, and harp that originates with the pre-Hispanic Wanka people of the Mantaro Valley of Peru. The traditionalist position is represented by an artist/intellectual who once resided in Europe and who decries modernization and seeks to preserve ancient practices. The modernist position is represented by a clarinet player and music teacher who believes that modern instruments such as the clarinet and the saxophone help to make traditional music sound better, and who claims that the modern is more useful for creating identity than the traditional. The radical position is represented by younger musicians aged 15 to 25 who are experimenting with replacing the harp with the electric bass and the violin with the synthesizer.

In the third approach, scholars view musical individuals as agents who give meaning to—and change—social, cultural, and musical systems in specific instances. Influenced by practice theory and related theories of agency (Ortner 2006:131–34), this position serves as an antidote to an earlier ethnomusicological theory that music and musicians merely reflect or participate in larger cultural and social systems and processes. This approach is also characteristic of musical ethnographies that attempt to account for the history of a tradition. One of the clearest examples in our corpus of musical ethnographies is Virginia Danielson's *The Voice of Egypt: Umm Kulthūm, Arabic song, and Egyptian society in the Twentieth Century* (1997). A star of the tradition is at the center of this study, and is construed by Danielson as an agent: "One wants to account for the impact of exceptional performers . . . on the culture of their societies without losing track of them as participants affected by their societies" (ibid.:15–16).

She claims that Umm Kulthūm helped to "constitute" cultural and social life, "advance an ideology of Egyptianess," and create a cultural and artistic world that was simultaneously Arab, Western, and cosmopolitan—and in line with the nationalist politics of the period.

The notion of agency is not restricted, however, to historical studies in which ethnomusicologists, like historical musicologists, treat individuals as the agents of stylistic change. Even in more synchronic studies, many ethnomusicologists work on the assumption that individual musicians are agents of social and cultural practices and that music is not merely a passive reflection of pre-existing social and cultural structures. For example, Jane Sugarman's *Engendering Song: Singing and Subjectivity at Prespa Albanian Weddings* (1997) provides richly detailed descriptions of how people at social gatherings in this conservative Muslim community choose whether to sing, what songs to sing, and the manner in which they will sing them. In a tour de force of cultural analysis, Sugarman demonstrates how such seemingly mundane choices create this community's sense of social identity; its sense of social organization around notions of patrilineality and gender; and its sense of "honor and moral order" (ibid.:182–97).

A fourth reason for placing individuals at the center of musical ethnographies is the reflexive turn in ethnomusicology, a direction that Gourlay (1978) anticipated with his call to place the encounter of ethnomusicologists with musicians in the field at the center of their narratives about musical cultures. As they engage in self-reflection about field encounters and as they write themselves into their narratives, they naturally write about the people they meet, not just about abstract features of music, culture, performances, or social structure. In thematic terms, these approaches to reflexivity include recognizing the dialogic achievement of knowledge in fieldwork; problematizing the researcher's social, political, or economic position; and using the self as a source of knowledge, especially in contexts of music learning. Anthony Seeger, for example, places his book *Why Suyá Sing* (1987) within the trend towards reflexive anthropology. Music making, for Seeger, is an important part of the "delicate" economy of knowledge that constitutes fieldwork. Seeger recounts that it wasn't until he and his wife began singing that the Suyá recognized their full value to the community (ibid.:19–21). The inclusion of this encounter in Seeger's narrative is doubly useful: it illuminates the complex negotiations involved in fieldwork and reveals something of the Suyá's value system. At a more general level, Seeger suggests that the ethics of reflexive anthropology are rooted in an intersubjective and dialogical approach to field research, one that sees people not as abstract objects, but as thinking subjects with whom ethnomusicologists share knowledge. A particular strength of this book, however, is Seeger's success in registering his own presence without making it a focal point of the entire narrative.

The Author's Encounter with the Individual

We use the term "encounter" to imply a relationship between researcher and subject that shapes the possibilities of research and the narrative that emerges from it. Accordingly, we placed each book into one of three categories based on the nature of the authors' encounters with the individuals they study: direct encounter, indirect encounter, or both direct and indirect encounter. Direct encounter refers to face-to-face interaction between ethnographer and subject, engaging the usual modes of fieldwork, including interviews and participant observation, as well as the collection of oral histories and the compilation of biographies (Keil 1979; Cooke 1986; Blau et al. 2002) and autobiographies (Mitchell 1978; Groemer 1999; Simonett 2001). Indirect encounter, in contrast, implies a degree of separation between the researcher and the individual subject. It may involve such historical research materials as correspondence, existing biographies, musical scores, recordings, and other secondary sources. And it may also make use of fieldwork methods in developing a picture of the social and ideological world in which the individual lives or lived (see Walser 1993, Stock 1996, and Danielson 1997 for examples of this methodologically hybrid indirect approach). Of the musical ethnographies in which individuals play a central role, our survey shows that over half use only direct methods, whereas a small number use only indirect methods (Becker 1980). A significant number use some combination of direct and indirect methods (Loza 1999).

Although ethnomusicologists often generalize about music and culture from encounters with a limited number of individuals (Shelemay 1997), few musical ethnographies contain detailed reflections on the nature of these relationships and how they impact research method, theoretical orientation, and narrative presentation. Individual-centered ethnographies, however, tend to deal with these issues more explicitly. Michael Bakan, in *Music of Death and New Creation: Experiences in the World of Balinese Gamelan Beleganjur* (1999), acknowledges the way in which his relationship with two Balinese composers, Asnawa and Sukarata, shaped his narrative. Asnawa serves more as a source of information, evident in the fact that he is frequently cited as a reference in the first three chapters. Sukarata, in contrast, is a focus of the study in the second half of the book, where Bakan recounts his experience studying drumming with him. Bakan discusses how his initial encounters with these composers shaped his theoretical orientation toward the individual and thus his approach to writing their biographies. For instance, his initial misreading of Asnawa's social status, which caused a significant miscommunication between the two, led him to investigate more thoroughly the composer's views of his own social position, as well as other peoples' views of Asnawa's status. In so doing, Bakan was able to construct a more nuanced picture of the individual as situated within a multifaceted social field. These composers, he discovered, define themselves and their artistic worlds, just as those worlds define them.

Narrative Strategies

Ethnomusicologists narrativize their encounters with individuals in many ways, with biographical writing being just one (Stock 2001). We extend Stock's argument by situating biography within a fuller typology of narrative strategies used in individual-centered musical ethnography. Our goal in this section is to show how ethnomusicologists have applied a range of narrative techniques, including but not limited to biographical writing, to the problem of situating the individual in musical ethnography. In doing so, we are suggesting a definition of biography that is simultaneously narrower and broader—that is, a more precise placement of what we call "biographical writing" within the ethnomusicology of the individual, and a broader definition of "musical biography" that includes a range of foci and rhetorical techniques.[2]

Focusing on the vast majority of books in this sample that represent individuals centrally or strongly, we have identified five narrative techniques commonly used to write the individual into musical ethnographies: biography, assisted autobiography, dialogue, polyvocality, and analysis of musical texts and performances. In practice, of course, these five techniques often overlap, but they are abstracted here for the sake of clarity. In providing examples of each from the literature, we illustrate not only their particular rhetorical aspects, but also the implications of each for theorizing the paradoxical position of the individual in ethnomusicology.

Biography

The first narrative strategy is biography—defined narrowly here as a monologic account of an individual's life and work, constructed from either historical research, fieldwork, or some combination of the two. Biographical writing takes at least three forms: book-length treatments of a single individual or family (Rice 1994; Porter 1995); formal and encapsulated biography, which may include isolated sections or chapters devoted to individuals (Berliner 1978; Keil 1979); and the character-driven narrative, in which biographies of many individuals are integrated into the storyline (Lortat-Jacob 1995; Berger 1999). Biographical writing, when approached from an ethnomusicological perspective, necessarily engages the researcher in a host of social, cultural, historical, and personal issues. In writing her book on Egyptian icon Umm Kulthūm, for example, Virginia Danielson was drawn not only to the life story and musical texts of this individual, but also to "larger questions about Egyptian and Arab culture and society" (Danielson 1997:3). As one of her consultants put it, "Egyptians not only like her voice, we respect *her* . . . We look at her, we see fifty years of Egypt's history. She is not only a singer" (ibid.:4; emphasis in original). The iconic performer, Danielson concludes, must be understood as shaped by the society (e.g., its institutions, aesthetics, and imaginative proclivities) that she in turn helped to reshape in innovative ways.

Chapter-length biographies, or those confined to a particular section of the book, such as those found in Paul Berliner's (1978) and Charles Keil's (1979) pioneering ethnographies, appear different in orientation from the book-length biography in that their primary goal is to add some color and specificity to a broadly drawn narrative of a musical culture (see also Capwell 1986). In other cases, biographical chapters or sections are integral to the construction of the narrative as a whole, and general arguments are advanced through these particulars (Kippen 1988; Turino 2000; Florine 2001).

Yet another approach to biography is the character-driven narrative, in which individual personalities move the storyline along just as they might in a work of fiction. Bernard Lortat-Jacob's *Sardinian Chronicles* (1995) is a classic example of this approach. The dissolution of concepts of culture and field, as well as abstract ideas such as "tradition" and "identity," are exemplified here in narrative form as a series of particular encounters between the author and the individuals whose music he is studying. Certain aesthetic preferences, repertory choices, types of musical experience, recognizable expressive and emotive qualities, and parameters of acceptable musical and social interaction are observable. But any totalizing vision of Sardinian "culture" or the research "field" is eschewed.

Assisted Autobiography

The second narrative strategy is "assisted autobiography" (Erdman 1997), in which individual recollections or oral autobiographies are recorded, transcribed, or reprinted by the author in extended form with little or no alteration, restructuring, or interpretive interruptions. Following Jeff Titon (1980) and Veit Erlmann (1996), we differentiate assisted autobiography or assisted life story from anthropological biography or life history primarily by the extensiveness and continuity of the quotations and by the emphasis on accurately presenting the individual's voice. Titon notes that a distinguishing feature of life story is the fact that it is first and foremost a *story*, a fiction that "affirms the identity of the storyteller in the act of telling. The life story tells who one thinks one is and how one thinks one came to be that way" (1980:290). Likewise, in assisted autobiography, the telling is just as important as the facts.

Perhaps the most extended work of assisted autobiography in this corpus is Frisbie and McAllester's oral history, *Blessingway Singer: The Autobiography of*

Frank Mitchell (Mitchell 1978), in which Mitchell himself is credited as author. The book consists primarily of Mitchell's own words, culled from extensive interviews conducted by Frisbie and McAllester. The book is much more than an autobiography, however. In footnotes, the editors give us a considerable amount of contextual information derived from historical and field research, including Mitchell's own correspondence and his comments to other researchers. The "assisted" in assisted autobiography points to the multiple layers of editorial choice and interpretation that are involved in capturing and textualizing an individual's "voice."

Dialogue

The third narrative technique is dialogue, a postmodern ethnographic technique used to de-center ethnographic authority by situating knowledge and historicizing the field encounter (Clifford and Marcus 1986; Marcus and Fischer 1986). This concept is a reaction to totalizing representations, such as the "ethnographic present," which render cultures as closed systems that stand outside of history. It is an approach that seeks to replace the "truth" claimed by an omniscient ethnographer with the "partial truths" generated in the research encounter. In musical ethnography, this takes the form of actual or constructed dialogue between ethnomusicologist and research consultant, and dialogue among research subjects that reveals the tone and content of local discourses about music. Such narratives are written in many ways, including with the use of extended interview transcripts, either standing alone or juxtaposed with an interpretative monologue by the author (Loza 1999; Browner 2002)—this latter technique is referred to as an "ethnographic pair" by Tara Browner (2002), who builds on the work of Mary Louise Pratt (1986) and James Clifford (1988). This approach facilitates the possibility of multiple interpretations by placing the author's monologic narrative directly alongside that of the subject's own words. Another strategy is to write "situated dialogue," distinguishable from interview transcripts by its more literary presentation and its placing of particular speakers within specific contexts. This may involve direct quotation (Levin 1996; Myers 1998) or the author's verbatim recollection of a certain conversation (Herbst 1997).

Another dialogic technique is implicit dialogue or "dialogue in monologic form" (Rice 1994:9–12), a monologue intended to evoke, though not necessariiy reproduce verbatim, the specificity of the fieldwork conversations that inspired it. This is an approach that Michelle Kisliuk (1998) considers carefully. She argues that because "there is no definable border between the 'field' and the space of writing," ethnographic writing is inevitably shaped by the field experience and vice versa. In order to capture this "immediacy and particularity," she adopts a dialogic approach in which "the ethnographer weaves a narrative based on the *conversations* within which she is engaged" (ibid.:14; emphasis in original). The problem of "voice" and representation cannot be solved, she argues, by placing "reams of direct quotes" into the text. What is required is sensitivity to the always shifting power relations involved in the research encounter, something she suggests is best done through this evocative dialogic approach.

Polyvocality

The fourth narrative technique used in individual-centered musical ethnography is "polyvocality" (Clifford and Marcus 1986:15). A well-worn idea in anthropological literary criticism, we define it for our purposes as a strategy for incorporating multiple voices into a narrative. It is distinguishable from biography and dialogue in that voices may not be anchored to particular life histories nor presented in the context of specific conversations or interviews. The emphasis is on individual voice, experience, knowledge, and worldview, any of which may or may not contain biographical information. Polyvocality in its realist form incorporates these multiple voices into an overarching monologic narrative (Monson 1996; Averill 1997). Mark Slobin (1989), in his ethnography of the American Jewish cantorate, chooses this strategy thoughtfully. He writes that he was interested in a "bottom-up" approach, a presentation of the "story" of the *hazzanim* as a "counterpoint of overlapping, sometimes dissonant voices" (ibid.:xi). He approaches the book as a "sourcebook"—an oral history of sorts that allows readers room to hear his informants voices, "enter their world," and form their own interpretations (ibid.:xii). He chose not to contextualize or identify the voices beyond general characteristics (e.g., male, female), because he felt that, in the absence of clearly defined patterns of relationships, it would confuse rather than clarify matters to provide biographical details on all of the speakers, and be too cumbersome to do so with such a large sample.

If realist polyvocality is a strategy for incorporating multiple voices into an otherwise monologic narrative, surrealist polyvocality treats the play and polyphony of voices as constitutive of the narrative itself.[3] This type of experimental technique is rather rare in musical ethnography (see, for example, Herbst 1997 and Myers 1998). Edward Herbst's *Voices in Bali* (1997) is one of the few books using this strategy, and he explicitly rationalizes the use of layered dialogue as an effective way of capturing the author's research process. The originality of his approach lies in its explicit attention to shifts in voice and perspective, the "ongoing continuum between inner experience and outer forms" (ibid.:xx), often marked in the narrative by changes in textual formatting and layout. What is important for Herbst is not only the incorporation of a variety of voices, but also a reflexive attention to shifts in the ethnographer's own voice or perspective. The ethnographer, too, speaks with multiple voices—the scholarly voice, the experiential voice, and the conversational voice, among others.

Analysis of Texts and Performances

The fifth narrative technique we wish to posit is the analysis of musical texts and observations of performances to paint a picture of an individual's life, work, and milieu, with or without explicit reference to biography or autobiography. David Coplan's (1994) study of South Africa's Basotho migrant "word music," or *sefela*, demonstrates how the deep study of texts and performances can reveal the personal aspects of cultural forms, as well as the inclination of individual artists to present their experience in social terms. Coplan's description of sefela captures this paradox neatly: "sefela is a poetic autobiography composed in social context, a personal odyssey of common travails and travels" (ibid.:88). He invokes Raymond Williams's concept of the "structure of feeling" to describe this imaginative process whereby individual artists articulate their own experiences as a finely balanced assessment of the real and ideal, of "social reality and social aspiration" (ibid.:28–29).

This process is what Jeff Titon (1988), in reference to the very different performative tradition of charismatic preaching, refers to as "allegoresis"—the interpretation of life events in terms of broad cultural patterns, belief systems, or community values. This process of allegoresis allows individual memory, through public performance, to become a means of articulating shared beliefs, values, and meanings in the remembered events of everyday life. Titon writes that the pastor Brother John "weld[ed] the church members into one through personal narrative, passing tradition through individual experience to forge communal truth" (ibid.:461). These reflections, along with many others in our corpus (e.g., Qureshi 1986, Shelemay 1998), demonstrate ways in which musical texts and performance analysis can be used to shed light on the seemingly paradoxical position of the individual in ethnomusicology. Musical texts, in these cases, are placed in dialogue with ethnographic observations to advance theoretical discussion of the relationship between individual, culture, society, and history.

Our aims in presenting this typology are both analytic and synthetic. On one hand, we parse ethnomusicological biography into its particular representational techniques and provide examples of the rationales that ethnomusicologists give for each. On the other hand, we treat biographical writing as but one narrative approach among several used to center the individual in musical ethnography. As part of a more broadly conceived ethnomusicology of the individual, we suggest that biography and ethnography are intertwined. Neither one represents a distinct set of research methods, nor an entirely different narrative focus. At the methodological level, the dividing line is unclear, since each may incorporate a combination of methods, including fieldwork and the study of documentary evidence. Nor is the division clear at the level of narrative. The notions of biographical writing as exclusively focused on the personal or unique and of ethnographic writing as denoting the cultural or general do not apply to the ethnomusicology of the individual. The two categories begin to blur as ethnomusicologists direct biography toward culture and society, and channel ethnography into the life experiences and perspectives of individuals.

Conclusions

In our survey of over one hundred book-length musical ethnographies published by ethnomusicologists (and a few fellow travelers) between 1976 and 2002, we found that the study of individuals is now a norm in the discipline even as ethnomusicologists retain an interest in broadly shared musical, cultural, and social processes within communities. It seems that Slobin's (1993) and Stock's (2001) calls for an ethnomusicology of the individual and Rice's (2003) proposal for a subject-centered musical ethnography are being answered within an overarching concern for music as a constituent element of shared culture. No matter how attentive they are to particular musicians in their writing, ethnomusicologists are always at pains to understand those individuals as embedded in or manipulating culturally shared ideas and practices.

The maintenance of a musical culture, however, is far from being a fully shared and coordinated community effort; it is often "intensely personal and idiosyncratic" in its workings, the result of specific relationships between particular teachers and students (Shelemay 1997:199). Kay Kaufman Shelemay has remarked that during field research, abstract concepts such as "culture" and "field" inevitably dissolve into "a stream of individuals" with whom the researcher becomes entangled (ibid.:201). Culture, she suggests, can no longer be thought of as located in a spatial "field" or place where ethnomusicologists study. Rather, culture and field are better thought of as constituted in and through the relationships of individuals. Bruno Nettl (1984) has gone so far as to suggest that the discipline of ethnomusicology is largely defined by these idiosyncratic relationships between master teachers and their ethnomusicologist students. He suggests that the musicians with whom ethnomusicologists study are more than just teachers of individual researchers; they are also "teachers of the field," the primary sources of insight into the relationship between music and culture. It seems clear that while ethnomusicology shares with anthropology an interest in the general and comparable features of culture and society, ethnomusicologists possess an acute awareness, perhaps resulting from the ethnographic method or from the same cultural tropes employed by historical musicologists, of the significance of individuals—including themselves—both to their field research and to the cultures they represent. Still, we aver that the converse of Shelemay's formulation is also true. Ethnomusicologists' engagement with individuals, an inevitable and necessary consequence of information-gathering during fieldwork, leads them into new entanglements with society and culture. Ethnomusicology's ongoing engagement with individuals has revealed the intensely personal aspects of culture, and the fundamentally social aspects of the individual.

This paradoxical situation is evident in our sample of musical ethnographies. In spite of their longstanding and continuing focus on the social life of music and musicians, ethnomusicologists throughout our survey period have included individuals prominently in their books. This corpus, in fact, displays an interesting "curve": at either end of the sample, books that ignore individuals entirely and those that focus the entire narrative on a single individual, family, or ensemble together represent only a small part of the corpus. The vast majority of books fall in the middle, using individuals in some important way for various narrative and theoretical purposes.

We found that the type of individual musician included in these books depends on the author's research goals. Studies of the history of traditions, including the encounter with modernity (about one quarter of the corpus), focus on innovators who made stylistic breakthroughs that dealt with new, emerging cultural, social, political, and economic realities. Fully half of the books deal with key figures, knowledgeable and articulate musicians who occupy respected positions within a tradition, and who help the author make general points about the musical culture. The remaining quarter deal with average musicians and nonmusicians, or they ignore individual musicians altogether. These are narratives animated by themes and issues that trump the particular qualities of innovative or key musicians.

Since fieldwork is the central method used by ethnomusicologists to gather knowledge about musical cultures, it is not surprising that nearly two-thirds of the books feature face-to-face, direct encounters with the individuals featured in the writing. But given what seems to be an increasing concern with the writing of musical histories in ethnomusicology, it is understandable that in about a third of these musical ethnographies the authors complement their fieldwork by researching individuals through printed, archival, and recorded sources.

This study illustrates that the apparent paradox of the individual in ethnomusicology represents not an irresolvable problem, but rather a challenge that has spurred a variety of methodological, theoretical, and narrative solutions. The inclusion of individual musicians may result from ethnomusicologists' attempts to reconcile the particulars of fieldwork with cultural generalization. Individuals may also be included because ethnomusicologists, in their field studies, have been exposed to concepts of selfhood that undercut Western notions of individual autonomy and free agency. The attention to individuals in ethnomusicology also reflects a broader shift in the social sciences towards theories of agency, practice, power, and historical change. Theories of culture that account for modernity and globalization are impetuses as well. The notion that musical cultures are fragmented and deterritorialized seems to drive the now common—indeed, practically unavoidable—ethnomusicological study of individuals. No matter the reason, our survey of musical ethnographies points to how ethnomusicologists seek to understand the cultures and communities they study by paying careful and respectful attention to the individual musicians they encounter in their research.

Notes

1. See Ortner 1984 and 2006 for valuable syntheses of these trends in the social sciences. The emergence of alternative theoretical foundations in ethnomusicology echoes developments in the social sciences during the 1970s and '80s, as outlined by Ortner, when critical theories of gender, race, class, and power dovetailed with a turn toward more historical and practice-oriented approaches to the study of cultures and societies. In a similar vein, see Abu-Lughod's 1991 essay "Writing Against Culture" for a valuable critique of the classic concept of culture.

2. The latter point was inspired by a personal conversation with A. J. Racy, who suggested that for musical biography to be truly ethnomusicological, it must incorporate a range of texts and perspectives—personal, historical, ethnographic, and musical.

3. See Clifford (1981:563–64) on "surrealist ethnography"; see Marcus and Fischer (1986: 45–76) for a discussion of realist, dialogic, and surrealist approaches to ethnographic writing; and see Tyler (1986) on the poetic and polyphonic character of what he calls "post-modern ethnography."

References

Abu-Lughod, Lila. 1991. "Writing against Culture." In *Recapturing Anthropology: Working in the Present*, edited by Richard G. Fox, 137–62. Santa Fe, NM: School of American Research Press.

Allgayer-Kaufmann, Regine. 1987. *O aboio: Der Gesang der Vaqueiros im Nordosten Brasiliens*. Hamburg: Karl Dieter Wagner.

Appadurai, Arjun. 1990. "Disjuncture and Difference in the Global Cultural Economy." *Public Culture* 2(2):1–24.

———. 1991. "Global Ethnoscapes: Notes and Queries for a Transnational Anthropology." In *Recapturing Anthropology: Working in the Present*, edited by Richard G. Fox, 191–210. Santa Fe, NM: School of American Research Press.

Averill, Gage. 1997. *A Day for the Hunter, a Day for the Prey: Popular Music and Power in Haiti*. Chicago: University of Chicago Press.

Baily, John. 2001. "Learning to Perform as a Research Technique in Ethnomusicology." *British Journal of Ethnomusicology* 10(2):85–98.

Bakan, Michael B. 1999. *Music of Death and New Creation: Experiences in the World of Balinese Gamelan Beleganjur*. Chicago: University of Chicago Press.

Becker, Judith. 1980. *Traditional Music in Modern Java: Gamelan in a Changing Society*. Honolulu: University of Hawaii Press.

Berger, Harris M. 1999. *Metal, Rock and Jazz: Perception and the Phenomenology of Musical Experience*. Middletown, CT: Wesleyan University Press.

Berliner, Paul F. 1978. *The Soul of Mbira: Music and Traditions of the Shona People of Zimbabwe*. Berkeley: University of California Press.

Besmer, Fremont. 1983. *Horses, Musicians, and Gods: The Hausa Cult of Possession-Trance*. South Hadley, MA: Bergin and Garvey.

Blau, Dick, Charles Keil, Angeliki Keil, and Steven Feld. 2002. *Bright Balkan Morning: Romani Lives and the Power of Music in Greek Macedonia*. Middletown, CT: Wesleyan University Press.

Bohlman, Philip V. 1989. *Land Where Two Streams Flow: Music in the German-Jewish Community of Israel.* Chicago: University of Illinois Press.

Brinner, Benjamin. 1995. *Knowing Music, Making Music: Javanese Gamelan and the Theory of Musical Competence and Interaction.* Chicago: University of Chicago Press.

Browner, Tara. 2002. *Heartbeat of the People: Music and Dance of the Northern Pow-wow.* Urbana: University of Illinois Press.

Capwell, Charles. 1986. *The Music of the Bauls of Bengal.* Kent, OH: Kent State University Press.

Chenoweth, Vida. 1979. The Usarufas and Their Music. Dallas: SIL Museum of Anthropology.

Clifford, James. 1981. "On Ethnographic Surrealism." *Comparative Studies in Society and History* 23(4):539–64.

———. 1988. *The Predicament of Culture: Twentieth Century Ethnography, Literature, and Art.* Cambridge, MA: Harvard University Press.

Clifford, James, and George E. Marcus. 1986. *Writing Culture: The Poetics and Politics of Ethnography.* Berkeley: University of California Press.

Cooke, Peter. 1986. *The Fiddle Tradition of the Shetland Isles.* Cambridge: Cambridge University Press.

Coplan, David B. 1994. *In the Time of Cannibals: The Word Music of South Africa's Basotho Migrants.* Chicago: University of Chicago Press.

Coppet, Daniel de, and Hugo Zemp. 1978. *'Aré 'aré: un peuple mélanésien et sa musique.* Paris: Éditions du Seuil.

Danielson, Virginia. 1997. *"The Voice of Egypt": Umm Kulthūm, Arabic Song, and Egyptian Society in the Twentieth Century.* Chicago: University of Chicago Press.

Erdman, Joan, with Zohra Segal. 1997. *Stages: The Art and Adventures of Zohra Segal.* New Delhi: Kali for Women.

Erlmann, Veit. 1996. *Nightsong: Performance, Power, and Practice in South Africa.* Chicago: University of Chicago Press.

Florine, Jane L. 2001. *Cuarteto Music and Dancing from Argentina: In Search of the Tunga-Tunga in Córdoba.* Gainesville: University Press of Florida.

Gourlay, Kenneth A. 1978. "Toward a Reassessment of the Ethnomusicologist's Role in Research." *Ethnomusicology* 22(1):1–35.

Groemer, Gerald. 1999. *The Spirit of Tsugaru: Blind Musicians, Tsugaru-Jamisen, and the Folk Music of Northern Japan.* With the Autobiography of Takahashi Chikuzan. Warren, MI: Harmonie Park Press.

Hagedorn, Katherine J. 2001. *Divine Utterance: The Performance of Afro-Cuban Santería.* Washington, D.C.: Smithsonian Institution Press.

Hayward, Philip. 1998. *Music at the Borders: Not Drowning, Waving and Their Engagement with Papua New Guinean Culture (1986–96).* London: J. Libbey.

Herbst, Edward. 1997. *Voices in Bali: Energies and Perceptions in Vocal Music and Dance Theatre.* Middletown, CT: Wesleyan University Press.

Keil, Charles. 1979. *Tiv Song: The Sociology of Art in a Classless Society.* Chicago: University of Chicago Press.

Keyes, Cheryl L. 2002. *Rap Music and Street Consciousness.* Urbana: University of Illinois Press.

Kippen, James. 1988. *The Tabla of Lucknow: A Cultural Analysis of a Musical Tradition.* Cambridge: Cambridge University Press.

Kisliuk, Michelle. 1998. *Seize the Dance: BaAka Musical Life and the Ethnography of Performance.* New York and Oxford: Oxford University Press.

Levin, Theodore. 1996. *The Hundred Thousand Fools of God: Musical Travels in Central Asia (and Queens, New York).* Bloomington: Indiana University Press.

Lortat-Jacob, Bernard. 1995. *Sardinian Chronicles.* Chicago: University of Chicago Press.

Loza, Steven. 1999. *Tito Puente and the Making of Latin Music.* Urbana: University of Illinois Press.

Marcus, George E., and Michael M. J. Fischer. 1986. *Anthropology as Cultural Critique: An Experimental Moment in the Human Sciences.* Chicago: University of Chicago Press.

Merriam, Alan P. 1964. *The Anthropology of Music.* Evanston, IL: Northwestern University Press.

Mitchell, Frank. 1978. *Blessingway Singer: The Autobiography of Frank Mitchell, 1881–1967.* Charlotte Frisbie and David McAllester, eds. Tucson: University of Arizona Press

Moisala, Pirkko. 1991. *Cultural Cognition in Music: Continuity and Change in the Gurung Music of Nepal.* Jyväskylä, Finland: Gummerus Kirjapaino Oy.

Monson, Ingrid T. 1996. *Saying Something: Jazz Improvisation and Interaction.* Chicago: University of Illinois Press.

Muller, Carol Ann. 1999. *Rituals of Fertility and the Sacrifice of Desire: Nazarite Women's Performance in South Africa.* Chicago: University of Chicago Press.

Myers, Helen. 1998. *Music of Hindu Trinidad: Songs from the Indian Diaspora.* Chicago and London: University of Chicago Press.

Nettl, Bruno. 1984. "In Honor of Our Principal Teachers." *Ethnomusicology* 28(2):173–85.

———. 2005. *The Study of Ethnomusicology: Thirty-One Issues and Concepts.* Urbana: University of Illinois Press.

Neuman, Daniel M. [1980] 1990. *The Life of Music in North India: The Organization of an Artistic Tradition.* Chicago: University of Chicago Press.

Ortner, Sherry B. 1984. "Theory in Anthropology Since the Sixties." *Comparative Studies in Society and History* 26(1):126–66.

———. 2006. *Anthropology and Social Theory: Culture, Power, and the Acting Subject.* Durham, NC: Duke University Press.

Pejcheva, Lozanka, and Ventsislav Dimov. 2002. *The Zurna Tradition of Southwest Bulgaria.* Sofia: Bulgarian Musicology Researches.

Peña, Manuel H. 1985. *The Texas-Mexican Conjunto: History of a Working-Class Music.* Austin: University of Texas Press.

Porter, James. 1995. *Jeannie Robertson: Emergent Singer, Transformative Voice.* Knoxville: University of Tennessee Press.

Pratt, Mary Louise. 1986. "Fieldwork in Common Places." In *Writing Culture: The Poetics and Politics of Ethnography,* edited by James Clifford and George E. Marcus, 27–50. Berkeley: University of California Press.

Quigley, Colin. 1995. *Music from the Heart: Compositions of a Folk Fiddler.* Athens: University of Georgia Press.

Qureshi, Regula Burckhardt. 1986. *Sufi Music of India and Pakistan: Sound, Context and Meaning in Qawwali.* Chicago: University of Chicago Press.

Rees, Helen, ed. 2009. *Lives in Chinese Music.* Urbana: University of Illinois Press.

Reily, Suzel. 2002. *Voices of the Magi: Enchanted Journeys in Southeast Brazil.* Chicago: University of Chicago Press.

Rice, Timothy. 1987. "Towards a Remodeling of Ethnomusicology." *Ethnomusicology* 31(3):469–88.

———. 1994. *May it Fill Your Soul: Experiencing Bulgarian Music.* Chicago: University of Chicago Press.

———. 2003. "Time, Place, and Metaphor in Musical Experience and Ethnography." *Ethnomusicology* 47(2):151–79.

Romero, Raúl R. 2001. *Debating the Past: Music, Memory, and Identity in the Andes.* Oxford: Oxford University Press.

Schade-Poulsen, Marc. 1999. *Men and Popular Music in Algeria: The Social Significance of Raï.* Austin: University of Texas Press.

Schechter, John Mendell. 1992. *The Indispensable Harp: Historical Development, Modern Roles, and Configurations in Ecuador and Latin America.* Kent, OH: Kent State University Press.

Seeger, Anthony. 1987. *Why Suyá Sing: A Musical Anthropology of an Amazonian People.* Cambridge: Cambridge University Press.

Shelemay, Kay Kaufman. 1997. "The Ethnomusicologist, Ethnographic Method, and the Transmission of Tradition." In *Shadows in the Field: New Perspectives for Fieldwork in Ethnomusicology,* edited by Gregory E. Barz and Timothy J. Cooley, 189–204. New York and Oxford: Oxford University Press.

———. 1998. *Let Jasmine Rain Down: Song and Remembrance among Syrian Jews.* Chicago: University of Chicago Press.

Simonett, Helena. 2001. *Banda: Mexican Musical Life Across Borders*. Middletown, CT: Wesleyan University Press.

Slobin, Mark. 1976. *Music in the Culture of Northern Afghanistan* (Viking Fund Publication in Anthropology No. 54). Tucson: University of Arizona Press.

———. 1989. *Chosen Voices: The Story of the American Cantorate*. Urbana and Chicago: University of Illinois Press.

———. 1993. *Subcultural Sounds: Micromusics of the West*. Hanover, NH: University Press of New England.

Stock, Jonathan P. J. 1996. *Musical Creativity in Twentieth-century China: Abing, His Music, and Its Changing Meanings*. Rochester, NY: University of Rochester Press.

———. 2001. "Toward an Ethnomusicology of the Individual, or Biographical Writing in Ethnomusicology. *The World of Music* 43(1):5–19.

Sugarman, Jane C. 1997. *Engendering Song: Singing and Subjectivity at Prespa Albanian Weddings*. Chicago: University of Chicago Press.

Titon, Jeff Todd. 1980. "The Life Story." *The Journal of American Folklore* 93(369): 276–92.

———. 1988. *Powerhouse for God: Speech, Chant, and Song in an Appalachian Baptist Church*. Austin: University of Texas Press.

Titon, Jeff Todd, ed. 1984. *Worlds of Music: An Introduction to the Music of the World's Peoples*. New York: Schirmer Books.

Turino, Thomas. 2000. *Nationalists, Cosmopolitans, and Popular Music in Zimbabwe*. Chicago: University of Chicago Press.

Tyler, Stephen A. 1986. "Post-Modern Ethnography: From Document of the Occult to Occult Document." In *Writing Culture: The Poetics and Politics of Ethnography*, edited by James Clifford and George E. Marcus, 122–40. Berkeley: University of California Press.

Vander, Judith. 1988. *Songprints: The Musical Experience of Five Shoshone Women*. Urbana: University of Illinois Press.

Vélez, Maria Teresa. 2000. *Drumming for the Gods: The Life and Times of Felipe Garcia Villamil*. Philadelphia: Temple University Press.

Walser, Robert. 1993. *Running with the Devil: Power, Gender, and Madness in Heavy Metal Music*. Hanover, NH: Wesleyan University Press.

Weisethaunet, Hans. 1998. *The Performance of Everyday Life: The Gäine of Nepal*. Oslo: Scandinavian University Press.

Appendix: Sample of Musical Ethnographies, 1976–2002

Agawu, Kofi. 1995. *African Rhythm: A Northern Ewe Perspective*. Cambridge: Cambridge University Press.

Askew, Kelly. 2002. *Performing the Nation: Swahili Music and Cultural Politics in Tanzania*. Chicago: University of Chicago Press.

Austerlitz, Paul. 1997. *Merengue: Dominican Music and Dominican Identity*. Philadelphia: Temple University Press.

Averill, Gage. 1997. *A Day for the Hunter, a Day for the Prey: Popular Music and Power in Haiti*. Chicago: University of Chicago Press.

Baily, John. 1988. *Music of Afghanistan: Professional Musicians in the City of Herat*. Cambridge and New York: Cambridge University Press.

Bakan, Michael B. 1999. *Music of Death and New Creation: Experiences in the World of Balinese Gamelan Beleganjur*. Chicago: University of Chicago Press.

Becker, Judith. 1980. *Traditional Music in Modern Java: Gamelan in a Changing Society*. Honolulu: University of Hawaii Press.

Berger, Harris M. 1999. *Metal, Rock, and Jazz: Perception and the Phenomenology of Musical Experience*. Middletown, CT: Wesleyan University Press.

Berliner, Paul F. 1978. *The Soul of Mbira: Music and Traditions of the Shona People of Zimbabwe.* Berkeley: University of California Press.

———. 1994. *Thinking in Jazz: The Infinite Art of Improvisation.* Chicago: University of Chicago Press.

Besmer, Fremont. 1983. *Horses, Musicians, and Gods: The Hausa Cult of Possession-Trance.* South Hadley, MA: Bergin and Garvey.

Blau, Dick, Charles Keil, Angeliki Keil, and Steven Feld. 2002. *Bright Balkan Morning: Romani Lives and the Power of Music in Greek Macedonia.* Middletown, CT: Wesleyan University Press.

Bohlman, Philip V. 1989. *Land Where Two Streams Flow: Music in the German-Jewish Community of Israel.* Chicago: University of Illinois Press.

Brinner, Benjamin. 1995. *Knowing Music, Making Music: Javanese Gamelan and the Theory of Musical Competence and Interaction.* Chicago: University of Chicago Press.

Browner, Tara. 2002. *Heartbeat of the People: Music and Dance of the Northern Pow-wow.* Urbana: University of Illinois Press.

Capwell, Charles. 1986. *The Music of the Bauls of Bengal.* Kent, OH: Kent State University Press.

Charry, Eric. 2000. *Mande Music: Traditional and Modern Music of the Maninka and Mandinka of Western Africa.* Chicago: University of Chicago Press.

Chenoweth, Vida. 1979. *The Usarufas and Their Music.* Dallas: SIL Museum of Anthropology.

Chernoff, John Miller. 1979. *African Rhythm and African Sensibility: Aesthetics and Social Action in African Musical Idioms.* Chicago: University of Chicago Press.

Cooke, Peter. 1986. *The Fiddle Tradition of the Shetland Isles.* Cambridge: Cambridge University Press.

Coplan, David B. 1994. *In the Time of Cannibals: The Word Music of South Africa's Basotho Migrants.* Chicago: University of Chicago Press.

Danielson, Virginia. 1997. *"The Voice of Egypt": Umm Kulthūm, Arabic Song, and Egyptian Society in the Twentieth Century.* Chicago: University of Chicago Press.

Diehl, Keila. 2002. *Echoes from Dharamsala: Music in the Life of a Tibetan Refugee Community.* Berkeley: University of California Press.

Ellis, Catherine J. 1985. *Aboriginal Music, Education for Living: Cross-Cultural Experiences from South Australia.* St. Lucia: University of Queensland Press.

Emoff, Ron. 2002. *Recollecting from the Past: Musical Practice and Spirit Possession on the East Coast of Madagascar.* Middletown, CT: Wesleyan University Press.

Erlmann, Veit. 1996. *Nightsong: Performance, Power, and Practice in South Africa.* Chicago: University of Chicago Press.

Feld, Steven. 1982. *Sound and Sentiment: Birds, Weeping, Poetics and Song in Kaluli Expression.* Philadelphia: University of Pennsylvania Press.

Fikentscher, Kai. 2000. *"You Better Work!": Underground Dance Music in New York City.* Middletown, CT: Wesleyan University Press.

Florine, Jane L. 2001. *Cuarteto Music and Dancing from Argentina: In Search of the Tunga-Tunga in Córdoba.* Gainesville: University Press of Florida.

Friedson, Steven M. 1996. *Dancing Prophets: Musical Experience in Tumbuka Healing.* Chicago: University of Chicago Press.

Goertzen, Chris. 1997. *Fiddling for Norway: Revival and Identity.* Chicago: University of Chicago Press.

Groemer, Gerald. 1999. *The Spirit of Tsugaru: Blind Musicians, Tsugaru-jamisen, and the Folk Music of North Japan.* With the Autobiography of Takahashi Chikuzan. Warren, MI: Harmonie Park Press.

Guilbault, Jocelyne. 1993. *Zouk: World Music in the West Indies.* Chicago and London: University of Chicago Press.

Hagedorn, Katherine J. 2001. *Divine Utterance: The Performance of Afro-Cuban Santería.* Washington, D.C.: Smithsonian Institution Press.

Hamilton, James Sadler. 1989. *Sitar Music in Calcutta: An Ethnomusicological Study.* Calgary: University of Calgary Press.

Hayward, Philip. 1998. *Music at the Borders: Not Drowning, Waving and their Engagement with Papua New Guinean Culture (1986–96).* Sydney: J. Libbey.

Herbst, Edward. 1997. *Voices in Bali: Energies and Perceptions in Vocal Music and Dance Theatre*. Middletown, CT: Wesleyan University Press.

Hernandez, Deborah Pacini. 1995. *Bachata : A Social History of Dominican Popular Music*. Philadelphia: Temple University Press.

Hopkins, Pandora. 1986. *Aural Thinking in Norway: Performance and Communication with the Hardingfele*. New York: Human Sciences Press.

Howard, James H., Victoria Lindsay Levine, and Bruno Nettl. 1997. *Choctaw Music and Dance*. Norman: University of Oklahoma Press.

Keeling, Richard. 1992. *Cry for Luck: Sacred Song and Speech among the Yurok, Hupa, and Karok Indians of Northwestern California*. Berkeley: University of California Press.

Keil, Charles. 1979. *Tiv Song: The Sociology of Art in a Classless Society*. Chicago: University of Chicago Press.

Keyes, Cheryl L. 2002. *Rap Music and Street Consciousness*. Urbana: University of Illinois Press.

Kingsbury, Henry. 1988. *Music, Talent, and Performance: A Conservatory Cultural System*. Philadelphia: Temple University Press.

Kippen, James. 1988. *The Tabla of Lucknow: A Cultural Analysis of a Musical Tradition*. Cambridge: Cambridge University Press.

Kisliuk, Michelle. 1998. *Seize the Dance: BaAka Musical Life and the Ethnography of Performance*. New York and Oxford: Oxford University Press.

Koskoff, Ellen. 2000. *Music in Lubavitcher Life*. Urbana: University of Illinois Press.

Lassiter, Luke E. 1998. *The Power of Kiowa Song: A Collaborative Ethnography*. Tucson: University of Arizona Press.

Levin, Theodore. 1996. *The Hundred Thousand Fools of God: Musical Travels in Central Asia (and Queens, New York)*. Bloomington: Indiana University Press.

Lewis, J. Lowell. 1992. *Ring of Liberation: Deceptive Discourse in Brazilian Capoeira*. Chicago: University of Chicago Press.

Lortat-Jacob, Bernard. 1995. *Sardinian Chronicles*. Chicago: University of Chicago Press.

Loza, Steven. 1993. *Barrio Rhythm: Mexican American Music in Los Angeles*. Urbana and Chicago: University of Illinois Press.

———. 1999. *Tito Puente and the Making of Latin Music*. Urbana: University of Illinois Press.

MacKinnon, Niall. 1993. *The British Folk Scene: Musical Performance and Social Identity*. Buckingham: Open University Press.

MacLeod, Bruce A. 1993. *Club Date Musicians: Playing the New York Party Circuit*. Urbana: University of Illinois Press.

Manuel, Peter. 1993. *Cassette Culture: Popular Music and Technology in North India*. Chicago: University of Chicago Press.

———. 2000. *East Indian Music in the West Indies: Tan-Singing, Chutney, and the Making of Indo-Caribbean Culture*. Philadelphia: Temple University Press.

McLean, Mervyn. 1996. *Maori Music*. Auckland: Auckland University Press.

Mitchell, Frank. 1978. *Blessingway Singer: The Autobiography of Frank Mitchell, 1881–1967*. Charlotte Frisbie and David McAllester, eds. Tucson: University of Arizona Press.

Moisala, Pirkko. 1991. *Cultural Cognition in Music: Continuity and Change in the Gurung Music of Nepal*. Jyväskylä, Finland: Gummerus Kirjapaino Oy.

Monson, Ingrid T. 1996. *Saying Something: Jazz Improvisation and Interaction*. Chicago: University of Chicago Press.

Moyle, Richard M. 1979. *Songs of the Pintupi: Musical Life in a Central Australian Society*. Canberra: Australian Institute of Aboriginal Studies.

———. 1986. *Alyawarra Music: Songs and Society in a Central Australian Community*. Canberra: Australian Institute of Aboriginal Studies.

Muller, Carol Ann. 1999. *Rituals of Fertility and the Sacrifice of Desire: Nazarite Women's Performance in South Africa*. Chicago: University of Chicago Press.

Myers, Helen. 1998. *Music of Hindu Trinidad: Songs from the Indian Diaspora.* Chicago and London: University of Chicago Press.

Nelson, Kristina. 1985. *The Art of Reciting the Qur'an.* Austin: University of Texas Press.

Nettl, Bruno. 1995. *Heartland Excursions: Ethnomusicological Reflections on Schools of Music.* Urbana: University of Illinois Press.

Neuman, Daniel M. [1980] 1990. *The Life of Music in North India: The Organization of an Artistic Tradition.* Chicago: University of Chicago Press.

Olsen, Dale A. 1996. *Music of the Warao of Venezuela: Song People of the Rain Forest.* Gainesville: University Press of Florida.

Pegg, Carole. 2001. *Mongolian Music, Dance, & Oral Narrative: Performing Diverse Identities.* Seattle: University of Washington Press.

Pejcheva, Lozanka, and Ventsislav Dimov. 2002. *The Zurna Tradition of Southwest Bulgaria.* Sofia: Bulgarian Musicology Researches.

Peña, Manuel H. 1985. *The Texas-Mexican Conjunto: History of a Working-Class Music.* Austin: University of Texas Press.

———. 1999. *The Mexican American Orquesta : Music, Culture, and the Dialectic of Conflict.* Austin: University of Texas Press.

Porter, James. 1995. *Jeannie Robertson: Emergent Singer, Transformative Voice.* Knoxville: University of Tennessee Press.

Quigley, Colin. 1995. *Music from the Heart: Compositions of a Folk Fiddler.* Athens: University of Georgia Press.

Qureshi, Regula Burckhardt. 1986. *Sufi Music of India and Pakistan: Sound, Context, and Meaning in Qawwali.* Chicago: University of Chicago Press.

Rees, Helen. 2000. *Echoes of History: Naxi Music in Modern China.* New York and Oxford: Oxford University Press.

Reily, Suzel. 2002. *Voices of the Magi: Enchanted Journeys in Southeast Brazil.* Chicago: University of Chicago Press.

Reyes, Adelaida. 1999. *Songs of the Caged, Songs of the Free: Music and the Vietnamese Refugee Experience.* Philadelphia: Temple University Press.

Rice, Timothy. 1994. *May It Fill Your Soul: Experiencing Bulgarian Music.* Chicago: University of Chicago Press.

Romero, Raúl R. 2001. *Debating the Past: Music, Memory, and Identity in the Andes.* Oxford: Oxford University Press

Roseman, Marina. 1991. *Healing Sounds from the Malaysian Rain Forest: Temiar Music and Medicine.* Berkeley: University of California Press.

Sakata, Hiromi Lorraine. 1983. *Music in the Mind: The Concepts of Music and Musician in Afghanistan.* Kent, OH: Kent State University Press.

Sarkissian, Margaret. 2000. *D'Albuquerque's Children: Performing Tradition in Malaysia's Portuguese Settlement.* Chicago: University of Chicago Press.

Schade-Poulsen, Marc. 1999. *Men and Popular Music in Algeria : The Social Significance of Raï.* Austin: University of Texas Press.

Schechter, John Mendell. 1992. *The Indispensable Harp: Historical Development, Modern Roles, and Configurations in Ecuador and Latin America.* Kent, OH: Kent State University Press.

Seeger, Anthony. 1987. *Why Suyá Sing: A Musical Anthropology of an Amazonian People.* Cambridge: Cambridge University Press.

Shelemay, Kay Kaufman. 1998. *Let Jasmine Rain Down: Song and Remembrance among Syrian Jews.* Chicago: University of Chicago Press

Simonett, Helena. 2001. *Banda: Mexican Musical Life Across Borders.* Middletown, CT: Wesleyan University Press.

Slobin, Mark. 1976. *Music in the Culture of Northern Afghanistan.* (Viking Fund Publication in Anthropology No. 54.) Tucson: University of Arizona Press.

———. 1989. *Chosen Voices: The Story of the American Cantorate.* Urbana and Chicago: University of Illinois Press.

———. 2000. *Fiddler on the Move Exploring the Klezmer World.* New York and Oxford: Oxford University Press.

Stock, Jonathan P. J. 1996. *Musical Creativity in Twentieth-century China: Abing, His Music, and Its Changing Meaning.* Rochester, NY: University of Rochester Press.

Stokes, Martin. 1992. *The Arabesk Debate: Music and Musicians in Modern Turkey.* Oxford: Clarendon Press.

Stone, Ruth M. 1982. *Let the Inside Be Sweet: The Interpretation of Music Event Among the Kpelle People of Liberia.* Bloomington: Indiana University Press.

Sugarman, Jane C. 1997. *Engendering Song: Singing and Subjectivity at Prespa Albanian Weddings.* Chicago: University of Chicago Press.

Summit, Jeffrey A. 2000. *The Lord's Song in a Strange Land: Music and Identity in Contemporary Jewish Worship.* Oxford and New York: Oxford University Press.

Sutton, R. Anderson. 1991. *Traditions of Gamelan Music in Java: Musical Pluralism and Regional Identity.* Cambridge: Cambridge University Press.

———. 2002. *Calling Back the Spirit: Music, Dance, and Cultural Politics in Lowland South Sulawesi.* Oxford: Oxford University Press.

Tenzer, Michael. 2000. Gamelan Gong Kebyar: *The Art of Twentieth-Century Balinese Music.* Chicago: University of Chicago Press.

Titon, Jeff Todd. 1988. *Powerhouse for God: Speech, Chant, and Song in an Appalachian Baptist Church.* Austin: University of Texas Press.

Turino, Thomas. 1993. *Moving Away from Silence: Music of the Peruvian Altiplano and the Experience of Urban Migration.* Chicago: University of Chicago Press.

———. 2000. *Nationalist, Cosmopolitans, and Popular Music in Zimbabwe.* Chicago: University of Chicago Press.

Vander, Judith. 1988. *Songprints: The Musical Experience of Five Shoshone Women.* Urbana: University of Illinois Press.

———. 1997. *Shoshone Ghost Dance Religion: Poetry Songs and Great Basin Context.* Urbana: University of Illinois Press.

Vélez, Maria Teresa. 2000. *Drumming for the Gods: The Life and Times of Felipe Garcia Villamil.* Philadelphia: Temple University Press.

Wade, Peter. 2000. *Music, Race, and Nation: Música Tropical in Colombia.* Chicago: University of Chicago Press.

Walser, Robert. 1993. *Running with the Devil: Power, Gender, and Madness in Heavy Metal Music.* Hanover, NH: Wesleyan University Press.

Waterman, Christopher Alan. 1990. *Jùjú: A Social History and Ethnography of an African Popular Music.* Chicago: University of Chicago Press.

Waxer, Lise. 2002. *The City of Musical Memory: Salsa, Record Groove and Popular Culture in Cali, Columbia.* Middletown, CT: Wesleyan University Press.

Weisethaunet, Hans. 1998. *The Performance of Everyday Life: The Gäine of Nepal.* Oslo: Scandinavian University Press.

Williams, Sean. 2001. *The Sound of the Ancestral Ship: Highland Music of West Java.* Oxford: Oxford University Press.

Witzleben, J. Lawrence. 1995. *Silk and Bamboo Music in Shanghai: The Jiangnan Sizhu Ensemble Tradition.* Kent, OH: Kent State University Press.

Wong, Deborah. 2000. *Sounding the Center: History and Aesthetics in Thai Buddhist Performance.* Chicago: University of Chicago Press.

Yung, Bell. 1989. *Cantonese Opera: Performance as a Creative Process.* Cambridge: Cambridge University Press.

Zanten, Wim van. 1989. *Sundanese Music in the Cianjuran Style: Anthropological and Musicological Aspects of Tembang Sunda.* Providence, RI: Foris Publications.

PART II

Recent Trends in Ethnomusicology

Mieczyslaw Kolinski / University of Toronto
Toronto, Ontario, Canada

M usic has been created by man and constitutes an essential facet of his cultural manifestations; therefore, it cannot be properly investigated if approached as an isolated phenomenon. While it is to be welcomed that, in principle, this concept has been more and more widely recognized, its one-sided application tends to confuse rather than to clarify the real issue. The study of the vital part that music plays in the cultural life of many societies is a fascinating and rewarding objective; an excellent example of this kind of research is John Blacking's brilliant paper on "The Role of Music in the Culture of the Venda of the Northern Transvaal" (Blacking 1965). However, the general views expressed by that author at the outset of his article, and shared by a number of present-day scholars, call for a reexamination of the problems involved.

Blacking contends that "The roots of musical variety are to be found in culture and not in music, and in the human organization of sound rather than in its natural qualities. . . . There may be universal laws of sound, but there are unlikely to be universal laws of music-making. . . ." He concludes that "Two musical styles may have similar patterns of rhythm and melody, but unless we know their cultural background, we cannot postulate any but the most superficial relationship between them" (p. 20). However, extensive comparative studies of the musical styles of many societies around the world have disclosed that the startling variety of musical idioms is contained within the boundaries of certain basic principles of sound construction which function regardless of the cultural context and which, evidently, are deeply rooted in the structure of the central nervous system of *homo sapiens*. To support his thesis that "the roots of musical variety are to be found in culture and not in music" (p. 20), Blacking discusses a few instances of "cultural determinants of musical structure" in Venda music (pp. 47–48). But in substance he merely reaffirms a matter which has never been

From *Ethnomusicology*, Vol. 11, No. 1 (Jan. 1967), pp. 1–24 seriously questioned: the importance of a thorough investigation of the inter-dependence of music and dance on the one hand, and of music and language on the other, particularly in the case of languages with speech-tones such as the Venda.

Perhaps the most significant recent work based on the assumption that only culture determines musical structure is Alan P. Merriam's *Anthropology of Music* (1964). In the chapter "Toward a Theory for Ethnomusicology" he states that "the sounds of music are shaped by the culture of which they are part. . . . Music depends on pitch and rhythm, but only as they are agreed upon by members of the particular society involved" (p. 27). Merriam discusses the antithesis of "the study of music in culture" (1960:112) and of an approach which treats music "as an isolable value in itself" (1964:29). While the author's rejection of the latter concept is perfectly justified, unless its meaning is distorted by an arbitrary interpretation, his assumption that "the study of music in culture" represents the only alternative has to be challenged because it leaves no room for the investigation of the above-mentioned general trends of sound construction which are conditioned by the biological constitution of the brain and which function regardless of cultural context. Biology and culture cannot be divorced from each other. "The fact which must be stressed, because it has frequently been missed or misrepresented, is that the biological and cultural evolutions are parts of the same natural process" (Dobzhansky 1962:22).

Before analyzing the nature of the impact of the biological factor on musical structure, it seems necessary to further examine Merriam's views on the theoretical foundation of ethnomusicology. Starting from the premise that "the dual nature of ethnomusicology is clearly a fact of the discipline," the author attempts to arrive at a synthetic concept merging the anthropological and musicological aspects of the discipline into a homogeneous whole. He emphasizes that "such a fusion is clearly the objective of ethnomusicology and the keystone upon which the validity of its contribution lies" (1964:17). But in spite of the author's sincere desire to do equal justice to both musicology and anthropology, his whole approach denotes a completely anthropological orientation towards the problems involved in ethnomusicological studies. In fact, a major part of his book perfectly fulfills the reader's expectation raised by its title; it is, indeed, an outstanding contribution to "The Anthropology of Music." This situation leads to the question whether a balanced fusion of musicological and anthropological elements on the basis of Merriam's "music in culture" concept is possible or even desirable. Referring to Kunst's recommendation that the discipline of comparative musicology be rechristened "ethnomusicology," Merriam claims that its quick acceptance stresses "the fact that music does not exist by and of itself but is part of the totality of human behavior" (1960:108); however, the only argument given by Kunst in favor of the suggested change is the fact that the discipline "does not compare any more than any other science" (1955:9).

It might be added that a factor which probably contributed to the more or less general acceptance of the term was the last-minute change—following a suggestion of mine—of the originally planned name from "The American Society for Comparative Musicology" to "The Society for Ethnomusicology." The subsequent choice of the name of "Ethnomusicology" for the official Journal of the Society was also instrumental in the acceptance of the new name for the field.

At the outset of this article I stressed, in agreement with Merriam and other ethnomusicologists, the importance of the thesis that music cannot be approached as an isolated phenomenon; however, Merriam's extreme and one-sided contention that "music is a . . . phenomenon which exists only in terms of social interaction" (1964:27) seems untenable. Without attempting to find a universally valid definition of what music is, it may be said that music, being created by man, is a product of his general physio-psychological constitution, motivated and diversified both by individual or collective inventiveness and by cultural environment. Paradoxically, Merriam calls "music" what in reality constitutes its social framework, and consistently speaks of "music sound" when dealing with actual musical creation; as a result, he strongly advocates the primacy of "folk evaluation" over "analytical evaluation" (1964:31–32). These terms refer to two kinds of information sources available for the study of a musical style: folk evaluation obtains the data from the people who created the music, analytical evaluation from an analysis of the music itself. The author insists that "the folk evaluation is a necessity to the investigator, for without it he cannot know whether his analysis is present in the data or whether he has himself inserted it. This is not to say that the investigator puts nothing more into his materials than he takes out from the folk evaluation; to the contrary, it is his job to do so. But what he puts into the data must be built upon what he first learns from the culture at hand about its music and its music system, taken in the broadest sense. He is then in a position to generalize about that system from his broader knowledge of music systems in general" (p. 32}.

The gathering and assessing of data obtained from the "folk evaluation" of a musical style certainly contributes to an understanding of the cultural orientation of the society involved, but this kind of information source can hardly serve as a basis for the structural analysis of its music. Merriam contends that in order to carry out such an analysis it is necessary to know what the members of the particular society consider to be "music on the one hand, and noise, or non-music, on the other"; he deems this information "basic to the understanding of music in any society" because "what is considered to be music or non-music sound determines the nature of music in any given society" (p. 63). In support of his thesis he discusses the folk evaluation of music by the Basongye, one of the populations among whom he has conducted his major field research in problems of ethnography and ethnomusicology. As a result of "detailed questioning and observation" as well as of an interpretation of aphorismic statements such as 'When you are content, you sing; when you are angry, you make noise," the author arrives at the following three-part "theory" of noise and music as held by the Basongye: "In the first place, music for the Basongye always involves human beings. . . . No informant classifies the sound of 'singing' birds as music, nor does the wind 'sing' in the trees. . . . The second point in the Basongye 'theory' of what constitutes music sound is that such sound must always be organized. . . . The third criterion . . . is that to be music the sounds must have a minimal continuity in time" (pp. 64–66). This Basongye "theory" is highly interesting in that it implies an extremely broad definition of music; it states in fact that music is a human creation of sound organized in time. However, one is at a loss trying to discover in what respect this folk evaluation could be of any value for the transcription and structural analysis of the music of the Basongye. The same problem arises with regard to many other data presented by Merriam concerning folk evaluation of music. At best, they may provide adjunctive rather than essential information about musical structure. So we see that Merriam's insistence on the primacy of folk evaluation over analytical evaluation is justified only with regard to matters of essentially anthropological and not of essentially musicological concern. This dichotomy calls for a reexamination of the meaning of Merriam's basic premise that "the dual nature of ethnomusicology is clearly a fact of the discipline" (p. 17). In order to approach this question in an objective way it seems advisable: 1) to disregard for a moment the existence of ethnomusicology, no matter what is meant by this term; 2) to determine the place that music holds within the scheme of anthropological investigation; and 3) to delimit the scope of musicological research. In reference to point 2) it is evident that the study of the role which music plays in the culture of man is an important facet of anthropological investigation; this all the more since, as Merriam states in another context, "music is interrelated with the rest of culture; it can and does shape, strengthen, and channel social, political, economic, linguistic, religious, and other kinds of behavior" (p. 15). This intrinsic and significant function of music in culture makes it requisite to include musical anthropology within the curriculum of general cultural anthropology. With regard to point 3) it might here suffice to mention that musicology should embrace two interrelated branches: the study of idiocultural and of allocultural music. These terms refer to the music of one's own culture, respectively to that of foreign cultures. They have been chosen to avoid Western ethnocentricism; for example, to the Japanese musicologist the study of Western music is, of course, allocultural. There is a marked difference between the anthropological and the musicological approach to music, although it is a difference in focus and emphasis rather than in substance. While the anthropologist's interest in music concentrates upon its function within the complexity of man's culture, the same area of investigation represents to the musicologist merely one of several facets of contextual subject matters relative to the study of music itself. As Charles Seeger precisely and concisely states: "music is the 'text' of musicology" (1963:215). He refers to its context "as defined by the various sciences and critiques that concern themselves with the environment of music and musicology, viz.: physics, physiology, psychology, anthropology, aesthetics, philosophy, general value theory, etc." (*ibid.*). The thesis that music itself constitutes the essential object of musicological study by no means implies that music should or could be treated as an isolated phenomenon. Merriam is mistaken when he contends that "music sound has been treated as a closed system which operates according to principles and regularities inherent in itself and quite separate from the human beings that produce it" (1964:29). No musicologist is so foolish as to ignore that music is a human creation. But this fact is so self-evident that, as a rule, a musicologist who analyzes musical structure and attempts to determine certain "principles and regularities" inherent in a particular musical style or reflecting more general trends of musical construction hardly feels the need to remind us that these traits emanate from the human beings which produce the music.

One of the most ambitious objectives of musicological research is the comparative analysis of the known musical styles of the world's peoples designed to establish their distinguishing features and, ultimately, to search for universals providing a common basis for the immense variety of musical creations. The most appropriate term for this field of study appears to be *comparative musicology*. While it is true that comparison is a characteristic feature of every scholarly investigation, the epithet *comparative* emphasizes the broad comparative vistas involved. This terminology is in line with the unchallenged use of the same epithet for a great number of other disciplinary subdivisions, such as comparative literature, comparative phonetics, comparative psychology or comparative anatomy.

The previous discussion will enable us to reassess Merriam's premise that "the dual nature of ethnomusicology is clearly a fact of the discipline." Two basic questions have to be answered: 1) Is the nature of ethnomusicology dual? and 2) can ethnomusicology be considered as one discipline? Among the various approaches to ethnomusicology two stand out as the most significant; they are precisely those two fields of study that have been previously characterized as *musical anthropology* and *comparative musicology*; so the claim of a dual nature of ethnomusicology seems perfectly justified. It has been shown that musical anthropology forms an integral part of general anthropology to the same extent that comparative musicology forms an integral part of general musicology: therefore, the fusion of these two subject matters into one autonomous discipline seems inconceivable. This, however, does not at all mean that ethnomusicology has no *raison d'être*; to the contrary, a broad area of common concern urgently calls for a close cooperation between musical anthropologist and comparative musicologist; but the crucial point is that ethnomusicology should be conceived as a cross-disciplinary field of study rather than as one single discipline.

An acceptance of this concept would noticeably advance the cause of ethnomusicology: it would insure a sound balance between relative autonomy and interdependence of musical anthropology and comparative musicology; it would stimulate meaningful teamwork and mutual appreciation; and it would dispense the comparative musicologist and the musical anthropologist from the often unachievable, and therefore quite discouraging, obligation to become both a proficient anthropologist and musicologist as well as an accomplished expert in the highly technical and intricate task of transcribing recorded music, in particular with regard to allocultural musical styles.

It might be useful to evaluate some aspects of Merriam's fusion theory in the light of the above outlined cross-disciplinary concept of ethnomusicology. Most surprising is the striking opposition between Merriam's aim to arrive at a balanced merger in which neither the anthropological nor the musicological element gains ascendancy, and between the fact that his approach has not only an entirely anthropological orientation but also strongly discriminates against that essential facet of musicological research which has previously been characterized as comparative musicology. Paradoxically, Merriam criticizes this field of study as being "descriptive" and uses the epithet in a pejorative sense. Since the primary interest of comparative musicology, just as of musicology in general, is focused on music itself and not on its social and cultural context, Merriam deplores that "much of ethnomusicology has not gone beyond the descriptive phase of study" (1964:29–30). Thus, he does not seem to realize that the analysis of a single musical style is descriptive, no matter whether it is carried out from a primarily musicological or from a primarily ethnological angle; nor does he seem to admit that, for example, a cross-cultural study of the shape of melody is just as broadly comparative as, let us say, a cross-cultural study of "folk evaluation" of the standards of excellence in performance. At the root of this sort of discrimination lies a basic misconception in the judgment of which fields of study are broad, important and meaningful, or limited, unessential and technical. Merriam does not recognize the fact that musical aspects which appear limited, unessential and technical to the anthropologist might be of broad and meaningful significance to the musicologist. He degrades, indeed, the whole musicological discipline, both in its historical and comparative division, to an auxiliary branch of musical anthropology when he declares that "while the study of music as a structural form and as an historic phenomenon is of high, and basic importance, in my own view it holds this position primarily as it leads to the study of the broader questions of music in culture" (1960:113). This misconception brings about an unfounded indictment of the practice of transcribing and analyzing music recorded in the field by someone else. Merriam distinguishes three types of ethnomusicological investigation: field work, laboratory analysis, and armchair analysis. While there is general agreement that the main objective of the field worker should be "the study of music in culture," Merriam's dichotomy of the "homework" into laboratory and armchair analysis calls for a comment. According to Merriam, the laboratory phase of study has to be carried out by the field worker himself and should include: 1) "the collation of ethnographic and ethnologic materials into a coherent body of knowledge about music practice, behavior, and concepts in the society being studied . . ."; and 2) "the technical laboratory analysis of the music sound materials collected, and this requires special techniques and sometimes special equipment for the transcription and structural analysis of music" (1964:7–8). It is obvious that the cultural data have to be analyzed by the field worker himself; the same could be said with regard to the transcription and analysis of the music, if the field worker is apt to accomplish this task. However, since the latter is supposed to be a full-fledged cultural anthropologist, his chances of being capable to competently handle such a highly specialized and involved matter are rather slim. Referring to "the regrettable tendency to resort to armchair analysis" (p. 39), Merriam states that "the day of the 'armchair ethnomusicologist' who sits in the laboratory and analyzes the music that others have recorded . . . is fast passing in our discipline" (p. 113). Supposing this activity has become a thing of the past, would the situation be as ideal as Merriam anticipates? Quite to the contrary, its consequences would be most harmful for the future development of ethnomusicology, both in its comparative-musicological and anthropological branches. Thorough and competent transcription and analysis of available dependable field recordings of traditional music is one of the cornerstones of ethnomusicological research; but unfortunately only a small portion of this phonographic material has, thus far, been investigated. This unbalanced situation existed even in the early period of comparative musicology when as little as a couple of minutes of music could be recorded on one wax cylinder; and of course the breath-taking progress in the field of recording devices, culminating in the tape recorder era, strongly contributed to the broadening of the gap. So it is obvious that this discrepancy would take alarming proportions if anthropologists transcribing their own field recordings were considered the only legitimate analysts of allocultural music. Under these circumstances, anthropologists with some musical background, but without specific qualification, would be tempted to transcribe their own material; on the other hand, comparative musicologists would want to do field work and to collect recordings without the thorough anthropological training necessary for a successful investigation of the multifarious phenomenon of music in culture.

If, however, we recognize the cross-disciplinary nature of ethnomusicology, it becomes apparent that the only workable approach to the problem under discussion is a close cooperation between the musical anthropologist and the comparative musicologist, representing a team which combines the comprehensive resources of cultural anthropology and musicology with the musical ability and technical skill needed for an adequate transcription and analysis of allocultural music. The stages of a joint project designed to explore the music of a certain area can be outlined as follows: if the team has been established in advance, a preliminary mutual contact might be useful, giving the musicologist an opportunity to suggest to the prospective field worker the investigation of certain problems of primarily musicological interest not requiring any particular musical training. With regard to the general methods and techniques to be employed in the field, the musical anthropologist will find ample, valuable, and stimulating recommendations in Merriam's *Anthropology of Music*. The "laboratory" phase of the ethnomusicological project will start with the evaluation by the anthropologist of the data gathered by himself during the field work. The results obtained will be communicated to the musicologist who will study them and decide which aspects of the findings might be useful for the transcription and/or analysis of the field recordings. In turn, the analysis of the notated phonographic material, though based upon musicological methods, might well corroborate (or challenge) assumptions put forward by the anthropologist.

From an ethnomusicological point of view the situation is not too different when the field work is carried out by an anthropologist investigating the whole complex of cultural manifestations of a people, because the scope of his research will certainly encompass the study of music in culture. As an illustration of this kind of teamwork may be mentioned my collaboration with the late anthropologist Melville J. Herskovits involving the transcription and analysis of approximately one thousand songs recorded during his field trips to West Africa, Haiti, and Dutch Guiana. The choice of these areas was motivated by Herskovits' concern with the problem of the survival of African Negro culture traits in the Western Hemisphere. A comparative stylistic evaluation of the music corroborated and broadened Herskovits' ethnological findings (Kolinski 1936:515–520).

Within the framework of the cross-disciplinary concept of ethnomusicology the anthropological facet might best be defined as "the study of music in culture." This phrase has, of course, been borrowed from Merriam's general definition of ethnomusicology as "the study of music in culture." It must be made clear, however, that the meaning of the phrase markedly differs in the two contexts. In the cross-disciplinary concept it stands for one of two subject matters of equal importance, the other being comparative musicology, while in Merriam's fusion theory it means a complete subordination of the whole musicological discipline to an anthropological concept (see above). There is no doubt that Merriam's work comprises an impressive range of valuable information stimulating the anthropological branch of ethnomusicology; however, his above-mentioned attitude toward musicology, coupled with his adherence to an extreme behavioral school of thought denying any impact of psycho-physiological factors upon musical structure, does not serve the cause of comparative musicology and, therefore, of ethnomusicology in general.

What is urgently needed is the formulation of concepts and methods designed to bring about an objective, thorough, and meaningful analysis of musical structure. We cannot accept or reject *a priori* the contention that all musical structure is culturally derived unless we have examined all available pertinent data. As previously mentioned, such a large-scale investigation was carried out and resulted in the formulation of the thesis that the immense structural variety of musical styles represents a culturally derived diversification of psycho-physiological universals.

I dealt with the different aspects and implications of this thesis in a series of papers to which I wish to refer the reader (Kolinski 1957a, 1957b, 1959, 1960, 1961, 1962, 1964, 1965a, 1965b): therefore, I want now to limit myself to the discussion of one basic point.

Nature provided man with a melody instrument of greatest possibilities ages before his material culture permitted him to concern himself with the construction and the use of melody instruments. So the existing, well-organized tonal patterns of tribal vocal music took shape without instrumental prototypes. Since the human voice is able to produce with equal facility a virtually unlimited number of pitch shades within the natural limits of its range, we are faced with the crucial problem of: 1) what causes the singer to select certain tones out of this pitch continuum and to organize them into coherent structures; and 2) why similar patterns of tonal construction can be found in widely separated areas and in strongly contrasting cultures, such as the so-called halftoneless pentatonic scale (for example, C D E G A) which "Europe shares with a large part of the world, particularly with Northern Asia, with American Indians, and with Negro Africa" (Nettl 1965:41).

Before answering these questions it seems necessary to reexamine the current concepts on the main properties of sound that the human ear is able to discern. It is generally taken for granted that these properties are: pitch, loudness and timbre, with frequency, amplitude and wave form as their physical correlates. Loudness and timbre may be disregarded as determinants of tonal structure in tribal vocal music, so the only remaining property that could possibly be considered as a determinant would be pitch. But since the gamut of pitch shades represents a continuum which gradually changes from the lowest to the highest register, comparable to the gradual change from black to white through the gamut of shades of gray, intervals would have to be defined, measured, and classified exclusively in terms of their size. This would preclude any crystallization of certain intervals into distinct entities. It would indeed be absurd and futile to attempt, for example, to interpret the tonal structure of the following Deer Society song of the Pawnee Indians as a complex of distances chosen out of the indistinct continuum of pitch shades (Fig. 1; Densmore 1929:song 22):

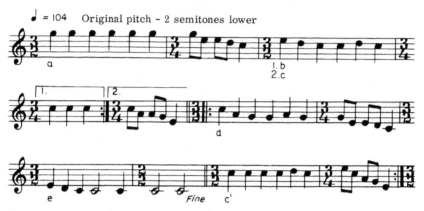

Figure 1. Pawnee Indians. Song of the Deer Society.

On the other hand, intervals are often described in terms of vibration ratios, and the fact that approximations to simple ratios, such as 1:2, 2:3 and 3:4, produce intervals which are structurally prominent in tribal vocal music raises the question whether the human ear may perceive another property of sound which, contrary to the pitch continuum, is capable of investing certain intervals with specific distinguishing characteristics. Whenever men and women intend to perform a tune in unison, they sing it, as a rule, in parallel octaves. We deal here with a universal which can be observed in the most contrasting cultural environments. The question of whether octave tones are to be conceived as identical phenomena has been extensively discussed. While it is true that the component tones of an octave appear identical in a certain respect, this identity refers to none of the currently recognized properties of sound, that is, neither to pitch nor to loudness or timbre. In fact, there is a considerable opposition between the pitch shades of the component tones of a simple octave, and an extreme contrast with regard to multiple octaves; on the other hand, even a complete identity in both loudness and timbre of the component tones of non-octave intervals, such as a major seventh or a minor ninth, yields nothing comparable to the phenomenon of octave identity. So we see that the property of sound which is identical in octave tones and different with regard to other intervals constitutes another dimension of aural perception clearly distinct from the dimensions of pitch, loudness, and timbre. I have suggested the term *tint* for this property of sound; for example, the tint C would be the property common to all C's, the tint

D the property common to all D's, etc., while C and D would represent different tints. As a matter of fact, this term would simply replace the vague and ambiguous term *tone*, often used in the same sense. For example, a penta*tonic* scale is characterized by a combination of five tints rather than of five pitches; so the pentatonic structure C D E G A C D E G of the above-mentioned Pawnee song comprises five tints and not five pitches, just as the Western twelve-*tone* system comprises twelve tints and not twelve pitches.

A comparison with corresponding properties of visual perception may further clarify the nature of tint. Sensory psychology distinguishes between achromatic and chromatic colors. The former comprise the continuum of shades of gray gradually leading from black to white; as already mentioned, that dimension of color experience may be likened to the pitch continuum gradually leading from the lowest to the highest register. The chromatic colors are those comprised in the solar spectrum, or rather in the so-called *color circle* which includes the purples between the red and violet ends of the spectrum. "The circumference of the color circle describes one dimension of color experience, *hue*—the technical term for the quality of redness, blueness, yellowness, or greenness that differentiates one color from another" (Hilgard 1962:229). While intersense analogies are always limited to a certain extent, there is a close correlation between some aspects of the visual property of hue and of the auditory property of tint. For example, the following series of ascending octaves,

Figure 2.

which represents the tint C on five pitch levels, is comparable to one hue, let us say red, produced in five levels of brightness, that is, very dark, medium dark, medium, medium clear, and very clear. On the other hand, the interval of a minor second, which consists of two different tints located on mutually close pitch levels, is comparable to two different hues of mutually close levels of brightness.

These two examples illustrate the fact that both hue and tint are properties of a distinctive-qualitative nature in contrast to the continuative-quantitative character of visual brightness and pitch. While it remains to analyze the relation between different tints, the preliminary answer to the question of what enables the tribal singer to select, without instrumental prototypes, certain tones out of the pitch continuum and why similar patterns of tonal construction can be found in widely separated areas and in strongly contrasting cultures, is precisely the aforementioned distinctive-qualitative nature of the auditory property of tint. Its opposition to the continuative-qualitative character of pitch is reflected in the opposition between the physical correlates of these two properties of sound: those of the pitch continuum are the gradually increasing or decreasing frequencies; those of tint identity and tint affinity are distinct simple vibration ratios such as 1:2 for the octave, 2:3 for the fifth, and 3:4 for the fourth. However, we cannot approach the highly complicated process of sensory perception from a purely arithmetical angle. So we have to take into account the general perceptual phenomenon known as the *difference threshold*; it refers to the minimum amount of difference among stimuli necessary before one can be distinguished from another. While there is, for example, a strict correlation between frequency and pitch, two different frequencies will produce an identical pitch perception if their difference is below threshold. Similarly, two intervals of different size will be identically perceived if the difference is below threshold. Let us suppose that one of these intervals is a perfect fifth characterized by a high degree of tint affinity and by the concomitant vibration ratio 2:3; in this case a subliminal alteration of its size would change this simple ratio into an irrational one without affecting its perception. Even perceivable deviations might not necessarily impair the structural impact of simple vibration ratios upon intervals, and it would be a serious mistake to ignore fundamental norms because of their relative flexibility. No less unjustified, on the other hand, would be an approach postulating *a priori* a particular system of vibration ratios, such as the one represented by the series of overtones, as a norm which organizes certain facets of auditory perception. Only by refraining from any kind of speculation and by objectively observing and analyzing all available relevant data is it possible to contribute to a clarification of the problems involved.

It has been mentioned that "whenever men and women intend to perform a tune in unison, they sing it, as a rule, in parallel octaves." To this statement it should be added that both in tribal and other music, including our own, the octave parallels are sometimes replaced by parallels in perfect fifths or fourths without an awareness by the singers that they do not perform in unison. This is a particularly strong evidence of the close tint affinity between the component tones of both the fifth and the fourth. The following youth initiation song of the Fuegian Indians, transcribed by Hornbostel (1948:99) may illustrate this kind of unintentional multisonance (a term designed to cover the harmonic, polyphonic and heterophonic facets of sound simultaneousness):

Figure 3. Fuegian Indians. Youth Initiation Song.

One of Hornbostel's basic premises is the thesis that tribal music discloses structural principles which are entirely opposed to those governing post-medieval Western music. As far as tonal structure is concerned Hornbostel draws a sharp line of demarcation between Western and non-Western music. To him "the main difference is this: our music (since about A.D. 1600) is built on harmony, all other music on pure melody. . . . Typically melodic steps are comparatively small, amounting, at most, to a major third or so. But within this group of small intervals no distinctions are made: a 'third' is not different in its function from a 'second,' and the width of an interval can vary time after time within wide margins" (1928:7). The only purely melodic intervals which are relatively stable are those "of perfect consonance (octaves, fifths, fourths, but not thirds); and even these need not be 'in tune'" (p. 9). According to Hornbostel not only octaves but also fourths and fifths "are too wide to be used in melodic sequence; one rarely leaps from a note immediately to its fourth or fifth" (p. 9). These considerations lead Hornbostel to the following interpretation of the almost universal phenomenon of halftoneless pentatonic patterns: two superimposed fourths form the tonal skeleton and either of these fourths is bridged by an intermediate step of indefinite size (p. 10).

Although this approach represents a serious and imaginative attempt to deal with strictly nonharmonic tonal structures such as those of tribal vocal music, it has to be rejected because essential facets of it are contradicted by strong factual evidence. The structural importance of the fourth and fifth in tribal vocal music is a well-known fact, provided, of course, that the tonal range reaches the size of one of these intervals; the same is true with regard to the octave. However, Hornbostel's claim that within the group of intervals smaller than a fourth "no distinctions are made" and that "a 'third' is not different in its function from a 'second,' and the width of an interval can vary time after time within wide margins" is in complete opposition to the real situation. While more or less noticeable intonational fluctuations can be observed within all types of unaccompanied vocal music, thousands of tribal songs could serve as examples demonstrating the tribal singer's ability to clearly distinguish between a minor second, a major second, a minor third, and a major third. These observations are corroborated, for example, by Nettl. Discussing the different intervals used in tribal songs he states that "these melodic intervals almost always approximate their Western equivalents. . . . Tonometric figures evidently give results which challenge this statement; they indicate a large number of melodic intervals absent from nonprimitive music. No doubt the discrepancy exists because the tonometer measures pitches to a point of accuracy far beyond that of the human ear; the *significant* primitive melodic intervals nonetheless correspond closely to Western ones" (1956:54). Because of Merriam's adherence to the general concept of music as learned behavior and to the specific one of intervals as "distances between tones" (1964:121), his following observations are particularly significant. Referring to the Basongye of the Congo, Merriam reports that "there is . . . a perfectly good ability to hear different intervals," that "every musician recognizes by ear that a major and minor third are not the same thing," and that "musicians are completely capable of distinguishing" major and minor seconds "*in abstracto*" (pp. 120–21). As far as seconds are concerned, tribal song not only clearly distinguishes between major and minor ones, but the presence or absence of the latter might constitute a characteristic stylistic feature. For example, a comparison between 307 Dahomean and 119 Ashanti songs showed that 84% of the Dahomean songs, but only 9% of the Ashanti songs, are completely halftoneless (Kolinski 1938:69). No less striking is, in many tribal vocal styles, the contrast between the frequency of the two types of seconds employed, the preference being always given to the major second. In a sampling which included the counting of steps employed in twelve Tuamotuan songs Burrows found 355 major seconds against 17 minor seconds (1933:78), while Merriam reports that in the Yovu songs from Ruanda 42.7% of all steps employed are major seconds against 3.8% of minor seconds (1957:940); simi-larly, in the Washo Peyote songs 46.9% of all steps employed are major seconds against 3.8% of minor seconds (Merrian and d'Azevedo 1957:634). Besides the major second, the minor third stands out as a melodic interval in tribal song. In many styles the two intervals constitute the majority of the steps employed. Sometimes the minor third is the most frequently used step; for example, in the songs of the Chukchansi Yokuts Indians the minor third leads with 42.8% of all intervals employed (Merriam and Spier 1958:617). In song styles such as that of the Navaho, where "the melodic intervals tend to be large, major and minor thirds and perfect fourths and fifth predominate, while leaps of an octave are not rare" (Nettl 1956:113). So we see that, contrary to Hornbostel's concept, the tribal singer is able to clearly distinguish not only between melodic fourths, fifths and octaves, but also between smaller intervals, and that the size of the latter also approximates that of the intervals employed in Western music.

Moreover, the study of tonal structure of tribal song discloses that the major second and minor third often rival the fourth and fifth in structural importance; to a somewhat lesser extent, this is also the case with the major third. A few Dahomean songs may illustrate the situation (Kolinski 1938:songs 123, 199, 193). In the Dahomean funeral song (Fig. 4) section I moves within the fourth E A, while section II is partly characterized by the interlocking of the fourth areas E G A and G A C; however, the dominating structural feature is the pendular minor third E G which accounts for two thirds of the song including the initial and terminal motives. Motive b represents an imitation, in the major second G A, of the preceding pendular minor third. In the Dahomean song for the Gods of Thunder (Fig. 5) the roles of the minor third and major second are reversed. With

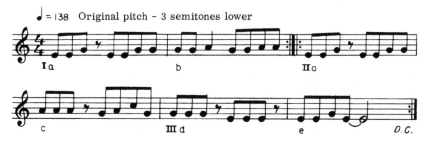

Figure 4. Dahomean Funeral Song.

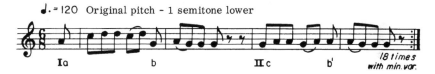

Figure 5. Dahomean Song for the Thunder God Bade.

the exception of the initial third step A C the song is composed of two pendular major seconds (C D and G A). The fourth and fifth are also structurally important: motive c is an imitation of motive a in the lower fourth, while the fifth step D G links the two pendulums. Perhaps the most striking feature of the Dahomean song for an Earth God (Fig. 6) is the pendular major third C E which forms the centerpiece of each 3/2 measure. This time no major seconds occur, while fourths and fifths are frequent. A replacement of high A by its lower octave is achieved through the replacement of the preceding ascending fourth E A in measure 1 by its inversion, the descending fifth E A in the subsequent measures.

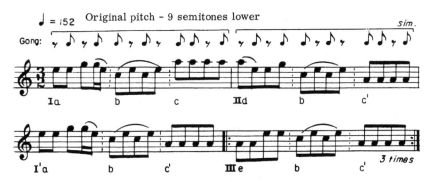

Figure 6. Dahomean Song for the Earth God Keledjegbe.

In the previous discussion of the distinctive-qualitative auditory property of tint it has been shown that octaves are characterized by tint identity, and fifths and fourths by a particularly close tint affinity. It remains now to clarify the nature of other tint relations. It is well known that the superimposition of fourths or fifths generates a series of new tones the number of which is virtually limited by the phenomenon of the cycle of fifths. Since each two tones adjacent in the cycle of fifths are correlated by the highest possible degree of tint affinity, it follows that tint affinity decreases with increasing distance in the cycle of fifths until tint affinity can no longer be observed. The following chart shows the grading of tint affinity of intervals and the correlated vibration ratios:

	Degree of tint affinity	Vibration ratio
Fourth, fifth CG	1st	2n:3
Major second Minor seventh C.D	2nd	2n:3²
Minor third Major sixth C..A	3rd	2n:3³
Major third Minor sixth C...E	4th	2n:3⁴

We see that all two-tint intervals of structural importance in tribal song, that is, the fourth, fifth, major second, minor third and major third, are distributed among the four categories of intervals characterized by tint affinity. These intervals function in tribal song as primary structural entities, and each category embraces intervals of a specific quality resulting from the degree of tint affinity between the two component tones. Occasionally a major second may derive from a combination of a fourth and a fifth progressing in opposite directions, or a minor seventh may have a double-fourth function. As a rule, however, no double, triple, or quadruple fourth-fifth relations are involved in the occurrence, in tribal song, of a major second or a minor or major third.

When intervals are simultaneously sounded and compared according to their placement in the cycle of fifths, one observes a gradual modification of their character from the hollowness of the 1st degree tint affinity of the fourth and fifth to the relative brilliance of the 4th degree tint affinity of the major third and minor sixth. However, one further step in the cycle disrupts this continuity so that no 5th or 6th degree tint affinity can be claimed for the minor second, the major seventh, and the tritone. The lack of tint affinity of these intervals apparently accounts for their structural irrelevance in tribal song.

The impact of the phenomenon of tint identity and tint affinity upon the tonal structure of tribal song is not limited to the selection of certain intervals out of the pitch continuum. More importantly, it determines the organic correlation of the structural elements involved. The tonal structure of a tribal song is often described in terms of the number of tones employed within one octave and is classified as tetratonic, pentatonic, etc. When a body of tribal vocal music is analyzed, the relative frequency of these categories as well as of the different tone steps employed are used as stylistic criteria. However, these features are of minor relevance because they do not reveal the essentials of tonal structure. For example, the following motives are both pentatonic, and the tone steps employed are 50% major seconds and 50% minor thirds:

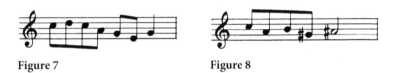

Figure 7   **Figure 8**

Yet the two tonal structures are quite dissimilar. The former belongs in the type commonly termed halftoneless pentatonic and virtually corresponds to the black keys of the piano, while the latter denotes a strictly chromatic tone material in spite of the nature of the tone steps employed. Nor is the absence of halftones the distinguishing feature of the halftoneless pentatonic scale since, for example, such a contrasting scale as F G A B C♯ is also halftoneless pentatonic. What significantly and unequivocally distinguishes this type of tonal structure from all others is the fact that it not only embraces all four categories of tint affinity but that all components of the underlying tint complex C G D A E are directly correlated: C-G, G-D, D-A and, A-E through 1st degree affinity; C-D, G-A, and D-E through 2nd degree affinity; C-A and G-E through 3rd degree affinity; and C-E through 4th degree affinity. It is this broadest possible realization of the principle of tint affinity resulting in an organic coherence of all structural elements involved which apparently accounts for the almost universal distribution of this pattern.

In addition to the 5-tint complex C G D A E, which forms the basis of the aforementioned type of tonal construction, all conceivable 3- and 4-tint complexes characterized by a direct correlation of their component tints are quite frequently found in tribal song. For example, the 4-tint complexes C G D A and C G A E are common in Dahomean songs, the former being represented by 14, the latter by 25 different scales (Kolinski 1961:44–47; see also Figs. 3–5). As for the 3-tint complexes, it seems worthwhile mentioning that two of them correspond to the major and minor triads C G E and C A E.

In view of the decisive impact of tint affinity upon tonal organization it seemed to me essential to work out a classification of tonal structures based primarily upon the different types of tint correlation. Only within the framework of these structural types can a subdivision according to the number of tints employed become meaningful. I want to refer the reader to this classification (Kolinski 1961) and to limit myself to a brief discussion of a few points. Since the placement in the cycle of fifths of the tints employed in a piece reflects the nature of their mutual correlation, the main types of tonal structure have been established according to the size of the section needed within the cycle of fifths to place the tints of a piece under analysis. For example, the tetra-type occupies a 4-tint section, that is, C G D A, and includes the 4-tint complex C G D A, the 3-tint complexes C G A and C D A, and the 2-tint complex C A; similarly, the aforementioned complex C G A E is classified as a pentatypic 4-tint complex, while the so-called halftone-less pentatonic scales represent pentatypic 5-tint structures.

The tint complexes belonging to the di-, tri-, tetra-, and pentatype are characterized by a direct tint affinity of their components. Realizing the resulting structural closeness of these complexes some scholars have termed the tri-, tetra-, and pentatypic 3- and 4-tint complexes "incomplete pentatonic." This approach is, however, just as unjustified as, for example, an interpretation of the pentatypic 5-tint scale as an incomplete diatonic one. Still more objectionable is the interpretation of the aforementioned structures as "pre-pentatonic" or "older than pentatonic" because it denotes a general evolutionary orientation culminating in such completely unfounded speculations as Wiora's concept of "The four world ages of music" (1961).

Two further types of tonal construction are quite frequent in tribal song: the hexa-type, requiring the cycle section C g d a e B, and therefore characterized by the presence of a minor second or a major seventh; and the hepta-type, requiring the cycle section F c g d a e B, and therefore characterized by the presence of a tritone. As mentioned before, the minor second, the major seventh, and the tritone consist of two tints each which are not directly correlated; nevertheless, through various kinds of indirect correlation these intervals are, in tribal song, perfectly integrated within the web of direct tint affinity. This integration is achieved through a direct correlation of the two mutually unrelated tints of a minor second, a major seventh or a tritone with a third tint or with a tint complex. fu fact, it is this kind of twin-tint correlation which results in the use of the aforementioned intervals either as actual tone steps or as part of the tonal structure. A few examples may illustrate these patterns. Let us start with a song of derision from the subtribe Ple of the Pygmoid Sakai of the Malay Peninsula

(Fig. 9; Kolinski 1930:629). It is performed by a male leader and contrapuntally imitated in the upper octave by a female chorus. It has a hexatypic 3-tint structure. The major third C E forms the tonal nucleus. However, the final C of the 3/2 motives is often not directly reached from the upper third E but through the detour of the descending fourth E B; so the halfstep B C results from the tint affinity of E to both B and C. Quite different is the function of the halfstep B C in the Samoan war song (Fig. 10; Kolinski 1930:644). Here the tetratypic 3-tint structure B D E forms the tonal nucleus; some of the nine renditions of the song are even completely tetratypic. The halfstep B C of the hexatypic tetrachord B C D E in the first measure is correlated through the tint affinity of D to both B and C. The scale E g b c e of the next example, a Dahomean lullaby (Fig.

Figure 9. Song of Derision of the Pygmoid Sakai of the Malay Peninsula.

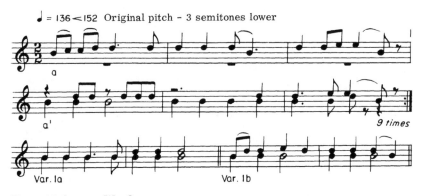

Figure 10. Samoan War Song.

11; Kolinski 1938:song 39), is one of the following 14 Dahomean scales based upon the hexatypic 4-tint complex C G E B:

Hexa-C-mode	Hexa-G-mode	Hexa-E-mode
g b C e	G b c e g b c	E g b c e
g b C e g	e G b c	c E g b
g b C e g b	e G b c e g	c E g b c e
e g b C e g b	e G b c e g b c	c E g b c e g
	c e G b c e	
	c e G b c e g	(Kolinski 1961:51)

Figure 11. Dahomean Lullaby.

In this example either of the two tints of the halfstep B C shows a direct tint affinity to both E and G, that is, C E, B E, G C, and G B. In the first section of a Dahomean Dokpwe work song (Fig. 12; Kolinski 1938:song 4) the hexatypic 5-tint scale a c D g a b results from a merger of the pentatypic 4-tint structure D g a b with the tetratypic 4-tint structure a c D g a:

$$D \quad g \quad a \quad b$$
$$a \quad c \quad D \quad g \quad a$$

Similarly, in the Dahomean religious song for Aiza (Fig. 13; *ibid.*: song 237) the heptatypic 7-tint scale a C d e f g a b c results from a merger of the hexatypic 6-tint structure a C d e g a b c of section I with the pentatypic 5-tint structure C d f g a of sections II and II'.

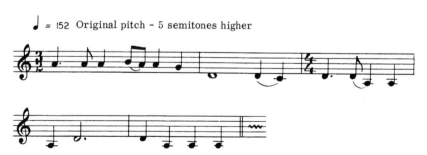

Figure 12. Dahomean Dokpwe Work Song.

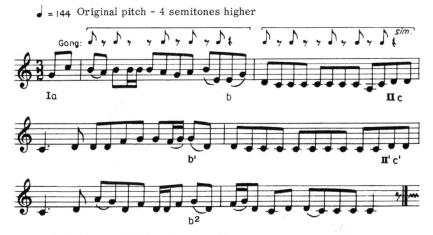

Figure 13. Dahomean Religious Song for Aiza.

It is significant that tint complexes of higher types rarely occur in tribal song in spite of the fact that no less than 208 different 4- to 7-tint complexes belonging in the octa-, ennea-, and decatype can be distinguished (Kolinski 1961:40–41).

It now remains to discuss the implications of the above demonstrated fact that the tonal structure of tribal song is determined by the phenomenon of tint identify and tint affinity. We saw that this phenomenon has a clearly circumscribed physical correlate, namely, the approximation to certain vibration ratios. This means that the property of tint is not culturally derived but, similarly to other properties of sound, is psycho-physiologically rooted and constitutes, therefore, an intrinsic facet of man's auditory perception. Consequently, the laws of tint identity and tint affinity represent universals, regardless of the degree and kind of their impact upon the tonal structure of the music of the world's peoples. We have to take this basic factor into consideration, in particular when dealing with the immense variety of instrumental patterns; and we should include within the framework of our investigations a thorough study of the nature of the relation between vocal and instrumental patterns which in different cultures may vary from strong opposition between the two media to marked convergence.

With regard to the Eastern and Western tone systems we may observe a complete integration of the phenomenon of tint identity and various degrees of compliance with the laws of tint affinity. This compliance is most conspicuous in systems based upon the cyclic principle where the tones are generated through continuous progressions in fifths and fourths, as in the case of the Chinese and the medieval Western tone systems. I have elsewhere shown that in spite of the gradual abandonment by post-medieval theorists of the "quintal" principle in favor of the so-called "natural" one and of the general acceptance of the latter up to the present day, it is the medieval quintal concept upon which our tone system is ultimately based (Kolinski 1962). This means that the dualistic major-minor principle of the past centuries is not sanctioned by nature but represents merely one among numerous possibilities of tonal construction derived from direct and indirect tint relations. It is the heptatypic 7-tint complex F C G D A E B which generated the major and minor modes as well as the so-called church modes, and the selection of major and minor out of the medieval modal system represents a historical and cultural development.

The early days of comparative musicology showed a strong tendency to discover in tribal music features of tonal construction reminiscent of Western patterns, and such matters as the possibility of a latent feeling for triadic harmony inherent in American Indian songs were seriously discussed. After the fallacy of this approach had been recognized, a strong reaction took place, and the general attitude of comparative musicology swung from one extreme to the other, denying any structural similarity between Western and non-Western musics. Neither of the two viewpoints is tenable, and the previous discussion has shown that the answer to the problem lies between the two extremes: for example, there is a culturally motivated striking opposition between the purely melodic tonal structure of American Indian song and the harmonic Western major-minor system; however, at the source of these two contrasting types of tonal construction lie the biologically rooted and, therefore, universally valid laws of tint relations.

The emphasis placed, in the previous discussion, upon these universals by no means tends to minimize the multifariousness of tonal structures due to cultural diversity. On the contrary, it is the awareness of the nature of the auditory property of tint which makes a meaningful and thorough investigation of the culturally derived diversification of tonal structures possible. The importance of the study of music as an integrated facet of the various cultural manifestations of a society has been justly stressed. Less clearly recognized is, however, the fact that an extensive and objective ethnological evaluation of musical structures, hinges on the establishment of a system of well-founded and detailed methods of musicological analysis. It is to be hoped that the realization of this ethno-musicological correlation will stimulate the comparative musicologist to continue the work already done in this direction and so to broaden the basis of cooperation between the musicological and ethnological branches of ethnomusicology.

References Cited

Blacking, John
    1965   "The role of music in the culture of the Venda of the northern Transvaal," *Studies in Ethnomusicology* 2:20–53.
Burrows, Edwin G.
    1933   *Native music of the Tuamotus.* Honolulu: Bernice P. Bishop Museum, Bulletin 109.

Densmore, Frances
   1929   *Pawnee music*. Washington: Bureau of American Ethnology, Bulletin 93.
Dobzhansky, Theodosius G.
   1962   *Mankind evolving*. New Haven: Yale University Press.
Hilgard, Ernest R.
   1962   *Introduction to psychology*. Third edition. New York: Harcourt, Brace, and World.
Hornbostel, Erich M. von
   1948   "The music of the Fuegians," *Ethnos* 13:61–102.
Kolinski, Mieczyslaw
   1930   "Die Musik der Primitivstämme auf Malaka und ihre Beziehungen zur samoanischen Musik," *Anthropos* 25:585–648.
   1936   "Suriname music," *in* Melville and Frances Herskovits, *Suriname folk-lore* (New York: Columbia University Press), pp. 489–740.
   1938   "Die Musik Westafrikas." Manuscript deposited at the Department of Anthropology, Northwestern University.
   1957a "The determinants of tonal construction in tribal music," *Musical Quarterly* 43:50–56.
   1957b "Ethnomusicology, its problems and methods," *Ethnomusicology Newsletter* 10:1–7.
   1959   "The evaluation of tempo," *ETHNOMUSICOLOGY* 3:45–57.
   1960   Review of A. M. Jones "Studies in African music," *Musical Quarterly* 46:105–10.
   1961   "Classification of tonal structures, illustrated by a comparative chart of American Indian, African Negro, Afro-American and English-American structures," *Studies in Ethnomusicology* 1:38–76.
   1962   "Consonance and dissonance," *ETHNOMUSICOLOGY* 6:66–74.
   1964   Transcription II in "Symposium on transcription and analysis: a Hukwe song with musical bow," *ETHNOMUSICOLOGY* 8:241–51.
   1965a "The structure of melodic movement; a new method of analysis" (revised version), *Studies in Ethnomusicology* 2:95–120.
   1965b "The general direction of melodic movement," *ETHNOMUSICOLOGY* 9:240–64.
Kunst, Jaap
   1955   *Ethno-musicology*. Second edition. The Hague: M. Nijhoff.
Merriam, Alan P.
   1957   "Yovu songs from Ruanda," *Zaire* 11:933–66.
   1960   "Ethnomusicology, discussion and definition of the field," *ETHNOMUSICOLOGY* 4:107–14.
   1964   *The anthropology of music*. Evanston, Ill.: Northwestern University Press.
Merriam, Alan P., and Warren L. d'Azevedo
   1957   "Washo Peyote songs," *American Anthropologist* 59:615–41.
Merriam, Alan P., and Robert F. G. Spier
   1958   "Chukchansi Yokuts songs," *Actas del XXXIIIᵒ Congreso Internacional de Americanistas* 2:611–38.
Nettl, Bruno
   1956   *Music in primitive culture*. Cambridge: Harvard University Press.
   1965   *Folk and traditional music of the Western continents*. Englewood Cliffs, N.J.: Prentice-Hall.
Seeger, Charles
   1963   "On the tasks of musicology," *ETHNOMUSICOLOGY* 7:214–15.
Wiora, Walter
   1961   *Die vier Weltalter der Musik*. Stuttgart: Kohlhammer.

Toward the Remodeling
of Ethnomusicology

TIMOTHY RICE

Ethnomusicology, like any academic field, is constantly being created and rec-reated through the research, writing and teaching of its practitioners. Direct action in the form of new data, interpretations, theories, and methods effectively defines the field. Modeling a discipline, on the other hand, requires a step back from direct engagement in research to ask the descriptive question, what are we doing?, and the prescriptive question, what ought we to be doing? The answer will surely depend on the intellectual and social matrix of the modeler (Blum 1975 and C. Seeger 1977) and the effectiveness of the model will depend either on the extent to which it captures simply and elegantly the current work being done in the field or provides a kind of "moral imperative" for future action.

Probably the best example of an effective model in the recent history of ethnomusicology is "Merriam's model" proposed in 1964 in the *Anthropology of Music*. His "simple model" . . . "involves study on three analytic levels—concep-tualization about music, behavior in relation to music, and music sound itself (p. 32)." The model is essentially circular in form (see fig. 1) with concept affect-ing behavior which produces the sound product. And he continues, ". . . There is a constant feedback from the product to the concepts about music, and this is what accounts both for change and stability in a music system" (p. 33). This model was seminal in the history of ethnomusicology and to that date was the most forceful and cogent statement of anthropological concerns with respect to music. The model defined ethnomusicology as "the study of music in culture" and that view—even as modified to "music as culture" and "the relationship between music and culture"—has remained one of the core concepts in the discipline ever since.

We can of course argue about the extent of its influence during the last twenty years, but there can be no doubt that it continues to be influential. It is

From *Ethnomusicology*, Vol. 31, No. 3 (Fall 1987), pp. 469–88

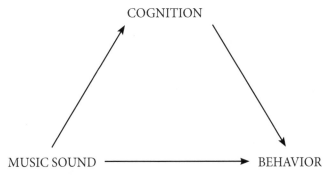

Figure 1. The Merriam Model

still frequently cited to contextualize particular research problems (for example, Yung 1984 and Sawa 1983), Bruno Nettl (1983) called it "definitive," not just of the study of music but apparently of music itself, and it provided the basic model for the recent collaborative textbook, *Worlds of Music* (Titan 1984). If that book's authors, coming from a very wide range of backgrounds, could agree on this model, then the continuing extent of its influence is clear-at least as an overall image or model of the field.

In addition to defining the field and being influential, Merriam's model also has three other attractive properties which make it a useful foil for the "remodeling" proposed here. First, it is a "simple model" with three "analytic levels." Part of the reason it has been influential is that it is easy to remember. Second, its levels seem to be relatively complete and inclusive. They cover a broad range of concerns. Third, it is a cogent model in the sense that its "analytic levels" are supposed to interrelate. In spite of these attractive properties, however, I acknowledge that not everyone has agreed with it, and we have certainly wrestled with it as much as we have embraced it. But because it is simple, inclusive, cogent, definitive, and influential, I am going to refer to it frequently in the "remodeling" that follows, partly because I hope the model proposed here has many of these same qualities.[1]

The first and most immediate effect of the Merriam model was to increase the amount and prestige of work done on social, physical and verbal behaviors associated with music. Its second effect was to set in motion a search for ways to relate these behaviors to the "music sound itself." Much of the subsequent work in "the anthropological study of music" (Blacking 1976b) can be interpreted as attempts to find the points of intersection, causation, or "homologies" between Merriam's "analytic levels."

In the search for those connections a number of social science paradigms have been borrowed and invoked over the last twenty years, including biological approaches (Blacking 1977), semiotics (Nattiez 1983), ethnoscience (Zemp 1978), ethnography of performance (Herndon and McLeod 1980) and communications (Feld 1984), structuralism (A. Seeger 1980), symbolic interactionism (Stone 1982), Marxism (Shepherd 1982), hermeneutics (Becker 1984) and an eclectic mix of a number of approaches (Feld 1982). Although these paradigms and methods are often seen as conflicting or mutually exclusive within anthropology and sociology, and certainly differ from the structural functionalism behind Merriam's *Anthropology of Music*, their application within ethnomusicology can be interpreted as an attempt to solve the central problem created by Merriam's model: how can we convincingly speak about the relationship between music and other human behaviors.

Although much of the "theory" developed in ethnomusicology over the last twenty years has addressed this question, there are obvious signs of resistance to the sought-after perfect union between so-called "musicological" and "anthropological" approaches. An incident from last year's annual meeting in Vancouver can serve to illustrate the divergence of opinion in the field and some of the continued resistance to anthropological approaches. During the discussion following Stephen Blum's paper, "The Ethnomusicologist vis-à-vis the Fallacies of Contemporary Musical Life," someone commented that in the paper and response and discussion to that point, he had not heard much reference to contemporary social theory, particularly coming out of anthropology, and worried that ethnomusicologists were perhaps twenty years out of date in their view of society and culture. The responses by prominent ethnomusicologists to this observation covered an astonishing range. Someone responded that she and probably others did keep up; someone else said she wished she could keep up but was so busy as a teacher covering "the whole earth" that she couldn't keep up; and two people responded essentially with, "Who cares if we keep up?" If anyone were laboring under the impression that ethnomusicology was a unified discipline or even that there was widespread agreement that it represented a union of anthropological and musicological approaches, this interchange would have been illuminating and perhaps discouraging.

In addition to this lack of agreement about the methods and disciplinary roots of our field, there is evidence of pessimism about what we have achieved in the way of a union between anthropological and musicological approaches even by those deeply committed to such a union.[2] Gerard Behague (1984: 7) recently wrote that "our analytical tools for establishing that relationship [between "social context" and "music sound-structure"] unequivocally lack in sophistication." Herndon and McLeod (1979: iii), in the late seventies, still complained that "the wholeness . . . which gives equal consideration to the music, itself, and the behavior surrounding its origin, production, and evaluation still eludes us." Ruth Stone (1982: 127), whose innovative approach to event analysis is designed to solve this problem, admits that "it is not yet possible to achieve the ideal unitary analysis."

Thus ethnomusicology seems to be in a rather odd position. On the one hand, we have an old model which continues to exert a fair bit of influence and to define the core problem for the field. On the other hand, there is pessimism about the extent of our achievements in solving the problem, continued open resistance to anthropological models,[3] and competition among a host of social science paradigms rushed into the breach in an attempt to solve all or some of our problems. In this context I think it is time to rethink the relationship between ethnomusicology and its cognate disciplines and perhaps, like an old house, remodel it along lines that describe and prescribe what we actually do rather than what particular scholarly traditions tell us we ought to do.

Some might argue that modeling a discipline is not necessary. Obviously research will continue largely along lines dictated by personal interest, intellectual training, traditions of scholarship, and social and institutional demands. Yet disciplinary models are attractive for a number of reasons.[4] They provide a kind of intellectual framework that helps us contextualize, interpret, classify and evaluate our work, and they can provide some sense of direction or purpose. Lewis Thomas (1974), the well-known essayist on biological topics, characterizes the scientific enterprise as analogous to the building of an anthill. He guesses that individual ants, like most scientists, have no idea of the shape of the anthill they are building. The combined intelligence of masses of ants and scientists achieves spectacular results even though individual ants and scientists cannot imagine exactly to what purpose their work is directed. Modeling is an attempt to imagine the shape—however hazy—of the metaphorical anthill that we are building.

The Model

There are two immediate, personal sources for the model presented here. One comes from my teaching experience, the other from reading in the secondary literature. First, I teach an introductory course to all first-year students in a large conservatory-style music program at the University of Toronto. The course treats all kinds of music (Western and non-Western, classical, folk, popular and so on) as a prelude to a more detailed study of Western classical music. The course description, generated in committee, reads, "Formative processes in music cultures of the world." Thus, I have been forced to wonder in a very practical, pedagogical context just what the formative processes in music are. Are they melody, harmony, and rhythm as some of my colleagues at the Faculty of

Music seem to imagine? Or are they the relationship between music and politics, economics, social structure, music events, and language as ethnomusicologists have claimed in the last twenty years? Was there a way to pull some semblance of order out of the long lists one could make? Was there a way of reconciling the music structural concerns of many music history courses with the anthropological concerns of many ethnomusicology courses?[5]

I developed various ways to deal with this problem, and then about four years ago, while rereading Clifford Geertz's *The Interpretation of Cultures,* I was struck by his claim that "symbolic systems . . . are historically constructed, socially maintained and individually applied" (pp. 363–364). Instantly I recognized these as the "formative processes" that I had been searching for. Here was a three-part model, analogous to Merriam's, that was easy to remember and that seemed to balance social, historical and individual processes and forces in ways that seemed immediately and intuitively satisfying. The Merriam model, or at least its working out over the last twenty years, has tended to lead to an emphasis on social processes and as a consequence alienated ethnomusicology from the concerns of historical musicology. How could one teach about all music when the perspectives brought to bear on different musics seemed so different?

I would like to examine the implications of a slightly modified form of this statement by Geertz as a "model for ethnomusicology." Simply put, I now believe that ethnomusicologists should study the "formative processes" in music, that they should ask and attempt to answer this deceptively simple question: how do people make music or, in its more elaborate form, how do people historically construct, socially maintain and individually create and experience music?[6]

It is hard to capture the overlapping strands of theory and practice as they currently operate in our field, but if this statement by Geertz struck a responsive chord in me, then it probably is because this sort of thinking is "in the air." When I looked more closely at recent literature with this model in mind I did indeed find "preechoes" of it in the writing of a number of our colleagues.[7] For example, Herndon and McLeod ask this same question, how does man make music, in their book, *Music as Culture,* but do not then go on to make the coherent series of claims that this model does. John Blacking has argued perhaps most persuasively for the emphasis on process, as opposed to product, that is modeled here.

Probably the place where the general emphases of this model are currently being worked on most clearly is in the area of performance practice or ethnography of performance and communications. Steven Feld (1984: 6), for example, argues for a focus on listeners "as socially and historically implicated beings"—a statement that captures the three poles of this model. Bonnie Wade (1984: 47) points out that "creativity in the performance practice of Indian art music . . . involves . . . the role of the individual performer, how he sees his own creativity in relationship to his musical tradition, to his fellow performers, and to his audience." Creativity as individual experience, history as tradition, and social processes involving musicians and audience represent one of many ways that the three parts of this model can be interrelated to tell an interesting story. That story gets at fundamental musical processes without belaboring points about homologies between musical and cultural forms, and yet manages to integrate the study of music into the study of history, society, and cognition.

Kenneth Gourlay (1982: 413) came very close to modeling the field along these lines. "Gourlay's A.B.C" calls for "a humanizing ethnomusicology with three distinct, if related, fields of inquiry." A, for Armstrong's affecting presence, involves the study of "how musical symbols operate to produce their effect or meaning, and what effects they produce." B stands for Blacking's model of change, and C, for condition, context, and conceptualization. He does not go on to show, however, how the three fields can be related.[8]

Thus, the general outline of the model proposed here is clearly "in the wind." But this relatively recent "atmosphere" in the field has yet to be developed into a simple, cogent and inclusive model, and to have its implications for the field examined.

The Parts of the Model

First, the model needs to be explained in terms of how it organizes the welter of "issues and concepts," to use Nettl's (1983) phrase, generated by ethnomusicologists.

"Historical construction" comprises two important processes: the process of change with the passage of time and the process of reencountering and recreating the forms and legacy of the past in each moment of the present.[9] In synchronic, "in-time" studies of music in a particular place at a particular time, the study of historically constructed forms as a legacy of the past finds a place here. Jean-Jacques Nattiez (1983: 472) has deplored what he calls the synchronic "cultural-ism" of much current ethnomusicology and argues for a greater emphasis on diachronic approaches to musical form. However, he concludes that "music generates music." I prefer this model's claim that people generate music at the same time that it acknowledges the formative power of previously constructed musical forms. Individuals operating in society must come to grips with, learn, and choose among a host of previously constructed musical forms. Although this process is normally acted out in specific instances of learning, listening and playing using the medium of music itself, analogous behavior in the speech domain requires musicologists to describe the intricacies of forms in words. Both operations—musician/performers making music for musician/listeners and musicologists writing or speaking to their readers or audience—require a sophisticated encounter with historically constructed forms.[10]

Historical construction can also be interpreted as the diachronic, "out-of-time" study of musical change or the history of music. In spite of the notorious difficulty of constructing music histories in many of the cultures we typically consider, ethnomusicologists have been fascinated by the issue of change. It would be descriptively accurate and therefore useful to have a model of our field that reflects the central importance of change, of historical processes. For us history or "historical ethnomusicology," to use Kay Shelemay's phrase, does not, in fact, seem to be one of many issues, but a primary issue, a fundamental process, a given of music making, and this model acknowledges that by elevating the study of change to the highest analytical level of the model.[11,12]

Processes of social maintenance have been particularly well documented by ethnomusicologists in the years since Merriam's *The Anthropology of Music*, and it is easy to construct at least a partial list of the way music is sustained, maintained, and altered by socially constructed institutions and belief systems: ecology, economics and the patronage of music; the social structure of music and musicians; protest, censorship and the politics of music; performance contexts and conventions; beliefs about the power and structure of music; music education and training; and so on. The study of the processes by which these social systems impact music and, conversely, how music impacts these systems has been one of the most fruitful areas of research in the last twenty years, whether expressed in terms of context, causal relations, homologies, or deep-structural relations.

Emphasis on the individual is probably the most recent and as yet weakest area of development in ethnomusicology. While the study of individual composers and individual acts of creation is well-entrenched in historical musicology, such studies have remained until very recently suspect in ethnomusicology. The antagonism and even fear of humanistic, historical or individual approaches is exemplified in this statement of Judith and A. L. Becker (1984: 455):

> A move toward the study of particularities nudges ethnomusicology away from the social sciences into the realm of the humanities where uniqueness is legitimate. Our discipline has historically been allied with the social sciences; we take our paradigms from the social sciences. Any step toward the humanities also feels like a step toward the approaches of traditional historical musicology with its outworn methodology and unexamined assumptions.

They then invoke another paradigm they call literary criticism, ironically an approach deeply rooted in the humanities but that has recently been taken over by social science. The interpretive anthropology of Geertz and others seems to move the social sciences in the direction of the humanities, and drastically reduces the need for the "fear and trembling" one senses on both sides of this apparently once formidable division. This model, in fact, does move ethnomusicology closer to the humanities and historical musicology (and might have the effect of moving historical musicology closer to ethnomusicology), but without giving up an essential concern for the social bases of musical life and experience or a general scholarly concern for generalization and comparison.

John Blacking has emerged as a clear advocate of approaches to the study of the individual in a number of recent articles, but he too betrays a fear of individuality when he argues that it is not Mozart's uniqueness but his capacity to share that is important (1976b). A balanced approach must be willing to acknowledge the extent and importance of individuality and uniqueness in particular societies, and finding a balance between historical, social, and individual processes should be an important part of "the interpretation of [musical] cultures." The recent work of Ellen Koskoff (1984), Dane Harwood (1976), Bruno Nettl (1983), Klaus Wachsmann (1982), Steven Feld (1984) and the writers of *Worlds of Music* (1984) has moved us substantially in the direction of increased consideration of individual creativity and personal experience as legitimate objects of scholarly enquiry.

Some of the issues that might be discussed under individual creativity and experience include: composition, improvisation and performances of particular pieces, repertories and styles; perception of musical form and structure; emotional, physical, spiritual and multisensory experience mediated by music; and individual cognitive structures for organizing musical experience and associating it with other experiences. If interest in the individual and individual experience continues to grow, then eventually the history of ethnomusicology might be interpreted as having moved successively through the three stages of this model from a concern with historical and evolutionary questions in its early "comparative musicology" stage to a concern for music in social life after *The Anthropology of Music*, to a concern for the individual in history and society in the most recent or next phase.

In fact the work actually being done in the field today is rather well balanced between these approaches. The articles in *Ethnomusicology* in the eight-year period from 1979 to 1986 contain a good balance among these approaches. The largest group predictably emphasizes social processes but a perhaps surprising number look at individual processes as well:

general theory and method	13%
surveys	4%
music analysis	10%
history/change	22%
social processes	34%
individual processes	17%
Total	100%

Thus it seems that this model rather effectively reflects not just the current theoretical atmosphere in the field, but the balance in the actual work we are doing. It is an accepting model in which virtually everyone in the field can find a place for his or her work.

Interpretation in the Model

Perhaps the most exciting feature of this model is the richness of interpretation that it suggests, hardly surprising since it was originally sparked by a book entitled *The Interpretation of Cultures*. In fact, the model suggests four hierarchical levels of interpretation (see fig. 2).

To be effective a model ought to be dynamic or cogent, that is, it should imply or suggest ways to relate the parts of the model to one another. In fact, this model strikes me as particularly dynamic in the sense that its parts can so easily be shown to interlock and interrelate. If the levels easily interrelate, then the move from description to interpretation and explanation, which bedevils the Merriam model, should be straightforward and in fact a feature of this model.

The main interpretive problem set up by the Merriam model was to find ways to relate music sound to conceptualization and behavior, and I have already written about some of the pessimism about what we have achieved. A striking recent statement of the difficulty of interpretation presented by the Merriam model comes from *Worlds of Music*, which uses it. Speaking of dividing music cultures into "parts" along the lines of the Merriam model, they write: "... At best, isolating parts of a music-culture for study is an oversimplification; at worst, an untruth. But given the limitations of courses and textbooks, it is our only recourse" (p. 9).

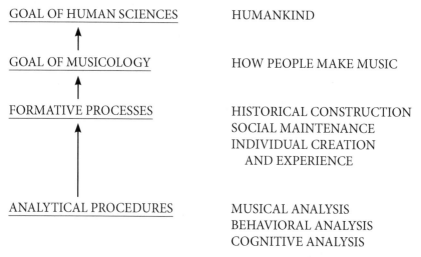

Figure 2. Hierarchy of levels in the model.

All of us sympathize with their dilemma precisely because it is not just a dilemma of courses and textbooks, but a dilemma for ethnomusicology as a whole. J. H. Kwabena Nketia (1985) recently called for "the development of an integrative technique that enables the scholar to group and regroup his data" (p. 15) and for "methods of synthesis that bring together the different aspects of music and music making in a meaningful and coherent manner" (p. 18). He called this a "challenge" for ethnomusicology, and this model is an attempt to respond to that challenge.

At the first and lowest level of interpretation, I suggest that instead of or in addition to seeking to relate the levels of Merriam's model to each other through cause, homologies, correspondences or what have you, that we embed them within the levels of this model and ask how they contribute to the formative processes we have identified (see fig. 3).

A rich story could presumably be told about how changes in sound, concept and behavior contribute to the historical construction of a particular kind of music (for example, Cavanagh 1982). Another story might revolve around the social forces that maintain sound structures, assign them meaning and value, and generate behaviors consistent across both musical and nonmusical domains. A third story might treat the range of individual variation in ideas, behaviors and music in a given musical culture. In this model, Merriam's analytic levels can still be used, but the way they are related to one another is a little more flexible and varied than a monolithic search for causes and homologies, and thus easier to achieve. Furthermore, instead of sanctioning formal descriptions of either sound, cognition or behavior, as interesting as they might be, this model demands an interpretation of what our descriptions imply about our knowledge of fundamental formative processes. For example, a formal analysis of the "music sound itself" might yield interpretations of a piece's importance in the historical construction of the style, of individual creative processes as evidenced in the piece or performance, or of elements in the cultural or social system that

Figure 3. Merriam's levels embedded in this model.

affected elements of form. Good writing in ethnomusicology already does these sorts of things, and that is why I claim that the interpretations demanded by this model are relatively easy and enormously varied. It is a rich model allowing for a variety of perspectives, not a narrow model with a single perspective.

Moving to a second, higher level in this model, we can ask how its parts interrelate to generate interpretations. Two main structural problems with Merriam's model have led to problems of interpretation, whereas this model solves them. First, in the Merriam model music sound is directly contrasted to behavior and cognition. Having separated music from context in this artificial way, we have struggled ever since to put this particular Humpty-Dumpty back together again. In the model proposed here, the analysis of music, the study of the "music sound itself," is demoted to a lower level of the model, while people's actions in creating, experiencing, and using music become the goal of the enquiry. Instead of trying to find homologies between unlike things—sound, concepts and behaviors—this model tries to integrate and relate like things, namely three formative "processes."

The second structural problem with Merriam's model is that the relations between his analytic levels go only in one direction and relate one level to only one other (see fig. 1). In this model, on the other hand, each level is connected to the other two in a dialectical, or two-way, relationship. There are simply more relationships in this model and thus more possibilities for interpretation. Each process can thus be explained in terms of the other two (see fig. 4). Historical construction can be explained in terms of both changes in patterns of social maintenance and individual creative decisions. Individual creation and experience can be seen as determined partly by historically constructed forms

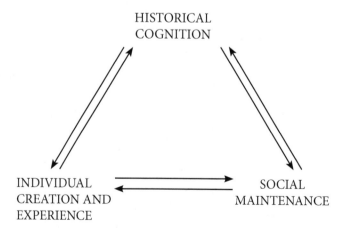

Figure 4. Relationships in the model.

as learned, performed, and modified in socially maintained and sanctioned contexts. Social maintenance can be seen as an ongoing interaction between historically constructed modes of behavior, traditions if you will, and individual action that recreates, modifies and interprets that tradition. Thus, the levels in this model are on a metaphorical "rubber band," which can be pulled apart to analyze, but which keep wanting to snap back together. This gives the model a certain dynamic, interpretive energy, to extend the metaphor, and allows the telling of many interesting stories. In general, application of this model demands a move from description to interpretation and explanation and provides a flexible, varied and rather easy way to do it, or at least to imagine how to do it.

If we are able to identify and relate fundamental formative processes in particular ethnographic situations, then this should lead us to the third level of interpretation in the model, which is a concern for general statements about how people make music. The model thus leads us to a comparative stance with respect to music. If we can keep before us an image of fundamental formative processes that operate in many cultures, this should lead us to create microstudies that can be compared to other microstudies, as opposed to the detailed, independent and insular studies that seem to proliferate in the ethnomusicological literature at present.

One example of how the model was used in a particular situation and had a comparative effect was a paper by Stephen Satory, a graduate student at the University of Toronto, who decided to use the model in his report of field work in the Hungarian community in Toronto for the 1985 Niagara chapter meeting of SEM. Subtitling his paper, "The role of history, society and the individual," he analyzed the musical life of Hungarians in Toronto, and particularly the position and importance of the dynamic revival movement involving improvised dancing called *tanchaz* or "dance house," begun in the early '70s in Budapest. Although he could have focused on any part of the model, he chose to address all three parts of it. Having committed himself to the model, he was constantly forced by it to move beyond a description of what he had observed to interpretations of broader processes. In his discussion of historical construction he periodized immigration patterns, discussed the rise of community social institutions in Toronto to support cultural expression and distinguished five types of transmission of the tradition, many of them involving specific individual actions. As for social maintenance he compared this tradition in three locales: in the villages of Transylvania where the forms originated, in Budapest and in Toronto. He interpreted its lack of popularity in Toronto, compared to its importance in Hungarian venues, as a consequence of the differing political, social and intellectual climate in the three places, concluding among other things that the unstructured, improvisational aspects of the tradition do not correspond to the goal and work-oriented values of Hungarian immigrants to Toronto. In spite of its lack of popularity and community support, however, the tradition lives in Toronto through the agency of a relatively small number of individuals who value it variously as a means of ethnic group identity, nostalgia for village life, a source of friendships, exercise, and the aesthetic pleasure of skill and virtuosity. Using the model allowed Stephen to rework his material from a number of different perspectives, and the interpretations he made of his particular data linked his work to the work of many others.

At the Niagara meeting his paper was one of four papers on immigrant musical traditions in North America. In the discussion that followed, Stephen's paper became the focus of comment not because it was the best researched, or had the richest data or concerned the most colorful tradition, but because it was the only paper that went beyond description to interpretation. The interpretations linked his specific research to wider issues that all of us were interested in and could discuss. Perhaps we should not ask much more from a model than that it increases the possibilities for communication among us.

The fourth level of interpretation would eventually identify what is shared and what is unique about music in the repertoire of human behaviors. Something like this level was suggested by Blacking (1976b: 11): "the aim of ethnomusicological analysis is to reveal what is peculiar to the process of making and appreciating music, as distinct from other social activities." At this level ethnomusicology would contribute to comparative studies in many cognate fields and to our knowledge of humankind in general. If the fundamental "formative processes" in music are conceived as historical, social, and individual, then the eventual identification of "musical processes" will connect music to the rest of human behavior and music study to the rest of the academic world.

Relations to Other Disciplines

Finally, this model of an ethnomusicology that includes historical, anthropological and psychobiological components and concerns could be a model for a unified, rather than a divided, musicology. This is a satisfying conclusion because it reflects the direction in which some ethnomusicologists have wanted to move for years. Ethnomusicologists often possess a sort of missionary zeal that they have a corner on the best and most proper and widest perspective on music and that ethnomusicology is in fact musicology.[13] But it is not helpful to downplay or ignore the significant achievements of historical musicology in favor of a claim that we have all the right answers. Historical musicologists have much to teach ethnomusicologists about historical and individual creative processes, just as we have much to teach them about the powerful forces of contemporary culture on musical sound structures and the social and cognitive bases of musical experience.

When ethnomusicologists speak of musicology, they seem to regard its primary methodological stance as analytical and product-oriented (for example, Qureshi 1981), but at least some historical musicologists seem to work from perspectives not incompatible with those of ethnomusicologists. Anthony Seeger (1985: 349), in his review of the *New Grove* coverage of the many "ologies" of music, points out that Vincent Duckles, in his article on musicology, "at least raises the serious possibility that . . . all musicology becomes ethnomusicological in focus" and calls part of the article "an excellent summary of an important ethnomusicological perspective." As he points out, "no single perspective [on music] will ever be more than a perspective" (p. 351). The model proposed here may solve this problem of isolation and of unitary perspective by demanding the integration of perspectives at one level of interpretation.

The historical musicologist Richard Crawford likens his approach to that of a mapmaker in search of it all, as opposed to a prospector in search of a few treasures,[14] and Friedrich Blume, in his 1972 essay on "Musical Scholarship Today," defines a musicology that "embraces all fields of musical activity in all periods of history and all peoples and nations" (p. 16). He regards himself as a historian and musicology as a branch of history in much the way that many ethnomusicologists regard themselves as anthropologists, with ethnomusicology as a branch of that discipline. As a consequence of his view that musicology is a branch of a discipline with much wider social and cultural concerns, in his case history, he speaks about a musicology that has a broad reach, rather than a narrow analytic focus. Among other things, he calls for a study of "the mental processes shaping [sounds]" (p. 16) and regards as "dangerous" an isolated view of music that forgets "the impact of music in our social life and the role played by music in humanity" (p. 27).

If historical musicologists with deep roots in the discipline of history have such ethnomusicologically orthodox views, it would seem to follow that a complete musicology—one concerned with integrating our knowledge of music into our knowledge of mental, social, historical, and spiritual processes and with all the music of all peoples and nations—might best be imaged with roots in three far-reaching disciplines: history, anthropology, and psychology. Claims about whether the resulting discipline is humanistic or scientific in its orientation could perhaps be left aside once and for all. Blacking and Gourlay, in their search for what is life-enhancing about music, Feld in his search for the sources of emotional content in music, the Beckers, in their desire to interpret rather than explain musical cultures, have adopted value-based, personal, and difficult-to-compare orientations traditionally associated with the humanities. Some historical musicologists, on the other hand, perhaps taking their cue from developments in history generally and also in ethnomusicology, write about studying music "in the past" rather than "of the past" (Treitler 1982), the "vast masses" and their lives and music as well as the Great Heros and Great Masters, and the social life and mental processes of music—orientations traditionally associated with the social sciences. We seem to be living in an ecumenical age when the disciplines to which we are "sub" are moving closer together. Musicology must take part in that movement. We can both benefit from it and contribute to it. Such a musicology also has a much better chance than our present divided versions of making significant contributions to our knowledge of humankind.

If we are able to create a unified musicology willing to make bold interpretive statements about the nature of the "formative processes" in music, the result would be a new and stronger discipline.[15] Musicology, which now has a rather limited profile and impact in the wider academic world, could take its proper place alongside its cousins in the other humanities and social sciences as a discipline making engaging and coherent claims about people and their artistic, social and intellectual behaviors.

Acknowledgements

This paper and the accompanying responses were originally presented at the 1986 annual meeting of the Society for Ethnomusicology in Rochester, N.Y., October 19, 1986. I am grateful to the respondents for agreeing to participate in this "symposium" and to Bruno Nettl for both his able moderating of the panel and his helpful comments before and after the paper was delivered. To preserve something of the character of the event, the paper and responses are presented with only slight alterations from their original spoken form. At Rochester the responses were followed by comments from the floor, whereas here there is a short response from me.

Notes

1. For a recent list of "research models" in ethnomusicology, see Modir 1986.
2. Carol Robertson (1984: 450) complained recently of the "dozens of dissertations" that comment on "ecology, geography and history without tying these introductory chapters into subsequent chapters on musical sounds."
3. Larry Shumway (1986) criticizes *Worlds of Music* for a "social science orientation" with not enough emphasis on aesthetics and the personal experience of music, a sign that he and others still resist the emphases of much recent research and writing.
4. While the best writers in any field probably have no need of simple models, it strikes me that models may be particularly helpful to students and others trying to find a context for their work. I did a casual survey of dissertations completed in the last seven years at U.S. schools of ethnomusicology and was surprised to find—perhaps naively—that few contextualized their work even perfunctorily within a general theoretical framework in ethnomusicology, but simply considered a particular musical tradition and previous scholarship on it. (The exceptions tended to be work on ethnicity and identity, for which there is a clear and identifiable body of literature.) In effect, ethnomusicology does not exist as a discipline in these dissertations. If they can be taken

as an indicator of the field, then ethnomusicology is, as Blacking (1971: 94) has lamented, "little more than a meeting ground for those interested in the anthropology of music and in music of different cultures." A model, particularly an inclusive one of the sort being suggested here, might allow a higher percentage of students and scholars than at present to imagine the general shape of the field and the place of their work in it.

5. While the perspectives brought to bear on Western and non-Western music often seem different, that does not imply, as Kerman (1985: 174) has suggested, that, "Western music is just too different from other musics, and its cultural contexts too different from other cultural contexts" to allow ethnomusicological research to "impinge directly on the study of Western music." It is not the music and contexts which are so different as too preclude comparative study, so much as the mainstream approaches and values in the two areas that often seem to be at odds.

6. Another slightly more cumbersome way to articulate the question might be:

$$\text{how do people} \quad \left\{ \begin{array}{l} \text{historically} \\ \text{socially} \\ \text{individually} \end{array} \right\} \quad \left\{ \begin{array}{l} \text{create/construct} \\ \text{maintain} \\ \text{experience} \end{array} \right\} \quad \text{music?}$$

The question might also be phrased, how and why do people make music, but the answer to the why question may follow rather naturally from a consideration of how. In any case, Herndon and McLeod and McLeod (1979), Erdman (1982) and Idries Shah among others have all retreated from asking why to asking how. Blacking (1976b: 4) has pointed out that there are important senses in which music makes man, but while this is an engaging aphorism, I prefer the notion that man is always the active agent in the creation, experience and maintenance of music.

7. J. H. Kwabena Nketia (1981, 1985) has recently struggled with the problem of defining the field in two interesting articles. Among other things he is critical of a shift of emphasis from musical experience to the behavior that surrounds music and the assumption "that there is a one-to-one correspondence and a relationship of causality between aspects of music and aspects of culture and society. . . . The assumption is not easily demonstrated even for individual cultures" (1981: 24–25). In his 1985 study he complains that "current approaches in ethnomusicology tend to be monistic or characterised by one dimension of music" (p. 12). He then goes on to call for "the development of an integrative technique that enables the scholar to group and regroup his data" (p. 15) and "developing methods of synthesis that bring together the different aspects of music and music making in a meaningful and coherent manner" (p. 18)—precisely the kind of approach being modeled here. He goes on to construct a categorization of the field based on "three cognitive dimensions of music" (p. 14), which really are more like three methodological stances vis-à-vis music: as culture; as the object of aesthetic interest; and as language. He claims that his cognitive dimensions provide scope for this integrative approach, but without demonstrating how this might happen, leaving it as a "challenge" for ethnomusicology. In fact, it may be precisely this sort of methodological classification, which seems to separate rather than unite us, that may have to be overcome or altered.

8. The thrust of this model may, at first glance, appear to be insular and academic, in comparison to Gourlay's simultaneously pessimistic and activist "humanizing ethnomusicology." In fact, the model has as an important component of its social matrix the teaching enterprise. What are the important lessons about music that we want to convey in the course of a pedagogical process that, at its best and most optimistic, ought to be "humanizing"? I see a great potential for a model like this at least to "humanize" the environments in which we work and the students and colleagues whom we teach.

9. A third approach to historical issues is Kay Shelemay's (1980: 233) notion of "historical ethnomusicology," which involves "the potential that a synchronic study holds for illuminating the historical continuum from which it emerged," a remarkable reversal of the usual claims about the ability of history to illuminate the present. (For another recent reversal of the usual approach to history, see Yung's (1987) notion of "historical interdependency" as a process by which the new affects the perception, construction and revision of the past.) Shelemay thinks that "the lack of

emphasis on historical studies is the result of the break with historical musicology." The lack of emphasis, however, may be more in theory than in practice. Although our methods rest heavily on field work and an implicitly synchronic approach to the "ethnographic present," a large percentage of our published work focuses on processes of change, either directly observed or reconstructed from previously available data. We have, in practice, identified change and historical processes not just as one of many processes, but as a fundamental one. Probably historical processes and interpretations have been resorted to as convenient interpretive gestures when social and cultural processes and interpretations were not observed or were more problematic.

10. Gourlay (1982: 142) objects that analysis is not an approach "to understanding what happens when men and women make music," but it may be a key to understanding what happened when people made music, to reconstructing past experience, and to understanding musical creativity (for example, Cavanagh 1982).

11. Bielawski (1985) attempts to develop a full-blown theory of historical perspectives in ethnomusicology and emphasizes them—perhaps not surprising for an Eastern European—in his statement of basic goals for the field: "To study music from various historical points of view should be the aim of contemporary ethnomusicology" (p. 14). He goes on to argue that systematic and historical perspectives are "supplementary and interdependent," but like so many other claims along this line, he does not go on to say how precisely this might work.

12. McLean (1980: 53): "The one means of compiling a 'history' of Oceanic music is to begin with music styles as currently practised." The study and description of musical styles on the modern map is the beginning of an attempt to reconstruct history (see Nattiez 1982 for an example of a theoretical map with historical density).

13. What will this discipline be called? Gilbert Chase (1976), in a pointed and delightful polemic on the relationship between history, anthropology and musicology, decries the divisions within the discipline and points out a terminological shift since the days of Adler (1885) and Haydon (1941), and a significant retreat from the promise held out by the Harrison, Palisca, Hood volume of 1963 entitled simply, *Musicology*:

> "We have not yet—unfortunately—reached that point in time at which the term *musicology* is generally accepted as signifying the *total* study of music in human culture . . . *musicology*, without any qualifier, has been tacitly appropriated by the historical branch of that discipline" (pp. 231–32).

The terminological situation since the mid-seventies has not improved, although one could cite the 1977 IMS meeting in Berkeley and the *New Grove* as evidence of a theoretical improvement. If usurpation of the term "musicology" was tacit in the mid-70s, it is explicit in the '80s with the publication of Kerman's *Contemplating Music* and the formation in 1982 of the *Journal of Musicology*, which, although it has an ethnomusicologist on the editorial board, pointedly ignores ethnomusicological concerns in its statement of purpose: "A quarterly review of music history, criticism, analysis, and performance practice."

14. Richard Crawford (1985: 2), speaking for the field of American music studies, also carves out an orientation very close to ethnomusicological principles: "For scholars of American music in recent years have more and more looked beyond the selective, aesthetically dominated perspective of the concert hall and begun to consider any kind of music made in America as potentially significant. They have broadened their focus from Music with a capital M to *music-making*: in John Blacking's phrase, from product to process. . . ." He goes on to propose a journalistic who-what-where-when-how model, very similar to one proposed by Anthony Seeger (1980), that gets at issues dear to the hearts of ethnomusicologists.

15. Helen Myers (1981: 43) calls for a rigorous scientific approach based on Popper's notions of falsifiability. "What is required of us is to pose adventurous and imaginative conjectures and then strengthen them by systematically attempting to prove them false." While I share her enthusiasm for "adventurous and imaginative conjectures," the interpretive approach advocated here may not

lead to directly falsifiable statements (Dentan 1984), but rather to complex "stories" that can only be compared using criteria such as completeness, cogency, inclusiveness and so on.

References

Adler, Guido
    1885   "Umfang, Methode und Ziel der Musikwissenschaft," *Vierteljahrsscrift fur Musikwissenschaft* 1: 5–20.
Becker, Judith and A. L.
    1984   "Response to Feld and Roseman," *Ethnomusicology* 28(3): 454–456.
Behague, Gerard
    1984   "Introduction," Performance Practice: *Ethnomusicological Perspectives* (Westport, CT: Greenwood Press), pp. 3–12.
Bielawski, Ludwik
    1985   "History in Ethnomusicology," *Yearbook for Traditional Music* 17: 8–15.
Blacking, John
    1976a   "Introduction," *The Performing Arts: Music and Dance*. The Hague, pp. xiii–xxi.
    1976b   "The Study of Man as Music-Maker," ibid., pp. 3–15.
    1977   "Some Problems of Theory and Method in the Study of Musical Change," *Yearbook of the International Folk Music Society* 9: 1–26.
Blum, Stephen
    1975   "Toward a Social History of Musicological Technique," *Ethnomusicology* 19(2): 207–231.
    Blume, Friedrich
    1972   "Musical Scholarship Today," in Barry S. Brook et al., eds., *Perspectives in Musicology*. New York: Norton, pp. 15–31. Cavanagh, Beverley
    1982   *Music of the Netsilik Eskimo: A Study of Stability and Change*. Ottawa: National Museums of Canada.
Chase, Gilbert
    1976   "Musicology, History, and Anthropology: Current Thoughts," in John W. Grubb, ed., *Current Thought in Musicology*. Austin: University of Texas Press, pp. 231–246.
Crawford, Richard
    1985   *Studying American Music*. New York: Institute for Studies in American Music, Special Publications No. 3.
Dentan, Robert Knox
    1984   "Response to Feld and Roseman," *Ethnomusicology* 28(3): 463–466.
Erdman, Joan
    1982   "The Empty Beat: *Khali* as a Sign of Time," *American Journal of Semiotics* 1(4): 21–45.
Feld, Steven
    1982   *Sound and Sentiment*. Philadelphia: University of Pennsylvania Press.
    1984   "Communication, Music, and Speech about Music," *Yearbook for Traditional Music* 16: 1–18.
Geertz, Clifford
    1973   *The Interpretation of Cultures*. N.Y.: Basic Books.
Gourlay, Kenneth
    1982   "Towards a Humanizing Ethnomusicology," *Ethnomusicology* 26(3): 411–420.
Harrison, Frank LL., Mantle Hood, and Claude V. Palisca
    1963   *Musicology*. Englewood Cliffs, N.J.: Prentice-Hall.
Harwood, Dane
    1976   "Universals in Music: A Perspective from Cognitive Psychology," *Ethnomusicology* 20(3): 521–533.

Haydon, Glen
    1941   *Introduction to Musicology.* N.Y.: Prentice-Hall.
Herndon, Marcia and Norma McLeod
    1979   *Music as Culture.* Norwood, Pa.: Norwood Editions.
    1980   *The Ethnography of Musical Performance.* Norwood, Pa.: Norwood Editions.
Kerman, Joseph
    1985   *Contemplating Music.* Cambridge: Harvard University Press.
Koskoff, Ellen
    1982   "The Music-Network: A Model for the Organization of Music Concepts," *Ethnomusicology* 26(3): 353–370.
McLean, Mervyn
    1980   "Approaches to Music History in Oceania," *World of Music* 22(3): 46–54.
Merriam, Alan P.
    1964   *The Anthropology of Music.* Evanston, Il.: Northwestern University Press.
Meyers, Helen
    1981   "'Normal' Ethnomusicology and 'Extraordinary' Ethnomusicology," *Journal of the Indian Musicological Society* 12(3–4): 38–44.
Modir, Hafez
    1986   "Research Models in Ethnomusicology Applied to the *Radif* Phenomenon in Iranian Classical Music," *Pacific Review of Ethnomusicology* 3: 63–78.
Nattiez, Jean-Jacques
    1982   "Comparisons within a Culture: The Examples of the *Katajjag* of the Inuit," in Robert Falck and Timothy Rice, eds., *Cross-Cultural Perspectives on Music* (Toronto: University of Toronto Press), pp. 134–140.
    1983   "Some Aspects of Inuit Vocal Games," *Ethnomusicology* 27(3): 457–475.
Nettl, Bruno
    1983   *The Study of Ethnomusicology: 29 Issues and Concepts.* Urbana: University of Illinois Press.
Nketia, J. H. Kwabena
    1981   "The Juncture of the Social and the Musical: The Methodology of Cultural Analysis," *World of Music* 23(2): 23–31.
    1985   "Integrating Objectivity and Experience in Ethnomusicological Studies," *World of Music* 27(3): 3–19.
Qureshi, Regula Burckhardt
    1981   "Qawwali Sound, Context and Meaning." PhD Dissertation, University of Alberta.
Robertson, Carol
    1984   "Response to Feld and Roseman," *Ethnomusicology* 28(3): 449–452.
Sawa, George
    1983   "Musical Performance Practice in the Early 'Abbasid Era." PhD Dissertation, University of Toronto.
Seeger, Anthony
    1980   "Sing for your Sister: The Structure and Performance of Suya Akia," in Marcia Herndon and Norma McLeod, eds., *The Ethnography of Musical Performance* (Norwood, Pa.: Norwood Editions), pp. 7–42.
    1985   "General Articles on Ethnomusicology and Related Disciplines [in the *New Grove*]," *Ethnomusicology* 29(2): 345–351.
Seeger, Charles
    1977   "The Musicological Juncture: 1976," *Ethnomusicology* 21(2): 179–188.
Shelemay, Kay Kaufman
    1980   " 'Historical Ethnomusicology': Reconstructing Falasha Ritual," *Ethnomusicology* 24(2): 233–258.

Shepherd, John
  1982   "A Theoretical Model for the Sociomusicological Analysis of Popular Musics," in Richard Middleton and David Horn, eds., *Popular Music 2: Theory and Method*. Cambridge University Press, pp. 145–178.
Shumway, Larry
  1986   Review of *Worlds of Music*, *Ethnomusicology* 30(2): 356–357.
Stone, Ruth
  1982   *Let the Inside Be Sweet*. Bloomington, Indiana University Press.
Thomas, Lewis
  1974   *Lives of a Cell*. N.Y.: Viking Press.
Titon, Jeff Todd, general ed.
  1984   *Worlds of Music*. New York: Schirmer.
Treitler, Leo
  1982   "Structural and Critical Analysis," in D. Kern Holoman and Claude V. Palisca, eds., *Musicology in the 1980s* (N.Y.: Da Capo Press), pp. 67–77.
Wachsmann, Klaus
  1982   "The Changeability of Musical Experience," *Ethnomusicology* 26(2): 197–215.
Wade, Bonnie
  1984   "Performance Practice in Indian Classical Music," in Gerard Behague, ed., *Performance Practice: Ethnomusicological Perspectives* (Westport, CT: Greenwood Press), pp. 13–52.
Yung, Bell
  1984   "Choreographic and Kinesthetic Elements in Performance on the Chinese Seven-String Zither," *Ethnomusicology* 28(3): 505–517.
  1987   "Historical Interdependency of Music: Case Study of the Chinese Seven-String Zither," *Journal of the American Musicological Society* 40(1): 82–91.
Zemp, Hugo
  1978   "'Are'Are Classification of Musical Types and Instruments," *Ethnomusicology* 22(1): 37–67.

Whose Ethnomusicology?
Western Ethnomusicology
and the Study of Asian Music

J. Lawrence Witzleben / Chinese University of Hong Kong

This article grew out of a long-term particularized encounter between a Western ethnomusicologist and Asians who study and respond to the discipline.[1] Since 1988, I have been teaching graduate and undergraduate courses in ethnomusicology and Chinese music at the Chinese University of Hong Kong.[2] In the graduate seminars, I present a version of the Western ethnomusicological canon to students from Hong Kong, mainland China, and Taiwan who are preparing to start or continue research on some aspect of Chinese music. These seminars, along with various conferences where I have presented my own work and ideas and discussed them with Chinese scholars, have been central to the present discussion: the process of teaching and representing the discipline of ethnomusicology has necessitated a reevaluation of the field and my own relationship to it. Additional ideas have come from teaching "music in world cultures" and Chinese music topics including instrumental music, folk song, and twentieth century music history. In the latter type of courses, I have been primarily perpetuating another set of canons, those of my teachers at the Shanghai Conservatory and of other musicians and scholars in China.[3]

These various encounters have suggested the need for a reassessment of the nature of ethnomusicology and its suitability or transmutability for both the study of Chinese and other Asian musics (by anyone) and the training of indigenous researchers in Chinese and other non-Western societies. The present article is a personal response which is linked to the many Asian voices which have prompted such a response. It is both a critique and a defense of Western ethnomusicology: a critique of the Western-centered concerns which continue to shape the discipline, and a defense of the ideas, methods, and fundamental concerns which continue to invigorate it.

From *Ethnomusicology,* Vol. 41, No. 2 (Summer 1997), pp. 220–42

"Whose Ethnomusicology?" is a fundamental question for all participants in the dialogue between this discipline of European and American origins and the students and scholars elsewhere who study it, reshape it, or distance themselves from it. Since the days when ethnomusicology was known as comparative musicology, and despite continually changing definitions, models, and methodologies, the search to realize a field of study capable of encompassing all musics has remained a guiding principle of the discipline. This is evident in practical models such as the Sachs-Hornbostel scheme of instrument classification (Hornbostel and Sachs 1990) and Alan Lomax's studies of folk song style (1968, 1976), but no less so in conceptual models such as Alan Merriam's (1964) and its subsequent modifications by Timothy Rice and others (1987). Scholars such as Bruno Nettl (1964, 1983) and Mantle Hood (1982) have combined practical and conceptual elements in their overviews of ethnomusicology and ethnomusicologists. More recent summaries of the field show that while a diversity of subfields, methods, and regional or conceptual specializations are widely accepted, the idea of ethnomusicology as a cross-culturally valid discipline remains strong. However, for many scholars in Asia and elsewhere, ethnomusicology is still widely perceived as ethnocentric and predominantly oriented towards the study of "others'" music by Western scholars.

This article raises two fundamental questions for the discipline: (1) Is "ethnomusicology" as understood and practiced in the United States and Europe suitable for or appropriate to the needs of non-Euro-American scholars? and (2) How can we reconcile the universalistic ideals of ethnomusicology as an academic discipline with the specialized needs and established scholarly conventions of a particular culture and its musics? The issues raised here are discussed with particular reference to the cultures of Hong Kong and China, but they are by no means culture-specific. I will address these questions by looking at two themes which have been central to ethnomusicology in the West—cross-cultural fieldwork and multicultural music knowledge—along with several recent developments which are of particular relevance to the issues at hand. I will follow this with a brief discussion of recent music scholarship in China—most specifically, though not exclusively, what is referred to there as "ethnomusicology"—and its compatibility (or non-compatibility) with its Western counterpart. In conclusion, I will look at the implications of these issues as a case study in the possibilities and problems of developing a less Western-oriented ethnomusicology. Although the questions raised here have arisen primarily from interactions with students, colleagues, and counterparts whose primary interest is Chinese music, I have used the term "Asian" in the title and in certain other instances because many of the issues raised here concerning compatibility with Western ethnomusicology are relevant to many parts of Asia. More than in the use of musical notation (where China and India, for example, are quite different), I believe that the common ground lies in the extensive indigenous written traditions of talking about music: history, theory, aesthetics, and the relationship of musical traditions to cultural sensibilities and other art forms. This is not to say that the problems raised here are not applicable to non-Asian non-Western cultures vis a vis ethnomusicology. In this paper, however, I am focusing on the particular kinds of problems raised by the existence of long-standing written traditions of music scholarship.

Crossing Cultures

In their book *Anthropology as Cultural Critique,* George Marcus and Michael Fisher observe that "(T)he significance of the expectation that all neophyte anthropologists should be tested by fieldwork in a foreign language, culture, and living arrangement cannot be overemphasized, since whatever they go on to do later . . . an often romanticized ethnographic fellowship is what all anthropologists share" (1986:21). Whether we consider ethnomusicology to be a sub-discipline of either anthropology or musicology or—as I understand it—a syncretic discipline drawing from both, the central place of fieldwork is something which unites anthropology and ethnomusicology, and the idea of a "romanticized ethnographic fellowship" certainly has an ethnomusicological counterpart. When we look at the prominence of Asian and African scholars specializing in their own cultures' traditions and teaching in ethnomusicology programs in the United States and Europe, it would seem that the concept of an ethnomusicologist as someone who by definition studies the music of a culture other than his or her own has become something of an anachronism. However, the idea of studying "the other" as a norm continues to persist. For example, in the recent book *Ethnomusicology: An Introduction,* Helen Myers states that "(T)oday's student is expected to immerse himself or herself in the totality of a foreign culture, usually for a year or more, and experience music first-hand in its diverse settings" (1992:22). If taken as a normative description of "what ethno-musicologists do," this definition is questionable, but not indefensible; as a state-ment of the "character and purpose of ethnomusicological fieldwork" (ibid.:xxii), it is an unfortunate reaffirmation of the preeminence of the researcher—almost inevitably a Westerner—studying the music of a culture other than his or her own. Even if we accept the idea that cross-cultural fieldwork is no longer a categorical imperative for a would-be ethnomusicologist, it is undeniable that such experiences have shaped the development of the field. A glance at the list of authors of the other articles in *Ethnomusicology: An Introduction* or of the studies in collections such as Titon 1992 or Nettl et al. 1992 indicates that a high proportion of the recognized experts in the field continue to specialize in musics of other countries or other ethnic groups.

More germane to the present discussion is the fact that despite the prominent position of the indigenous scholar in ethnomusicology today, a bias in favor of cross-cultural fieldwork in a distant and difficult environment remains strong, and this bias (intentionally or not) sometimes marginalizes or even trivializes the increasingly prominent work of scholars studying their own culture's traditions. Colleagues and friends from Asia and elsewhere who have studied ethnomusicology in the United States have mentioned that many American students of ethnomusicology tend to look down on those doing fieldwork in their indigenous cultures, presumably because this type of research is not exotic or difficult enough to serve as a "rite of passage." This attitude illustrates a romanticized viewpoint in which more attention is given to the hardships overcome by the researcher than to the quality of the research produced. (It should also be noted that a foreign student participating in a Western ethnomusicology program may already have gained considerable experience in the problems of crossing cultures and dealing with hardships of a different kind.)

In the broader contemporary cultural and academic environment of the United States, the situation is somewhat different; a researcher studying the music of a given culture is often perceived not only as a scholar but as a spokesperson or advocate for that culture, and the cultural outsider may face questions of both credibility and entitlement. What is all too easily forgotten is that "insider" and "outsider" are multiplex and relative perspectives. Every researcher is an insider in some respects and an outsider in others: a "cultural insider" exists at many levels of specificity (ethnicity, language, dialect; country, region, village, or neighborhood of one's origin), as does a "musical insider" (general music knowledge, performer or theorist, knowledge of a specific instrument or tradition, level of performance skill). In addition, each individual has a unique combination of attributes which connect them to or distance them from a particular topic, group, or individual: these include gender, age, religion, economic or class background, education, and political orientation. Even in an ethnomusicology program whose purpose is to train "emic" researchers (in the broad sense of "Chinese people studying Chinese music"), insider/outsider issues are still highly relevant, as the people and traditions studied are in some respects inevitably "the other." The researcher's native dialect and the social system in which they have grown up (mainland China, Taiwan, Hong Kong, and so on) are obvious indicators of his or her relationship to the subject matter, but levels of musical knowledge may also be quite significant. In the words of one performer, scholars who have not learned to perform the music, even those from the same locale and dialect group, are all "standing outside the door" (*zhan zai men wai*). For many musicians, expertise in the performance of their tradition is the most important prerequisite to credibility.

In part, the perception that ethnomusicologists work in distant or foreign cultures derives from the many widely-read and evocative descriptions of such research. The more subtle layers of boundary-crossing faced by researchers studying musical traditions which are to some extent their "own" are still rarely elucidated, despite the increasing prominence of ethnomusicological studies by cultural insiders.[4]

Multicultural Music Knowledge

There is a broad consensus within the discipline that ethnomusicology's subject matter includes all (or nearly all, with Western art music being the most common exception) of the world's musics, but there is virtually no consensus on, or even serious discussion of, the minimum corpus of knowledge required of a specialist in our discipline: how many parts of this musical landscape should a professional ethnomusicologist be familiar with, and how much should he or she know about each of these parts? From an idealistic humanistic perspective, the answers are simple: "all parts," and "as much as possible." The implied and sometimes explicit credo is not only that all musics are equally deserving of study, but that anyone calling themselves an ethnomusicologist should have at least a basic knowledge of the world's main musical culture areas. In practice, a graduate student in the United States takes a mixture of survey courses of broad geographical scope, area studies of particular countries or regions, seminars which draw material from a wide variety of cultures, and perhaps performance training in non-Western traditions. As teachers, ethnomusicologists are typically expected to expand their knowledge to develop courses such as "Music in World Cultures" and area courses outside of their own regional specialization.

Since the early 1980s, several textbooks intended for undergraduate courses have appeared. The scopes and aims of these books are somewhat different: Elizabeth May's anthology intentionally omits Europe and non-Native North America, as material on these areas is readily available elsewhere (1980:xi); Jeff Titon's book is presented as a series of case studies rather than as a survey (1992:xxii); the collection by Bruno Nettl et al. combines overviews with a focus on "detailed description of a musical event which may be considered broadly representative of its cultural area" (1992:2). Nevertheless, the inclusions and omissions do tell us something about ethnomusicologists' musical map of the world (see Table 1). The areas shared among the three books are Sub-Saharan Africa, India, Indonesia, Japan, Latin America, and Native American music of North America. Perhaps not coincidentally, these areas include the primary research areas for a high percentage of the ethnomusicologists who have most influenced the field. These six areas can also be taken as one representative sampling of the world's music cultures; coincidentally or not, this list also includes so-called non-literate and literate cultures in a roughly equal mix.

Table 1: Comparison of Countries and Culture Areas Covered in *Worlds of Music* **(Titon 1992),** *Excursions* **(Nettl, Capwell, et al. 1992), and** *Musics of Many Cultures* **(May 1980).**

	Titon	Nettl et al.	May
Africa		Sub-Sahara	South of Sahara
			Ethiopia
	Ghana		Ghana (Anlo Ewe)
Asia		China	China
	South India	India	India (classical)
	Indonesia	Indonesia	Indonesia (3 islands)
	Japan	Japan	Japan
			Korea
			Thailand
Europe	Eastern Europe	Europe	
	(peasant cultures)	(Vienna, art music)	
Latin America		Latin America	
			South American Folk
			South American Indian
Middle East		Middle East	
			Arabic (secular classical)
			Iran (classical)
			Jewish Music
North America	Black America		
	Native America	North American Indian	Native America
			Alaskan Eskimos
		Old World Cultures	
Oceania			Australian Aborigine
			Polynesia

It would be unfair to read too much into the selection of cultures covered in the most recent collections of area studies (Titon, Nettl et al.), but their shared inclusions and omissions do reflect emphases which are common in the field of ethnomusicology: Indonesia (but not mainland Southeast Asia), Japan (but not Korea), and Oceania conspicuous by its absence. In an undergraduate survey course, a selective and arbitrary study of a few musical cultures is inevitable, but when we look at the more intensive coursework expected of graduate students in ethnomusicology, the lack of a shared corpus of knowledge becomes more prob-lematical. While virtually all ethnomusicology programs require some intensive study in areas other than the student's own specialization, the acquisition of this multicultural music knowledge is widely varied and even somewhat haphazard. For example, while at the University of Hawai'i (1978–81) I took area courses on the musics of Hawai'i, the Philippines, and India; other students during the same time frame took courses on Africa, Japan, and Oceania. Thus, while all students in a given program usually receive similar training in the methods and tools of ethnomusicology, their knowledge of particular musical cultures is much more diverse.

As writings on and recordings of the world's musical traditions proliferate, it becomes increasingly obvious that no individual can have expertise in the totality of any one musical culture, let alone multiple cultures. However, despite the increasing specialization of scholarly writing in our field, I believe that multicultural training remains essential for ethnomusicologists, if only to suggest the many possibilities of musical expression. Moreover, the problem of ethnocentrism is not limited to Western culture. Publications, conference papers, and statements by musicians, scholars, and students in China and Hong Kong indicate that many stereotypes about other countries and ethnic groups persist. Many portrayals of Chinese minority cultures by Han Chinese (the dominant majority ethnic group in China) may be seen as patronizing or exoticizing (see Rees 1995). As Stevan Harrell has noted, this "older brother-younger brother" view of more- and less-developed cultures reflects both Marxist-Leninist-Maoist and traditional Confucian values (1995:3–36).[5] One of the most positive attributes of ethnomusicology is its potential for fostering a sense of cultural relativism and respect for other musics and cultures. In a more practical sense, knowledge of each others' writings and music is one thing that brings some degree of unity to our diversity of backgrounds and interests within the field.

Despite the absence of a widely accepted corpus of knowledge, most Western ethnomusicologists view geographical breadth of musical knowledge as highly desirable, if not essential. The value of multicultural studies, however, is by no means universally acknowledged. In China, the serious study of Chinese music is perceived as a full-time and lifelong task. Among scholars of Chinese music, specialization in one of the subfields, distinguished either by genre (instrumental music, folk song, opera, narrative, song and dance), ethnic group, or orientation (theory, history, and so on), is the norm. Some knowledge of Western music is assumed or required, but the multicultural studies which are central to Western ethnomusicology are perceived as, at best, diversions.[6] However, the principle of cultural relativism is fundamental to the nature of ethnomusicology; if so-called "musicology" had treated Western art music as one musical system among equals rather than as the primary focus of the study of "music," there would have been less need to develop a "comparative musicology" or "ethnomusicology" to deal with all the musics excluded from the mainstream of musicology. Although no reasonable scholar would claim expertise in all of the world's musics, the best ethnomusicological scholarship is grounded in a broadly-based multicultural awareness of music. It is one thing to discuss a localized tradition of scholarship such as "Chinese ethnomusicology," quite another to use—or, as I see it, misuse—the word "ethnomusicology" to refer to scholarship which is solely concerned with the music of one country or cultural area.

Recent Issues in Western Ethnomusicology

Among the first generation of self-proclaimed ethnomusicologists, a fusion of the parent disciplines of musicology and anthropology was the norm, although individual scholars or specific studies naturally tended to gravitate more to one than to the other. In recent years, the anthropological orientation has become increasingly prominent. As Peter Manuel has observed, "musicological analysis has now tended to be overshadowed by ethnological studies, which draw more from anthropology than musicology. To some extent, the greater prominence of anthropological-oriented studies is due to the fact that they are inherently more readable and accessible, and therefore read by more people" (1995, paragraph 9). Nazir Jairazbhoy recently referred to this trend as the swing of a "pendulum," which will presumably return to a more musicological orientation at some point in the future (1995a). In fact, Jairazbhoy's own book on North Indian classical music is singled out by Peter Manuel as an example of a musicological approach. Manuel describes the book as a "brilliant" but "inherently difficult and esoteric" work, contrasting it with Steven Feld's more widely accessible anthropological orientation (Manuel 1995, paragraph 5, citing Jairazbhoy 1995b and Feld 1990).

Somewhat in contrast to Manuel's conclusions, Regula Qureshi suggests that ethnomusicology and musicology are becoming increasingly compatible: "Despite profound epistemological differences, however, musicologists—not anthropologists—have gradually proceeded to accommodate ethnomusicologists and their ahistorical ways; this academic coexistence is leading ethnomusicologists to an increasing engagement with musicological orientations. In academia, musical bonds have clearly proven stronger than disciplinary ones" (1995:332–33).

Obviously, both the perception of and reception given to ethnomusicologists by musicologists or anthropologists vary considerably. If, as Qureshi suggests, many anthropologists show little interest in the study of music (ibid.:333, note 7), other ethnomusicologists find that it is their colleagues specializing in Western music (including those from non-Western cultures) who tend to treat ethnomusicology and ethnomusicologists with condescension or even outright hostility.

In personal conversations and electronic forums, perceived or suggested directions in the study of ethnomusicology are often the subject of heated discussion. One particularly lively debate was touched off by Terry Miller's complaint that two recent collections of articles were unfairly dismissed by reviewers for being "methodologically weak": "What disturbs me is the trend I notice towards judgment of validity and worth in others' work . . . The alleged Scholastic Correctness movement that I see enveloping the field says that a writer who is not informed by someone else's paradigm may be methodologically weak . . . Writers who fail to invoke a methodology are sometimes cast into the scholar's hell with the judgment that his/her work is 'merely descriptive' or simply 'musical ethnography'" (1994).[7] He goes on to suggest that "ethnomusicology resembles more an intellectual Tower of Babel than a cerebral melting pot" (ibid.). Several other scholars responded with a defense of "theoretical and interpretive approaches," including the following: "[purely descriptive writing] leads to highly specialized and often mutually incomprehensible research because the writer has no larger frame in which to engage discussion. This, in my opinion, is a far worse intellectual Tower of Babel than anything Terry can evoke: let the Javanists talk matters of 'wilet' and 'garap' while others listen in mute amazement" (Lysloff 1994). The discussion became further complicated with the suggestion that culture-specific ideas about music are also a kind of theoretical approach: "May I ask on what ethnomusicological theory is to be based, if not on highly specialised, descriptive, detailed, analytical studies of individual musical cultures and musical systems? And do not concepts such as wilet and garap constitute theory—admittedly not the kind of theory generated by outside ethnomusicologists, but the kind actually used by musicians in the cultures we study?" (Widdess 1994).

To a student outside of the United States, these discussions are at best perplexing: what is to be gained by entering a discipline whose advocates are in such disagreement on the fundamental nature of the field? As one attempting to teach and promote the discipline to such students, I am bothered by the degree of intolerance which pervades this and many other current discussions among Western ethnomusicologists. All the scholars cited in the preceding paragraphs address issues of communication and accessibility, which are obviously important criteria for assessing any scholarly writing. However, ethnomusicological writers have always expected readers to deal with large quantities of unfamiliar terminology and concepts. Indigenous names and classificatory schemes, whether they refer to melodic frameworks (Jairazbhoy 1995), song and speech types (Anthony Seeger 1987), or birds (Feld 1990:44–85), are essential to our understandings of musics and cultures. Obviously, some writings will be comprehensible primarily to specialists in music, while others are aimed at readers familiar with other branches of scholarship; this is endemic to an interdisciplinary field such as our own. However, the traditional tension between anthropological and musicological approaches seems to have become augmented by new ways to categorize or stigmatize ethnomusicologists and their work: the "area specialist" (whose purely descriptive studies, filled with foreign terms, are incomprehensible to all but others specializing in the same area) and "cultural theorist" (whose writings, filled with jargon from other specialized disciplines, are incomprehensible to those not already conversant in those disciplines) have come to represent diverging, and at times oppositional, tendencies within the discipline of ethnomusicology.

Despite some dissension within the ranks of ethnomusicologists, inter-disciplinary cooperation on a variety of fronts is increasing. Joint conferences held by ethnomusicologists in conjunction with specialists in disciplines such as folklore and performance studies (discussed in Lysloff 1984) have become commonplace events. As ethnomusicologists become increasingly concerned with the historical component of their study, musicologists are expanding the cultural aspects of their own discipline. In part, this development has been influenced by a rapprochement between history and anthropology, which has in turn influenced many aspects of music scholarship (see Qureshi 1995). The confluence of history and anthropology can also be observed in Timothy Rice's revision of Merriam's model for the study of music; a key element in Rice's new model is the incorporation of historical processes, as developed from the ideas of anthropologist Clifford Geertz (Rice 1987:473, citing Geertz 1973:363–64).

One other recent development is a modest return of "comparative musicology" as an approach within or related to ethnomusicology. Although the latter term has become the preferred name (at least in the United States) for a disci-pline which includes all of the world's musics, the former is by no means extinct: many prominent scholars contributed to the volume *Comparative Musicology and the Anthropology of Music* (Nettl and Bohlman 1991), and other recent studies explicitly emphasize comparative study as a methodological framework. Thomas Turino's explanation of the values of comparative research is framed with references to Merriam and Nettl, and is consistent with the ideals of earlier scholars: "comparison is potentially positive insofar as it broadens the boundar-ies of what we are able to think by giving us alternative ideologies, discourses, and experiences to think with. From my perspective, this is a major object of ethnomusicological work in general and this book in particular" (1993:6). In contrast to the global ambitions of earlier scholars such as Hornbostel, Lomax, and Sachs, recent comparative studies tend to focus on closely related cultures (such as Anglo and Anglo-American) or different locales or traditions within a single culture. Turino, who examines Peruvian music and musicians in differ-ent locales, describes his approach as "explicitly comparative, grounded ethno-graphically at the local level" (ibid.:7).

Although a considerable amount of literature comparing musical cultures exists, there has been rather little serious comparison of traditions of discourse and scholarship. Despite increasing interaction with scholars outside the Euro-American traditions, we know far more about the different ways of making music than of our different ways of researching and writing about music. Pri-mary source materials are certainly available in Western language translations (Lee 1981 and Becker and Feinstein 1984–88, for example), as are studies of non-Western developments in music scholarship (such as Wong 1991) and of the problems arising in cross-cultural clashes between different traditions of scholarship (such as Racy 1991). In terms of the development of our discipline, however, Western ethnomusicologists are much more likely to draw methodological inspiration from other branches of Western scholarship than from other cultures' traditions of music scholarship. We are certainly aware of the existence of alternative canons of study and of their differentness; Bruno Nettl has noted the significance of non-Western traditions of study (see 1983:267–68, for example), but even he indirectly acknowledges the preliminary nature of our understanding of these traditions: "there is a long-standing tradition of musical scholarship in India, and Indian scholars publish widely. While it is difficult to characterize, their work has a unique flavor and character" (ibid.:267). If Indian musical scholarship, a considerable amount of which is written in English, remains unknown to most Western ethnomusicologists, it is hardly surprising that the scholarly traditions of the rest of Asia have not been given their due.

Ethnomusicology and Music Scholarship in China

Since the 1980s the term *minzu yinyuexue*—literally, the study of the music of peoples or ethnic groups—has been used both as a translation for the English word "ethnomusicology" and as the name of an indigenous branch of musical scholarship in China. Not all scholars using this term consider themselves "ethnomusicologists" in the Western sense, and not all Chinese scholars who do consider themselves ethnomusicologists use the term *minzu yinyuexue*. The directions and branches of music scholarship in China have been summarized elsewhere (Zhang 1985, Wong 1991), and recent developments deserve discussion which is far beyond the scope of the present article. However, in order to examine the problems of applying or teaching Western ethnomusicology in Hong Kong or China, some discussion of contemporary Chinese scholarship is necessary.

Isabel Wong (ibid.) has discussed twentieth-century musicology in China in terms of six historical stages, and includes discussion of ethnomusicology within this framework. Concentrating specifically on the development of ethnomusicology in China, Shen Qia (1996) suggests that the discipline's evolution can be divided into four periods. The first period (1924–39), "comparative musicology" (*bijiao yinyuexue*), includes the work of Wang Guangqi, who studied with Carl Stumpf, Erich von Hornbostel, and Curt Sachs, and of Liu Tianhua, best know as a composer of music for the *erhu* and *pipa*, but also an active collector of folk music. The second period (1939–50), "folk music research" (*minjian yinyue yanjiu*), although framed by domestic and international turmoil, saw considerable activity in folk song collection and Chinese music scholarship, including the emergence of Yang Yinliu as this century's preeminent scholar of Chinese music (the contributions of Wang Guangqi, Liu Tianhua, and Yang

Yinliu are discussed in Wong 1991). The period from 1950 through 1980 was dominated by "Chinese (or 'ethnic') music theory" (*minzu yinyue lilun*), while "ethnomusicology" (*minzu yinyuexue*) has emerged as a major development from 1980 on.

The term *minzu* means "a people" or "ethnic group"; according to Shen Qia (1996:5–9), early proponents of *minzu yinyue lilun* such as Shen Zhibai conceived it as a discipline which was multicultural in scope. However, as it developed in the post-1950 period, *minzu yinyue lilun* came to refer more specifically to the study of Chinese music, including genres (instrumental music, folk song, and so on) and musical forms and structures. *Lilun* ("theory") is actually used in a much more expansive sense than the English term implies; at the Shanghai Conservatory, for example, courses taught under this label also include historical and cultural aspects of music, form and analysis, aesthetics, and learning to perform the musics studied. The term *minzu yinyuexue* was introduced by Luo Chuankai (Shen 1996:9), who borrowed the ideographs from the already accepted Japanese translation of "ethnomusicology," *minzoku ongakugaku*. However, since *minzu yinyue* had already become widely understood as referring to "Chinese traditional music," the addition of the syllable *xue* ("study," widely used in the same way as the suffix "-logy" to indicate a branch of study) to refer to "ethnomusicology" has caused, and continues to cause, a great deal of confusion. Not all contemporary scholars in China accept the name or even the concept of *minzu yinyuexue*/ethnomusicology, which continues to co-exist with *minzu yinyue lilun* and a variety of other names for and approaches to the study of Chinese music. The term *yinyuexue* (musicology) is also widely used. Conservatories and research institutes vary widely in the names used for disciplines and sub-disciplines; depending on the context or institution, *yinyuexue* may refer either specifically to the study of Western art music or to a more comprehensive Seegerian musicology which includes Chinese music as one branch of study.

The emergence of ethnomusicology as a distinct discipline of music research in China is linked to the use of the term *minzu yinyuexue* as the title of a major conference held in Nanjing in 1980. The resultant published papers (Zhongguo 1981) do not show an obvious break from the scholarship of "Chinese music theory"; in fact, modern Chinese researchers have always done a great deal of "what ethnomusicologists do": many scholars have conducted extensive fieldwork, and the concept of music in (or as) culture has been integral to their work. However, unlike the Western version of ethnomusicology, the articles from this collection are almost exclusively concerned with Chinese music. Fieldwork experience notwithstanding, performance context and the perspectives of performers are rarely discussed in any detail.

Since the early 1980s, *minzu yinyuexue* has begun to emerge as a more distinct branch of scholarship. Translations of Western ethnomusicological writings have become available, including selections from scholars such as Nettl, Merriam, Hood, and Jaap Kunst (Shanghai 1984, Dong and Shen 1985) and Nketia's book *Music of Africa* (1982), and their ideas and techniques have been borrowed, adapted, or debated. Although economic and other factors make extended fieldwork overseas difficult to impossible, a growing number of studies on cultures other than China or the West have been produced (Shen 1996:13 lists over twenty such studies). Non-Western-non-Chinese music is often collectively referred to as *Ya Fei La yinyue,* a contraction of the words for Asia (Yazhou), Africa (Feizhou), and Latin America (Lading Meizhou).

Many of the scholars in China whose ideas and interests are closest to Western ethnomusicology are Han Chinese working in one or more of the minority cultures. In a sense, their work is cross-cultural and often multicultural as well, since they often investigate the traditions of many different minority peoples (as in Du 1993, for example). Thus, they face many of the same tasks and problems as Western ethnomusicologists: they must cope with unfamiliar environments, language acquisition, oral traditions (though not exclusively so), and are perceived to a certain extent as cultural outsiders. Not surprisingly, these Chinese ethnomusicologists are quite interested in etic/emic issues (see Shen 1993, for example).

Chinese ethnomusicology's relationship to the related disciplines of anthropology and musicology is rather different from the situation found in the West. Concepts such as cultural relativism and the anthropological components of Western ethnomusicology have influenced a good number of Chinese scholars, but anthropology itself has had little direct influence on music research. Anthropology has had somewhat of a turbulent history in China: ethnology in particular has often been denounced as fundamentally colonial and imperialistic in nature, and much of the ethnographic study that has been sanctioned has occurred within the purview of "minority studies."[8] While some specific topics or directions in music scholarship have at times met with severe ideological criticism and even persecution, the study of music in general and Chinese music in particular has been far less controversial than anthropology, and it should come as no surprise that scholars of Chinese music have not universally championed the incorporation of a significant anthropological dimension into music research. More practically, music research in China occurs primarily in conservatories and arts institutes, so that anthropology coursework for music students or even regular interaction with anthropologists is far more complicated than in Western countries.

As in the West, in China the relationship between ethnomusicology and Western musicology is often problematical. In many ways, the hegemony of Western art music is even stronger in China than in contemporary Western culture. This problem is compounded by a highly restrictive view of "Western music" (essentially common-practice Western art music) which has shaped Chinese music education and scholarship. Tuning systems outside of twelve tone equal temperament are widely viewed as "backward" or "unscientific"; even though many ethnomusicologists and other scholars are aware of the flaws in such a viewpoint, serious investigation of regional tuning systems is still relatively rare. Similarly, discussion or teaching of traditional improvisational practices has been hampered by the idealization of the "correct" version of a written score.[9] Still, the dominance of Western-based ideas about music bothers many Chinese scholars, just as it has been an ongoing irritant to Western ethnomusicologists.

Toward a Multicultural Ethnomusicology

Like their counterparts in many other places, students in Hong Kong vary considerably not only in their academic and musical backgrounds, but also in their attitudes towards ethnomusicology as practiced in the West; some uninformed, others already knowledgeable and enthusiastic to learn more, still others suspicious of what they already do know about the field. In the processes of discussing ethnomusicology with Chinese students and colleagues and re-reading the discipline's literature in light of their reactions, the issues raised above have been recurring themes. Despite the universal aims and ideals of ethnomusicology, the discipline as practiced in the West continues to be pervaded with the perspectives and problems of Western scholars studying traditions other than their own, and this is exemplified by the continuing emphases on cross-cultural fieldwork and oral traditions. Nevertheless, I believe that many of the concerns of Western ethnomusicologists are also quite relevant to the indigenous scholar in an Asian or other non-Western culture. Every researcher must deal with "insider" or "outsider" perspectives, although their nature and scope are naturally quite different when working in a familiar culture and environment. Methods developed for the study of non-literate cultures are not fundamentally different from those appropriate for written traditions; they simply must be supplemented by study of the relevant indigenous scholarship and the integration of oral and written resources.

The question of specialized needs and scholarly conventions of a particular culture and its musics is more problematical. In the specific case which prompted this article, the ethnomusicology program at the Chinese University of Hong Kong, all ethnomusicology graduate students are specializing in some aspect of Chinese music, and their future credibility as scholars in a Chinese society will stem primarily from their knowledge of Chinese music and music research. This differs markedly from the situation in the West, where expertise in a specific culture area is often secondary to the ability to teach about and supervise research on the music of most or all of the the non-Western world.

Even within an ethnomusicology program with a strong regional focus, considerable diversity exists. Studying one's "own" music may be understood both in a local sense of "Hong Kong people studying Hong Kong's music" and in a pan-Chinese sense of "Chinese people studying China's music." At the Chinese University of Hong Kong, more than a third of the graduate students in ethnomusicology are from mainland China and Taiwan. While many Hong Kong students focus on traditions indigenous to their own Cantonese dialect region, others have conducted their research in mainland China or Taiwan, including Chinese minority cultures. Still, although the regional emphasis of an ethnomusicology program such as that in Hong Kong will naturally be somewhat stronger than that of its counterpart in the West, the need for an understanding of "music" (let alone "ethnomusicology") that transcends the study of one's "own" music is no less imperative in a Chinese society than it is elsewhere.[10]

Ideally, intensive study of both Western ethnomusicology and indigenous Chinese scholarship on music can lead to a truly multicultural approach to the study of music. Despite the differences between Western ethnomusicology and Chinese music scholarship pointed out above, many areas of compatibility already exist: to cite just a few examples, Wang Yaohua's research on the Chinese sanxian and its counterparts in Okinawa and Japan (1991) has much in common with the new comparative musicology developing in the West; Qiao Jianzhong's work in establishing regional stylistic areas for Chinese folk song (Miao and Qiao 1987) has parallels with ethnomusicological scholarship on European, African, and Native American cultures; Li Minxiong's studies of tune derivations (1983) are intellectual cousins of Charles Seeger and "Barbara Allen" (1977). In fact, culturally grounded intra-cultural comparative study has been at the forefront of modern Chinese music scholarship, and this is a development we can all learn from. The integration of music history with contemporary practice found in much Chinese scholarship is also something we are still struggling to achieve in the West. Finally, although they rarely make an issue of this fact, many contemporary scholars in China, like their Western ethnomusicological counterparts, have done extensive and meticulous fieldwork.

I am arguing here that music scholarship in China is essentially compatible with and complementary to Western ethnomusicology. The anthropological component of ethnomusicology strikes me as the aspect which may be most directly applicable to the study of Chinese music, since China already has well-developed indigenous musicological traditions. Although an emphasis on "music sound" rather than contextual or conceptual aspects of music is somewhat out of fashion in contemporary Western ethnomusicology, even most anthropologically-oriented ethnomusicologists, from Alan Merriam to Anthony Seeger, have viewed it as an essential part of our discipline. It is often stated that the study of music sound alone is inadequate for any understanding of a musical tradition, but Merriam and Seeger are equally adamant that the study of sound must not be neglected:

> The music product is inseparable from the behavior that produces it; the behavior in turn can only in theory be distinguished from the concepts that underlie it; and all are tied together through the learning feedback from product to concept . . . if we do not understand one we cannot properly understand the others; if we fail to take cognizance of the parts, then the whole is irretrievably lost. (Merriam 1964:35)

> The illusion that music can exist separately from its performers and audiences has led to confusion, long debate and a tendency to treat ethnomusicology as a divided field in which writers either analyse sounds or analyse social and cultural features of music making . . . Studies of musical products—sounds—often have not seriously investigated the interaction of the sounds with the performers and audiences. Studies of performers, audiences, and action have sometimes completely ignored the sounds produced and appreciated. (Seeger 1992:89)

Ethnomusicology developed as a reaction to the limitations of traditional musicology, and many of the canons of ethnomusicology clearly set it apart as a distinct field, or at least as a branch requiring specialized areas of knowledge such as fieldwork, transcription, and multicultural music studies. Less attention has been given, however, to several fundamental ways in which ethnomusicology differs from anthropology.

Firstly, the study of music allows the possibility of a high degree of participation, which may significantly alter the power relationships between the researcher and the culture studied. Bruno Nettl has quite accurately observed that so-called "informants" are in fact the "principal teachers" of many ethnomusicologists (1984), and a deferential attitude is common (though by no means universal) in both fieldwork situations and the resultant writings. By the very nature of the study of music, ethnomusicology has thus avoided some of the problems which anthropology as a whole has inherited. The concept of "bi-musicality" is perhaps unintentionally ethnocentric in nature,[11] but its true legacy is the development of the study of performance as research method, which continues to be an integral part of many respected ethnomusicological studies. Musical performance is clearly within the anthropological concept of participant-observation, but the extent and type of participation available to ethnomusicologists far exceeds the possibilities found in most types of anthropological research.

Secondly, at least in the United States, ethnomusicology is no longer a discipline taught and studied by Euro-Americans interested in "other" musical cultures; Asians and Africans, along with Asian Americans, African Americans, and scholars from a wide variety of other national and ethnic backgrounds, are teaching and researching the musics of their own—as well as other—cultures. The emergence of Western-language studies by knowledgeable, culturally "emic" scholars of non-Western traditions is a significant development in our field; in practice—if still not in theory—ethnomusicology in the West has already become multicultural in both persona and approaches.

In recent years, Western scholars have paid considerable attention to the legacies of ethnocentrism, colonialism, and imperialism and their implications for anthropology, ethnomusicology, and other disciplines. However, the postcolonial self-awareness and self-critiques which have shaken up these fields are a response to a "crisis" which was essentially created and inherited by Western scholars. James Clifford, whose writings and ideas have had considerable impact on American ethnomusicology, states this clearly in his introduction to *The Predicament of Culture*: "This book is concerned with Western visions and practices" (1988:9).

Postmodernist consciousness at large can also be viewed as a Western development: a fundamental tenet is that "the ideas of progress, rationality and scientific objectivity which legitimated Western modernity are no longer acceptable in large part because they take no account of cultural differences" (During 1993:170). In Japan, the problems inherent in the modernist vision are widely acknowledged, but Japanese scholars also point out that "postmodernism is a Western event" (Miyoshi and Harootunian 1989:vii) and suggest that "to confuse Japan's non-modernity with the West's 'postmodernism' is perhaps a serious error. The two versions are differently foregrounded in history" (ibid.:xi). China and some other Asian cultures continue to embrace their own versions of modernism and progress, sometimes in complex forms such as the combination of Marxist-Leninist-Maoist rhetoric with the apparent full-blown capitalism espoused in slogans such as "to get rich is glorious." These notions are certainly subject to critique, but a Western version of multiculturalism is hardly likely to be the key to the future development of Chinese ideas about their own culture. Ironically, postcolonial developments in Western scholarship may be perceived as the latest chapter in the saga of cultural imperialism, where truly meaningful commentary on music or other aspects of culture can only be provided by the scholar conversant with the current concerns and terminology of intellectual discourse in Western society. We—Western scholars in general and ethnomusicologists in particular—continue to be far more interested in Westerners' readings of the "texts" of other cultures and musics than in the complexities of "textual criticism" represented by indigenous non-Western traditions of scholarship. This is not to suggest that the approaches or ideas of scholars such as Clifford or recent developments in critical and cultural theory have nothing to offer to scholars of music in, for example, China. They are, however, developments within the traditions of Western academic and intellectual culture; like ethnomusicology itself, their relevance, suitability, or adaptability for scholars outside of these traditions should be examined rather than assumed.

This article is intended to raise issues and questions rather than to promote a particular conception of what ethnomusicology is or should be. Repeated defenses of the inclusion of "musicological" or "music sound" components within the ethnomusicological canon may misleadingly suggest a bias towards this type of research.[12] In fact, in the study of Chinese music, I suggest that the anthropological aspects of ethnomusicology are generally much more directly applicable than the musicological ones, since the principles and characteristics of Western art music have little in common with most Asian traditions. Elsewhere, I have lamented the fact that ethnomusicology has become such a specialized discipline that scholars or musicians with many common interests and experiences are not even aware of its existence (Witzleben 1991). However, I also believe that the tendency of many contemporary ethnomusicologists to disparage musicologically-oriented studies—by extension, including a great deal of the scholarly traditions practiced in Asia—as somehow less worthy or more old-fashioned is not only counterproductive but also potentially alienating for non-Western scholars who would otherwise perceive some degree of common ground with their own traditions of studying music. The choice between anthropological or musicological orientations is a false one, and represents either a misunderstanding of the bi-disciplinary nature of the field of ethnomusicology or a conscious rejection of this legacy: in fact, virtually every ethnomusicologist cited here has at some point written about both anthropological and musicological issues. The "hundred flowers" approach to intellectual development has become an over-familiar cliché in the West, but as an ideal, I would suggest that it is also quite suitable for the field of ethnomusicology.[13] In a discipline such as ours that has been notable for diversity in backgrounds, interests, and approaches, surely we can not only encompass widely varying schools of Western thought, but also include and be enriched by the ideas and traditions of other continents and peoples.

Appendix: Chinese Terms

bijiao yinyuexue	比較音樂學
minjian yinyue yanjiu	民間音樂研究
minzu yinyue	民族音樂
minzu yinyue lilun	民族音樂理論
minzu yinyuexue	民族音樂學
Ya Fei La yinyue	亞非拉音樂
yinyuexue	音樂學

Notes

1. Some of the ideas herein were first presented at the 1993 ICTM World Conference in Berlin, under the title "Ethnomusicology in Hong Kong or a Hong Kong Ethnomusicology? The Challenges of an 'Ethnomusicology at Home.'" At various stages in the revision process, I have received valuable criticism and suggestions from many people. In particular, I am grateful to Shen Qia, James Cowdery, Bell Yung, Helen Rees, Barbara Smith, and the anonymous readers for *Ethnomusicology* for their detailed comments. The article's title is partly inspired by Shepherd et al. 1977.

2. In recent years, there have typically been approximately one hundred twenty music majors at the Chinese University, almost evenly divided between the full-time daytime and part-time evening programs. Virtually all undergraduate music majors specialize in Western music, but they are required to take at least three courses in Chinese music and ethnomusicology. In the graduate music program, a majority of the students are in the ethnomusicology program. Their previous studies included Chinese literature and communications, along with a variety of specializations in music; many have considerable experience as performers of Chinese music, and a few have already written about and published on Chinese music.

3. In these courses I have been using the textbooks and other writings of my teachers Li Minxiong (1982, 1983) and Jiang Mingdun (1982), along with the work of Yuan Jinfang (1987), Miao Jing and Qiao Jianzhong (1987), and others. I have also drawn heavily on the ideas about Chinese musical aesthetics and performance styles passed on to me by my teachers of Chinese instrumental and vocal traditions.

4. Linda Fujie is one scholar who has explored these subtleties, in her discussion of dissertation research as a Japanese American in Japan (1986).

5. At the Post-Conference Symposium held in Guangzhou following the 1991 ICTM World Conference in Hong Kong, the Ghanaian ethnomusicologiest J. H. Kwabena Nketia gave an impromptu lecture in response to what he perceived as offensive portrayals of Chinese minority musical cultures. According to one scholar, despite considerable respect in China for Nketia's work, his views were not universally welcomed, and some influential scholars still uphold the "politically correct" principle of higher and lower stages of cultural development.

6. As a student at the Shanghai Conservatory, I was often questioned about music studies in the West, and one common response to my revelations was amazement that my department (the University of Pittsburgh at that time) had only one person (Bell Yung) responsible for covering all of Chinese music. Needless to say, the idea of teaching courses on the music of more than one culture was even more baffling.

7. The citation of electronic media references in a printed article is still relatively rare in ethnomuiscological scholarship, and the reader should be aware of the ad hoc nature of much of this form of communication. Since pagination of electronic journals varies according to the format used in printing a hard copy of the document, line numbers or paragraph numbers, rather than page numbers, are given in the citations.

8. Although somewhat unbalanced, Gregory Guldin's history of anthropology in China (1994) is extremely informative.

9. For example, aside from the historically-oriented discussion of "Theory and Notation," none of the Chinese contributors to the forthcoming *Garland Encyclopedia of World Music* include any discussion of temperament or tuning systems. Few Chinese scholars are quite concerned with topics such as non-equal-tempered tunings and improvisation, however. I was struck by the positive response to a conference paper (Witzleben 1994) in which I pointed out examples of other Asian societies whose traditional music was changing and flourishing, but still use indigenous tuning systems (Indonesia) or improvisational practices (India).

10. This is my personal view as a scholar and educator; it is reflected both in my teaching of ethnomusicology and in the philosophy of the discipline which I represent in my interactions with colleagues at the Chinese University of Hong Kong. As René Lysloff has quite correctly pointed

out to me, to suggest that everyone in China should immediately become musically multicultural would simply be one more example of claiming that a Western conception of the nature of music study is universally valid (pers. com. 1996). However, many ethnomusicologists in China also stress the need for a multiculturally-grounded approach to the study of Chinese music.

11. The implication of becoming "bi-musical" is that the ethnomusicologist already "speaks" Western music and must learn another tradition. By extension, *pipa* players or *gamelan* musicians would have to study Western (or some other "foreign") performance before undertaking ethnomusicological study of what they already know, a suggestion which should strike most readers as patently absurd.

12. In my own work, I am particularly interested in the area of concepts about music, especially the ideas and words of performers and their relationship to written scholarship (see for example chapter 8, "Aesthetics," in Witzleben 1995). Ethnography, performance study, and the study of written sources quite naturally all play a part in research on these themes.

13. Mao Zedong's exhortation to "let a hundred flowers blossom and a hundred schools of thought contend" led to an unprecedented outpouring of criticism by intellectuals in the 1950s. Although this "hundred flowers movement" was followed by a harsh crackdown in the subsequent "Great Leap Forward," it represents a still-viable ideal.

References

Becker, Judith O., and Alan H. Feinstein, eds. 1984–88. *Karawitan: Source Readings in Javanese Gamelan and Vocal Music.* 3 Vols. Ann Arbor: University of Michigan Center for Southeast Asian Studies.

Clifford, James. 1988. *The Predicament of Culture: Twentieth-Century Ethnography, Literature, and Art.* Cambridge, MA: Harvard University Press.

Dong Weisong and Shen Qia, eds. 1985. *Minzu Yinyuexue Yiwenji* [Collected translations in ethnomusicology]. Beijing: Zhongguo Wenlian Chubanshe.

Du Yaxiong. 1993. *Zhongguo ge Shaoshu Minzu Minjian Yinyue Gaishu* [An overview of the folk music of China's various minority peoples]. Beijing: Renmin Yinyue Chubanshe.

During, Simon, ed. 1993. *The Cultural Studies Reader.* London and New York: Routledge.

Feld, Steven. 1990 (second edition). *Sound and Sentiment: Birds, Weeping, Poetics, and Song in Kaluli Expression.* Philadelphia: University of Pennsylvania Press.

Fujie, Linda Kiyo. 1986. *Matsuri-bayashi of Tokyo: The Role of Supporting Organizations in Traditional Music.* Ann Arbor: University Microfilms International.

Geertz, Clifford. 1973. *The Interpretation of Cultures.* New York: Basic Books.

Guldin, Gregory Eliyu. 1994. *The Saga of Anthropology in China: From Malinowski to Moscow to Mao.* Armonk, NY: M. E. Sharpe.

Harrell, Stevan, ed. 1995. *Cultural Encounters on China's Ethnic Frontiers.* Seattle: University of Washington Press.

Hood, Mantle. 1982 [1971]. *The Ethnomusicologist.* Kent, Ohio: The Kent State University Press.

Hornbostel, Erich M. von, and Curt Sachs. 1990 [1914, 1961]. "Classification of Musical Instruments." Trans. by Anthony Baines and Klaus P. Wachsmann. In *The Garland Encyclopedia of Readings in Ethnomusicology.* edited by Kay Shelemay. New York and London: Garland Publishing, V.6:119–45.

Jairazbhoy, Nazir A. 1995a. Charles Seeger Lecture (keynote speech at the 40th Annual Meeting of the Society for Ethnomusicology, Los Angeles, October 21).

———. 1995b. *The Rags of North Indian Music: Their Structure and Evolution.* Bombay: Popular Prakashan.

Jiang Mingdun. 1982. *Hanzu Minge Gailun* [A survey of the folk songs of the Han Chinese]. Shanghai: Shanghai Wenyi Chubanshe.

Lee, Hye-Ku. 1981. *Essays on Korean Traditional Music.* Translated by Robert C. Provine. Seoul: Royal Asiatic Society, Seoul Computer Press.

Li Minxiong. 1982. *Minzu Qiyue Gailun* [A survey of Chinese instrumental music]. Mimeographed. Shanghai Conservatory of Music.

———. 1983. *Chuantong Minzu Qiyuequ Xinshang* [Appreciating traditional Chinese instrumental repertoire]. Beijing: Renmin Yinyue Chubanshe [People's Publishing Company].

Lomax, Alan. 1968. *Folk Song Style and Culture.* Washington: American Association for the Advancement of Science.

———. 1976. *Cantometrics.* Berkeley: University of California Press.

Lysloff, René T. A. 1994. "Scholastic Correctness." *Ethnomusicology Research Digest* 155 (May 3): lines 105–81. Electronic file retrievable by ANONYMOUS FTP or TELNET as ERD 155 (ERD 94-155) from inforM.umd.edu (128.8.10.29), directory inforM/Educational_ Resources/ReadingRoom/Newsletters/EthnoMusicology/Digest.

Manuel, Peter. 1995. "New Perspectives in American Ethnomusicology." *TRANS 1: Transcultural Music Review* (June). Department of Musicology of the C.S.I.C. (Barcelona). Electronic file retrievable at http://www.uji.es/trans/trans1/manuel/html.

Marcus, George E., and Michael M. J. Fisher. 1986. *Anthropology as Cultural Critique.* Chicago: University of Chicago Press.

May, Elizabeth, ed. 1980. *Musics of Many Cultures: An Introduction.* Berkeley: University of California Press.

Merriam, Alan P. 1964. *The Anthropology of Music.* Evanston, Illinois: Northwestern University Press.

Miao Jing and Qiao Jianzhong. 1987. *Lun Hanzu Minge Jinse Secai Qu de Huafen* [A discussion on differentiating "similar color areas" in the folk songs of the Han Chinese]. Beijing: Wenhua Yishu Chubanshe [Culture and Arts Publishing Co.].

Miller, Terry E. 1994. "Confessions of an American Ethnomusicologist." *Ethnomusicology Research Digest* 154 (April 29): lines 55–133. Electronic file retrievable by ANONYMOUS FTP or TELNET as ERD 154 (ERD 94-154) from inforM.umd.edu (128.8.10.29), directory inforM/ Educational_Resources/ReadingRoom/Newsletters/EthnoMusicology/Digest.

Miyoshi, Masao, and H. D. Harootunian, eds. 1989. *Postmodernism and Japan.* Durham and London: Duke University Press.

Myers, Helen, editor. 1992. *Ethnomusicology: An Introduction.* New York and London: W. W. Norton & Co.

Nettl, Bruno. 1964. *Theory and Method in Ethnomusicology.* New York: Free Press.

———. 1983. *The Study of Ethnomusicology: Twenty-nine Issues and Concepts.* Urbana, Chicago, and London: University of Illinois Press.

———. 1984. "In Honor of Our Principal Teachers." *Ethnomusicology* 28:173–85.

Nettl, Bruno, and Philip V. Bohlman, eds. 1991. *Comparative Musicology and the Anthropology of Music: Essays on the History of Ethnomusicology.* Chicago: University of Chicago Press.

Nettl, Bruno, with Charles Capwell, Philip V. Bohlman, Isabel K. F. Wong, and Thomas Turino. 1992. *Excursions in World Music.* Englewood Cliffs, New Jersey: Prentice-Hall.

Nketia, J. H. Kwabena (transliterated as En-ke-di-ya). 1982. *Feizhou Yinyue* [African music]. Beijing: Renmin Yinyue Chubanshe. Translation of *Music of Africa.* 1974. New York: W. W. Norton.

Qureshi, Regula Burckhardt. 1995. "Music Anthropologies and Music Histories: A Preface and an Agenda." *Journal of the American Musicological Society* 28(3):331–42.

Racy, Ali Jihad. 1991. "Historical Worldviews of Early Ethnomusicologists: An East-West Encounter in Cairo, 1932." In *Ethnomusicology and Modern Music History.* edited by Stephen Blum, Philip V. Bohlman, and Daniel M. Neuman. Urbana and Chicago: University of Illinois Press, 68–91.

Rees, Helen. 1995. "Domestic Orientalism: The 'Motif of the Music-Making Minority in China.'" Paper presented at the 40th Annual Meeting of the Society for Ethnomusicology, Los Angeles, October 19.

Rice, Timothy. 1987. "Toward the Remodeling of Ethnomusicology." *Ethnomusicology* 31(3): 469–88.

Seeger, Anthony. 1987. *Why Suyá Sing: A Musical Anthropology of an Amazonian People*. Cambridge: Cambridge University Press.

———. 1992. "The Ethnography of Music." In *Ethnomusicology: An Introduction*. edited by Helen Myers. New York, W. W. Norton, 88–109.

Seeger, Charles. 1977 [1966]. "Versions and Variants of 'Barbara Allen' in the Archive of American Song to 1940." In *Studies in Musicology* Berkeley and Los Angeles, University of California Press, 273–320.

Shanghai Yinyue Xueyuan Yinyue Yanjiusuo, Anhui Sheng Wenxue Yishu Yanjiusuo [Shanghai Conservatory Music Research Institute and Anhui Province Literature and Arts Research Institute]. 1984. *Yinyue yu Minzu: Minzu Yinyuexue (Bijiao Yinyuexue) Yicong* [Music and peoples: collected translations in ethnomusicology (comparative musicology)]. Shanghai and Anhui Province: Shanghai Conservatory of Music and Anhui Province Literature and Arts Research Institute.

Shen Qia. 1993. "Minzu Yinyue zhi 'Dao': Guanyu 'Junei he Juwai Ren' de Sikao" [The 'Tao' of ethnomusicology: thoughts on 'insiders' and 'outsiders'"]. *Yinyue Bijiao Yanjiu* [Comparative Research on Music] 1:26–31.

———. 1996. "Minzu Yinyue Xue zai Zhongguo" [Ethnomusicology in China]. Unpublished manuscript.

Shepherd, John, Phil Virden, Graham Vulliamy, and Trevor Wishart. 1977. *Whose Music? A Sociology of Musical Languages*. London: Latimer.

Titon, Jeff Todd, ed. 1992. *Worlds of Music: An Introduction to the Music of the World's Peoples* (second edition). New York: Schirmer Books.

Turino, Thomas. 1993. *Moving Away from Silence: Music of the Peruvian Altiplano and the Experience of Urban Migration*. Chicago: University of Chicago Press.

Wang Yaohua. 1991. *Sanxian Yishu Lun* [Essays of the art of the *sanxian*]. 3 Vols. Fuzhou: Haixia Wenyi Chubanshe [Straits literature and arts publishing company].

Widdess, Richard. 1994. "Scholastic Correctness." *Ethnomusicology Research Digest* 157 (May 13): lines 17–58. Electronic file retrievable by ANONYMOUS FTP or TELNET as ERD 157 (ERD 94–157) from inforM.umd.edu (128.8.10.29), directory inforM/Educational_Resources/ReadingRoom/Newsletters/EthnoMusicology/Digest.

Witzleben, J. Lawrence. 1991. Review of *Drumming on the Edge of Magic: A Journey into the Spirit of Percussion* by Mickey Hart, with Jay Stevens and Fredric Lieberman. *Ethnomusicology Research Digest* 36 (February 25). Retrievable as electronic file at http://www.inform.umd:8080/EdRes/ReadingRoom/Newsletters/EthnoMusicology/Archive/drumming-review.

———. 1994. "An Ethnomusicological Perspective on the Development of Chinese Instrumental Music." In *History of New Music in China: The Development of Chinese Music*. edited by Liu Ching-chih and Wu Ganbo. Hong Kong: University of Hong Kong Center of Asian Studies, 485–92.

———. 1995. *"Silk and Bamboo" Music in Shanghai: The Jiangnan Sizhu Instrumental Ensemble Tradition*. Kent, Ohio: The Kent State University Press.

Wong, Isabel K. F. 1991. "From Reaction to Synthesis: Chinese Musicology in the Twentieth Century." In *Comparative Musicology and the Anthropology of Music*. edited by Bruno Nettl and Philip V. Bohlman. Chicago: University of Chicago Press, 37–55.

Yuan Jingfang. 1987. *Minzu Qiyue* [Chinese instrumental music]. Beijing: Renmin Yinyue Chubanshe.

Zhang, Wei-hua. 1985. "Recent Development of Ethnomusicology in China." *Ethnomusicology* 29(2):264–71.

Zhongguo Yinyue [Chinese Music], eds. 1981. *Minzu Yinyuexue Lunwen Ji (The Selections of Ethnomusicology)*. 2 Vols. Nanjing: Nanjing Yishu Xueyuan Yinyue Lilun Jiaoyanshi [Nanjing Arts Institute Music Theory Teaching and Research Institute].

What Do Ethnomusicologists Do?
An Old Question for a New Century[1]

ADELAIDA REYES / Independent Scholar

Some questions refuse to die or be ignored, not because persistence is expected at some point to be rewarded with *the* answer, but because the ongoing dialectic between question and answer promises more fruit than the simple, linear question-answer process. Answers are impeachable; they have to be if knowledge is to grow. And so questions have to be asked, changing in form or using the same form but accommodating the changes that have taken place since those questions were last asked.

As practitioners, ethnomusicologists may see no need to inquire about what they do (though introspection on this subject can be beneficial), but the issue is often brought to our attention by non-ethnomusicologists when they discover that ethnomusicology is our profession. "Is that the study of ethnic music?" is the familiar refrain. Ethnomusicology is not recognizable to many—perhaps to most—non-ethnomusicologists. Is it recognizable to us?

The beginning of a new century is as good a time as any to return to the fundamental and persistent question of what we do. It is requisite to moving forward to the question of what we should or could be doing. But perhaps as necessary, if not more so, is a renewed appreciation for the importance of questions—not only those that are fresh incitements to research but those oft-repeated ones that try our patience but hold within them the core of our discipline.

More than a decade ago, Wim Kayzer, a Dutch journalist scribbled some questions on the back of an old hotel bill. "Why do we call grass green?" he wondered. "Why do some bamboos flower only once every 120 years, and how do the bamboos count the passing of the years?" Those questions became the seed that grew into a Public Television series which in 1995 became a book titled *'A Glorious Accident': Understanding Our Place in the Cosmic Puzzle*. The project was built around six participants, all eminent thinkers from different disciplines:

From *Ethnomusicology*, Vol. 53, No. 1 (Winter 2009), pp. 1–17 the philosopher Daniel C. Dennett, the physicist Freeman Dyson, the paleon-tologist Stephen Jay Gould, the neurologist Oliver Sacks, the biochemist Rupert Sheldrake, and the historian and philosopher of science Stephen Toulmin.

Through the entire series—one interview a week with each participant in turn, and a round-table bringing them all together on the final week—I was struck by at least two things. First, there was the almost incandescent importance of questions in the work and the achievements of the participating scholars. The philosopher Daniel C. Dennett may have been speaking for his colleagues when he noted that "our work is an extension of the children's questions which remain unanswered" (quoted in Kayzer 1995:xiii).

The second thing that I found striking was that forums such as this, though seeming to have no relation to ethnomusicology, actually have much to say to a discipline that prides itself on being multidisciplinary (this will become evident in the course of this paper). As questions ricocheted from one participant to the other, one popped up in my mind—the question that is this paper's title, which for decades has had an irritant as well as energizing effect on ethnomusicology: What do ethnomusicologists study? And/or what do they do?

There are surely many ways to go about addressing the question. But one route that I have some familiarity with begins on what is now an old, well-trodden, pot-holed road marked with conflicts, uncertainties, and unresolved issues that at times have made it look like a road to nowhere. Yet if one stays on it, goaded by questions that yield not conclusive answers but still more questions or refinements of old ones, one can be well enough rewarded to be willing to forget that the question that launched the construction of that road to begin with was that frustrating yet ever-challenging query: what is ethnomusicology?

The word "is" in that formulation covers a present tense of long duration. Its presentness stretches through time in a manner aptly described by the writer James Baldwin to the historian Eric Foner. "History," Baldwin said, "does not refer merely or even primarily to the past. On the contrary the great force [of history] comes from the fact that we carry it within us, [we] are unconsciously controlled by it in many ways . . . History is literally *present* in all we do" (2002:ix, emphasis in the original). The emphasis that Baldwin put on the word "present" calls attention to its two senses: its physical sense of here and its temporal sense of now.

This view of time as an agglomeration of past and present rather than as a linear, unidirectional sequence is the perspective from which I will explore events and activities that have helped shape ethnomusicology, and are likely to have an impact on what it will be. I focus on human acts rather than on faits accom-plis, borrowing from Thomas S. Kuhn who, in his classic work *The Structure of Scientific Revolutions* (1996) argued that the history of a discipline emerges less from a record of achievements, than from a record of research activities—less from the stasis of signal events now frozen in time than from the dynamism of ongoing action. Thus, the question, "what is ethnomusicology?" from which I derived "what do ethnomusicologists study?" quickly becomes "what do ethnomusicologists do when they study what they study?"

The transformations do not temper the strong, underlying definitional demands. In his long search for a key to defining ethnomusicology, Alan P. Merriam tried asking: "What do ethnomusicologists do?" a question he quickly abandoned as "uninformative" and "circular" (1977:189). But other questions followed, highlighting the value of well-formulated questions to the advancement of any search.

In tracing the transformations that the basic question—what is ethnomusicology?—has undergone, I hope to show that the persistence of the question comes not from sheer obstinacy but from a responsiveness to history's contingencies. The transformations offer clues to the developments in the discipline and to the thinking of its practitioners that make questions such as those we now ask continually necessary, reasonable, and fruitful. Just as important, the transformations, in summoning the past to the present, can help us envision a future for ethnomusicology that is historically anchored—one that retains a sense of rootedness even as it moves forward.

The "Preoccupation with Identity"

The question, "What is ethnomusicology?" was much on the minds of ethnomusicologists for most of the second half of the last century. In the mid-1950s when the U.S.-based Society for Ethnomusicology was being organized, definitions were debated, orally and in print, in the early issues of the *Newsletter* and in the journal, *Ethnomusicology,* into which the Newsletter had evolved. In 1977, Alan Merriam's "Definitions of 'Comparative Musicology' and 'Ethnomusicology': an Historical-Theoretical Perspective" sought an exhaustive treatment of the subject. In 1983, Bruno Nettl looked at what he called ethnomusicology's "preoccupation with identity" (Nettl 1983:3), and offered his own book-length "personal statement of what [he] think[s] ethnomusicology has been and is all about" (ibid.:x).

A major stimulus for all this definitional activity was the controversy over the assignment of value to "the music itself", i.e., to music as sonic phenomena on the one hand, and to music as a complex of human behaviors on the other. Alan Merriam, who pushed the latter to the forefront of ethnomusicological attention with the publication of his book, *The Anthropology of Music* (1964), was charged with splitting ethnomusicology into "two camps," one musicologically-oriented, the other anthropologically-derived. Vehemently declaring that "nothing could be farther from the truth," Merriam re-stated his position. The "major difficulty" for ethnomusicology, he argued, lies in finding a *modus vivendi* for the two disciplines that comprise it, namely musicology and anthropology (1969: 214, 226).

By Nettl's account, given in 2005 at the Society for Ethnomusicology's [SEM's] 50th Anniversary Celebration and published in the journal *Ethnomusicology* a year later, "the concept of two ethnomusicologies became widely accepted" (2006:186). By Bonnie Wade's account on the same occasion, the situation amounted to a "clear bifurcation." The divergent parts were in such "terrific competition," she reported, that "at moments it even felt like a struggle over the soul of the discipline" (2006:191).

Now we hear assurances that the duality and the bifurcation are at last behind us, that the discipline has now regained what is described as its "original, more unified perspective" (Nettl 2006:187). Yet, at conferences, meetings, symposia, and other forums for ethnomusicological exchange, the sounds of unresolved conflict linger on. Particularly outside the United States, works that are seen to stray too far from musical sound and its production and into the ethnographic or the social-scientific can be relegated to ambiguous categories, their disciplinary identity in doubt. They are given labels such as "anthropology of music" or "sociology of music" or "psychology of music." These were, for example, listed as "Interest Areas" in the 2002 *Membership Directory* of the Society for Ethnomusicology. Implicit in the labeling—and on occasion, explicitly expressed—is the question: "But is this ethnomusicology?"

Whether the consequence of the controversy over the anthropologically-derived and the musicologically-oriented was a split into two separate entities or a bifurcated discipline with some sort of dual-personality disorder, ethnomusicology apparently needs to better integrate its parts. In his Charles Seeger lecture, the centerpiece of the 2005 celebration of SEM's 50th anniversary, Anthony Seeger still saw as "one of the great challenges facing ethnomusicology . . . avoiding getting caught up in one facet or another of the music—the sociology without attention to sounds, analysis of performances without attention to social processes, the study of music that ignores movement, and so forth" (2006:229).

The impression I get from observing all the activity stirred up by this "preoccupation with identity" is the elusiveness of what is sought. As Merriam had pointed out, it is hard to pin down the commonalities that would unite what he described as "the extraordinarily mixed bag of interests" (1977:190) that are represented in ethnomusicological research. "What kind of field is it," he asked "that can encompass such variety and how can it possibly be defined?" (1977:19).

It sounds almost like a rhetorical question, but it raises two bonafide questions that deserve to be addressed: Does the apparent elusiveness of ethnomusicology's identity indicate nothing more than the growing pains of a relatively young discipline? Or is it a sign of maturity that a discipline can accept periods of instability, during which it can re-examine and redefine itself?

These are general questions that can be addressed to any discipline at certain points in its history. But they become specific to ethnomusicology when cast in terms of those contingencies that make the discipline's history its own. In that history then, might be found the source of those protean features that give the discipline's identity its apparent elusiveness. And in that capacity to assume forms that elude ready identification might be found, I suspect, some of the most interesting and challenging trajectories that can engage the discipline as it settles into the second century of its existence and as the twenty-first century moves on to complete its first decade.

For these reasons, Merriam's question, just quoted, deserves to be re-visited.

The Roots of Ethnomusicological Identity

In light of ethnomusicology's decades-long effort at self-definition, one is tempted to make the case that the discipline has been undergoing a rather protracted identity crisis or, alternatively, that it may, owing to the circumstances of its birth, simply be manifesting its proneness to such crises. It is perhaps indicative that in the hundred-some years of its existence, the discipline has undergone one major name change—from *vergleichende Musikwissenschaft* or comparative musicology to ethnomusicology—and has had one name adjustment—from a hyphenated version to its present hyphen-free incarnation. These changes may signal a condition that calls for corrective action, or they may represent the very attributes that account for the discipline's progress and growth. On these issues, history is an indispensable guide, and I will turn to it shortly after a slight digression the reason for which will quickly become apparent.

In his 1973 Jefferson Lecture in the Humanities,[2] the noted psychologist Erik Erikson (1974) argued that identity crisis is native to the United States. It is induced not just by external circumstances that bring in a continual infusion of new immigrants and new ways of life that must somehow find a place in American society and culture. Rather, it is induced as well by an internal force—the principle of diversity that came with the birth of the nation and, like part of an organism's genetic make up, is not easily excised. The diversity which is kept alive and is continually renewed as a result is thus a built-in, never-ending challenge to organize that diversity into a unitary identity. The tensions generated by the efforts to meet this challenge create an environment that not only favors identity crises but makes them inevitable or endemic as well as intrinsic to the identity and identity construction of the nation.

Is there something in Erikson's remarks that could be instructive for ethnomusicology? Is there something about the dynamics between a diversity of constituents and a unitary identity that vary when the diversity is systemic? A glance at the circumstances of the discipline's birth could be revealing.

We all know that *vergleichende Musikwissenschaft* or comparative musicology as ethnomusicology was initially known, was born as a subfield of musicology. Its identity—its distinction from its parent discipline and from its siblings, particularly historical musicology—was established through dichotomization, or through what linguists call complementary distribution: European and non-European music; the so-called cultivated and the presumed primitive; the written and documented on the one hand and the orally transmitted on the other; the culturally close and the culturally distant; and, in the context of the nineteenth century and the mind set prevalent then, the music of super-ordinate and that of subordinate cultures were the contrastive pairs. The second item in each pair characterized comparative musicology's musical domain.

Born with a culturally diverse study subject, comparative musicology was also born of mixed parentage. The new discipline was coaxed into existence by scholars who, by training and predisposition, came to their subject through different disciplinary lineages. Guido Adler, a musicologist, was also a psychologist. Carl Stumpf was a philosopher and psychologist. Erich von Hornbostel was trained in the Natural Sciences, earned a Ph.D. in chemistry, and worked in the Institute of Psychology at the University of Berlin. According to his friend, the ethnomusicologist Jaap Kunst, Hornbostel was also a composer and pianist. Alexander Ellis was a philologist, physicist, and music theorist.

The fathers of the discipline obviously considered their disciplinary differences an asset. Input from other disciplines was not only acceptable but expected. Guido Adler's 1885 article "Umfang, Methode und Ziel der Musikwissenschaft" which assigned *vergleichende Musikwissenschaft* its place within the broad category, "Musicology," offered a list of *Hilfswissenschaften* that included mathematics, pedagogy, psychology, aesthetics, and philology, among others.

With diversity built into it, comparative musicology thus started life with great potential for intellectual wealth—and great vulnerability to ambiguity. Both potentialities were embedded in the discipline's two core elements: its subject matter, and the methods for its study. The first, the subject for study, engages the intellectual curiosity and provokes the mind to ask questions; it is the core element that addresses that part of our question which inquires about what ethnomusicologists study. The second, the methods intended to reformulate questions in a manner that makes possible the creation of research strategies, responds to that part of our question which inquires about what ethnomusicologists do. These elements, each one internally diverse, is bound to the other by a shared conception of the nature of what is to be studied.

This conception enjoyed a general consensus on what comparative musicology's subject matter was, namely, "primitive," "exotic," non-European musics. These were, in Hornbostel's words, "genuine musical products of foreign cultures . . . [un]spoiled by Europeanisms" that could be collected like artifacts by travelers and brought back for study by experts ([1905] 1975:251). There was also a general consensus on the relations between object of study and investigator. Geographic distance was virtually imposed by the difficulty of doing work *in situ* at the end of the nineteenth century. But cultural distance was not merely a consequence of geographic distance. Cultural distance was presupposed; it governed the relations between the investigator and the music and musicians under study even when, as was the case, for example, in Carl Stumpf's study of Bella Coola Indians (1886) and their songs, the subjects were close at hand, and interaction between investigator and subject, face to face.

Distance, physical and cultural, was underscored by the state of recording technology at the time. Its primitive state meant that music for study was apprehended more often than not as either poorly recorded sound or as specimen frozen in essentially European notation by European investigators.

All these added up to a basic, commonly accepted concept of music as an autonomous and decontextualized object. This concept in turn, gave rise to two different methodological orientations.

One leaned heavily on the humanistic which took music to be a meaningful object in the nineteenth-century critic Eduard Hanslick's sense. "Music," he wrote, "refers to nothing but itself and thus . . . the 'meaning' of a piece is nothing but the music itself" (quoted in Hofstadter 1997:38). The object of musical analysis therefore was to discover the music's internal logic, to demonstrate how the music's parts relate to each other to form a coherent whole. Those with this orientation adopted methods then in use for the study of Western European music. European terminology and European systems of notation were the dominant descriptive, representational and analytical tools. Comparative musicological studies were thus undertaken with a European perspective on subject matter informed by a European world view.

The other orientation leaned more heavily toward the scientific, focusing on the physical and quantifiable properties of music. Standing at a cultural remove from their study object, investigators used experimental and measurement techniques from other disciplines to study such phenomena as tunings and pitch systems. An outstanding example of the results yielded by these methods was Alexander Ellis's groundbreaking article of 1885, "On the Scales of Various Nations." Its principal contribution was the substantial hole it blew in the assumptions of European musicology by demonstrating that "the Musical Scale is not one, not 'natural' nor even founded necessarily on the laws of the constitution of musical sound, so beautifully worked out by Helmholtz, but very diverse, very artificial and very capricious" (Ellis 1885:526).

The divergent methodological orientations, however, did not disturb the consensus on the nature of comparative musicology's study object. This was the period that Nettl might have been referring to in his 2005 Anniversary paper (2006:187) when he spoke of a "version" of the discipline with an "original, unified perspective." This period extended to the first quarter of the twentieth century, and comparative musicology's identity as a discipline based on what it studied remained virtually unquestioned a few decades more.

Against this background, which shows the discipline in a state of equilibrium, real or perceived, the duality or bifurcation that seized ethnomusicological attention in the second half of the twentieth century gains in significance. It triggered a re-examination of what ethnomusicology is about, of what ethnomusicologists do. It inspired efforts at definition of which Merriam's question, which initiated this section, was but one example. The duality/bifurcation debate amounted to the first serious challenge to the status quo. Its effects on the discipline have been wide-ranging and deep and its repercussions continue to be felt, tapping into both the discipline's potential for great intellectual wealth and its potential for ambiguity.

Growing Pains

The departure from the "unified perspective" was actually made inevitable by the convergence of many factors. The growing number of practitioners and the fact that many began to come from the same cultures as those to which the musics under study belonged, raised questions about the role of cultural distance in ethnomusicological study. So did the decline of colonialism and the consequent revisions in a hierarchical view of cultures and peoples. The growing ease of travel, the changes in world view wrought by two World Wars and by re-drawn geopolitical and ethnic boundaries, and the developments in technology all underscored with increasing intensity a changing musical universe. For those tracking developments in the discipline, these events altered the terrain in which questions of what ethnomusicology is and what ethnomusicologists do sought new meaning and relevance. But as in Erik Erikson's account of the United States' identity crises, the agents of change were not all external to the discipline. Internal factors were at work as well.

It is worth recalling that the use of Western European musicological concepts by comparative musicologists on the one hand, and by their counterparts in the other subfields of European musicology on the other, rested on very different grounds. European scholars studying European music, assumed that music is autonomous from their perspective as insiders to European culture with an insider's understanding of the music's cultural context. For comparative musicologists, however, the assumption that music was autonomous was an expediency. Absent or lacking information from the study object's culture of origin or innocent of the need to contextualize, comparative musicologists had little, if any, choice. What was expedient thus became normative. It became the basis for a common or standard set of practices that persisted even when the expediency that installed them no longer applied.

The tenacity of these practices despite the new realities resulted in a disconnect or a rupture between the demands of the subject matter and the methods used to address them. It was a rupture that grew as ethnomusicology's field of study began to expand and evolve. When folk and traditional music were introduced into the ethnomusicological domain, the effects on methodology were modest. But by the second half of the twentieth century, a shift in the formula for determining what qualified for ethnomusicological study made itself felt throughout the field and subsequently exposed significant inadequacies in method.

Willard Rhodes, with the strong support of Charles Seeger, both founding members of the Society for Ethnomusicology, insisted that ethnomusicology's subject for study was "the total music of man without limitations of time and space" (1956:460). Largely ignored when it was first formally proposed at the 1955 meeting of the American Anthropological Association, and later when it was published in *American Anthropologist* in 1956, the idea nonetheless began to gain momentum. By the 1970s, ethnomusicologists had begun to break away from the confines of the non-European and the so-called simple and self-contained societies. They began to work in Western urban areas and in complex societies in general. By the last quarter of the twentieth century, ethnomusicologists had just about overcome their reservations about working in their own backyard even as they continued fieldwork in distant places. The line that had kept the ethnomusicologist culturally distant finally grew slack and ineffectual.

At the same time, classificatory boundaries that were used to order the great variety of the world's music began to blur. Transmitted orally or through written or print media; popular, cultivated or art music; and supposedly-pure or "authentic" as well as hybridized musics were given a place at the ethnomusicological table. In short, Willard Rhodes' view of ethnomusicology's subject matter as "the total music of man" finally prevailed.

The effects went well beyond an expansion of musical terrain. Tantamount to opening the floodgates, this expansion washed away the dichotomies that had conferred on the discipline the unambiguous identity that derived from its subject matter and the way it was conceptualized. The impact was most telling, therefore, on the discipline's sense of itself. What the discipline gained in breadth came at the cost of its distinctiveness; hence, the "preoccupation with identity" that began in the 1950s and peaked in the last quarter of the twentieth century. Hence, too, the note of urgency that had developed in the search for identity in the face of a disturbing and potentially disruptive duality or bifurcation in the discipline. The content of the question, "what is ethnomusicology?" was shifting. Implicitly it was asking what ethnomusicology had become as it responded to new contexts and new contingencies.

The Critical Juncture

With the loss of the distinctiveness that came from ethnomusicology's subject matter—the music it studied, defined mostly by cultural origin and the type of society within which the music functioned—scholars turned elsewhere in the search for an ethnomusicological marker. They turned to what in the latter part of the twentieth century was commonly called the approach to subject matter.

In the early days of comparative musicology, when "primitive" and non-European cultures, and subsequently folk and traditional musics were presumed unchanging or were treated as though they were, different disciplinary approaches served to study the many facets of what was considered a well-delineated and relatively static subject. But with that subject becoming more inclusive, its forms more variable, method and its diversity began to pose serious problems.

In the 1960s the methods of musicology and of anthropology—both part of ethnomusicological method in principle if not in practice—came to be seen as competitive (e.g., Wade 2006). In 1980, David McAllester, echoing Merriam's 1969 view concerning the "major difficulty" of finding a *modus vivendi* for anthropology and musicology in ethnomusicology, characterized the pair—anthropology and musicology—as "uneasy bedfellows" within the ethnomusicological fold (McAllester 1980:306). Methods from other disciplines, notably linguistics, were subsequently embraced and then held at arm's length. So too were methods from sociology and related disciplines. In 2005, what Anthony Seeger saw as one of the great challenges facing ethnomusicology underscored the fact that reconciliation, balance, or integration, not just between the musicological and the anthropological but more broadly, between what comes from the humanities and what comes from the social sciences, has yet to be achieved. We are still quite a ways from "seeing music as *simultaneously* sounds . . . history and values" (Seeger 2006:229, emphasis added). The over-arching problem seems to boil down to this: an unbounded body of music—out of which ethnomusicologists carve out a study object—is to be served by an abstract methodological resource that is described rather vaguely as multidisciplinary.

This (admittedly oversimplified) description of a current dilemma in no way diminishes the outstanding research that ethnomusicologists have contributed and continue to contribute to scholarship. These works range across a stunning diversity of musics studied with a variety of methods that engage both the humanities and the sciences. But many of these works are instantiations; they are individual instances of well-executed research activities, their subject matter carefully delineated, the tools chosen from a rich storehouse of disciplinary possibilities, then carefully crafted and custom-made for the purposes of a given study. That many of these works are published in the journals of those disciplines from which they have drawn—anthropology, linguistics, sociology, psychology, and so forth—support their status as instantiations, identifiable as belonging to one discipline or another. These instantiations attest to the diversity of ethnomusicology's methodological resources. But a discipline's recognizability—its identifiability—calls for more than the sum of such instantiations. It calls for common ground, for a generalizability that those instantiations, by definition, tend to obscure.

Where then is that generalizability to be sought? Is that what the question, "What do ethnomusicologists do when they study what they study?" in fact asks?

At this stage in the discipline's development, the question reveals a complexity that was unforeseeable when the discipline was born. "The total music of man" as subject matter poses methodological challenges the magnitude of which one only glimpses when one confronts the need to translate that huge abstraction into delimited, concrete, observable forms that are amenable to study. In response to those challenges, multidisciplinarity offers a wide menu of options that imposes difficult criteria for choice. What has become clear is that the question no longer advances the inquiry if it were divided into two parts, each addressed separately, one part pertaining to what ethnomusicologists do, the other to what they study. Laden with history's encrustations, illumined by insights from history and transformed by the continuous influx of new data, the question may now point to what makes ethnomusicology recognizable only if addressed in full; for that recognizability lies neither on its subject matter nor on its methods. It lies rather on the relations between subject matter and methods as co-defining parts. This seems self-evident, needing no further comment. But history bears witness that the two can and do lose sight of each other.

The relations in question are not hierarchical or sequential as was suggested by Bonnie Wade's account (2006) of the dilemmas facing students as they confronted a bifurcated discipline. They had wondered whether one studied the culture first and then "plugged in" the music or whether it was the other way around. Nor are the relations that of parallel lines that may move in the same direction but do not meet, or that at some point are forced into a marriage of convenience, shoehorning ethnographic data, for example, into musical accounts.

The pertinent relations are those forged by the logic of means and ends. Subject matter, as the prod for asking questions, looks to methods as the strategy, first for delimiting and defining a study object that justifies investigation, and second, for providing a kind of road map that will get the study to its goal. The probability that the most efficacious methods will be devised rises in proportion to how well the questions we ask of our subject are formulated, how well the problems are defined. The relations between them—between study subject and method—should thus evoke a sense of inevitability. They should constitute an intrinsic connection that leads to statements that are not mere statements, but answers that, in addressing questions, feed or embody hypotheses. These, in turn, embody questions that are not mere rhetoric or matters of fleeting interest, but are questions that emerge from answers just delivered—questions that speak to the testability of new knowledge and are ready for use in the sustained guessing-testing-guessing chain that Charles Sanders Peirce saw as the mark of noteworthy science.[3]

These are, of course, general principles broadly applicable to all scholarly work. Toward more specificity, John Gray, professor of European Thought in the London School of Economics, provides a point of departure: "Social objects are not like stars or stones which exist independently of how humans think about them; social objects are partly created by human perceptions and beliefs. And when these beliefs and social perceptions change, social objects change with them . . . We can never have objective knowledge of society, if only because our shifting beliefs are continuously changing it" (2006:22).

By calling attention to the nature of social objects in particular, and to the relations of these to their investigators, Gray opens the door to considering ethnomusicology's subject matter—the total music of man—as social object. As such, it automatically addresses the ethnomusicologist's role vis-à-vis his or her subject and implicates the ethnomusicologist no longer as detached observer but as both participant in shaping the object and as strategist for its investigation.

Toward a Discipline Recognizable as Ethnomusicology

By the turn of the last century, ethnomusicology's resistance to considering music a social object had diminished substantially. To a large extent, ethnomusicology is now receptive to the idea that music is not only a human creation, but a social act. It implies human interaction. What Roman Jakobson says of language is equally true of music: *"we speak in order to be heard . . . and . . . we must take into account the meaning which* [the sounds of language] *carry, for it is in order to be understood that we seek to be heard"* (1978:12, emphasis in the original). Sound, at the service of language and music, is intended for human use, and can thus be made autonomous only for purposes of analysis, because their capacity to mean and to communicate becomes irrelevant if their nature as social act is denied.

Music as social object calls attention as well to an essential relationship between music and those who study it. Human perception and its effects on shaping the object perceived and on the scholar-researcher's responses to it, make of the object's representation in the study both objective and subjective reality. Niels Bohr, the Nobel Prize-winning scientist, saw himself as occupying an "obscure boundary between observer and observed, between subject and object." His task, therefore, is not "to find out what nature is . . . [but] what we can *say* about nature." (quoted in Rhodes 1992, emphasis in the original). The physicist, Freeman Dyson puts it more plainly: "Science is a human activity and the best way to understand it is to understand the individual human being who practices it" (1995:33).

These essential linkages—between music as social object and human agency—shed light on the study of music in general. Yet, they fall short of providing ethnomusicology with a distinctive marker. For this, one particular relationship needs to be explored: that between music and culture.

Music and Culture

Music in cultural context is one of ethnomusicology's most common concepts often serving as a shorthand definition. But translating it into practice is part of what drives the question, "what do ethnomusicologists do?" A major difficulty, to borrow from and elaborate on Merriam, lies in the lack of an internal cohesion that would protect music-in-cultural-context from dismemberment—the kind that led to the "two ethnomusicologies" idea or to the bifurcation of the discipline.

The introduction in the 1950s of the cultural as something separate from what has been called, by way of differentiation, "the music itself," has left the cultural open to being thought of as distracting, or as an inconvenient necessity—its function in the study of a music often murky and contested. There being no clear criteria for significance in the "extra-musical," another term with divisive or exclusionary connotations, the cultural can be treated like a prosthesis, to be attached to or detached from the study of "the music itself" at will. The value of the "extra-musical" to which ethnographic data is often relegated, can therefore swing from dubious, to interesting but non-essential, to indispensable.

But what if, to the concept suggested by the passage from Gray, one were to infuse the cultural? What if, to a concept that bound together study object, human agency, and methods, one were also to assume that the study subject is not just social object but part of expressive culture (as opposed to material culture or to the species-specific [Blacking 1973] and genetically-based [e.g., Sacks 2007:x–xiii])? As a mode of communication specific to a culturally-marked group, expressive culture requires not only a grasp of the rules that in language, for example, govern lexicon, grammar, and syntax, and in music govern the organization of pitch, time, and form. Expressive culture also presupposes a frame of reference that is historically constructed, a treasury of collective experience and associations from which members of the culture draw for meaning that transcends the merely literal or semantic to become cultural meaning. It is the kind of meaning that makes "inside jokes" intelligible only to those who have an insider's knowledge of the culture. It is the kind of meaning that music conveys, over and above the meaning made accessible by the discovery of the internal logic that makes the music coherent. It is the kind of meaning that responds to what Clifford Geertz (1983: 12; 98–100; 2000:209) called an ethnoaesthetic sensibility, the acquisition of which is part of what lends fieldwork, as part of ethnomusicological method, its strongest rationale.

Music as expressive culture differs from music in cultural context or similar formulations in its methodological implications. When conceived as expressive culture, music takes culture to be the necessary condition without which music is meaningless. The cultural thus enters an ethnomusicological study *at its conception*, setting up an ongoing and essential dialogue between the musical and the cultural, making one indispensable to the other.

Music as expressive culture thus helps bring to ethnomusicology what has eluded it for a long time—a distinctive marker. It distinguishes ethnomusicology from other disciplines that study music primarily as manifestations of individual creativity, as unique individual expression with a "voice" (in both the literal and literary sense) of his or her own. What Stephen Toulmin, in 'A Glorious Accident,' said of language, clarifies the distinction: language "is a social medium which we make our own as individuals but whose meaning entirely comes from its being in the public world" (1995:193). Music as expressive culture is in the public world, in what Geertz called "the common world in which men look, name, listen, and make" (1983:119).

Ethnomusicology's recognizability as a discipline could thus be served by a focus on this social object, this social medium that belongs first to a society, to a public within which it means and it functions, before individuals make it their own.

Much of this we owe to Franz Boas who had collaborated with Carl Stumpf in his 1885 study of the Bella Coola Indians.[4] Since the turn of the twentieth century, Boas had been insisting that art in general, like language, is not an autonomous whole but an external manifestation of the mental processes through which members of a culture view their world.

Perhaps it is not an exaggeration to say that ethnomusicology, for most of the twentieth century, had been grappling with the implications of Boas's ideas and those of others like him. But the problem has been converting those ideas into what these days it is fashionable to call "actionable" and generalizable.

That, I believe is one of the tasks that the past has put in front of us. And as we go about what can seem both prosaic (i.e., addressing long-standing questions such as those this article raises) and visionary (considering what doors those questions can open), it might be good to think of what the task requires of the investigator, the centrality of whose role (as I hope has been made evident above) has important methodological implications. What these are will emerge more fully as that role is better defined and realized. But what a number of natural scientists have to say has special weight because they have been customarily assumed and expected to be objective, and yet have become increasingly insistent on the human component of the scientific enterprise and of scholarly research in general.

Stephen Jay Gould, one of the contributors to 'A Glorious Accident,' notes, that "the mind is both an amazing instrument and a fierce impediment . . . we will always 'see' with the aid (or detriment) of conventions" (1995:18). The mind as double-edged sword had, in fact, long engaged Gould. Underscoring the other participants in 'A Glorious Accident,' to say nothing of other thinkers like John Gray and Niels Bohr, Gould delivers a message that speaks both to the present and the future: "Reality does not speak to us objectively and no scientist can be free from constraints of psyche and society. The greatest impediment to . . . innovation is usually a conceptual lock, not a factual lack" (1989:276).

Like Gould's—and Baldwin's—present tense, that of the question, "what do ethnomusicologists do when they study what they study?" is also of long duration. Never ceasing to ask and never losing sight of the dialectics between question and answer are parts of a legacy that ethnomusicologists would do well to treasure and to act upon.

Notes

1. This paper is a revised version of a keynote address given at the MACSEM Conference at Columbia University in New York on March 29, 2008.

2. The Jefferson Lecture is "the highest honor the United States Federal Government confers for distinguished intellectual achievement in the Humanities" (www. Neh.gov/).

3. The formulation, "guessing-testing-guessing . . . " (Sebeok and Sebeok 1983:23) is a nutshell formulation of a methodology that Charles Sanders Peirce developed over his extensive philosophical writings. Sebeok and Sebeok's reduction traces a process that begins with abduction which Peirce describes variously as a guess, a conjecture, the "only kind of argument which starts a new idea" (in Sebeok and Sebeok 1983:18), and through the guessing-testing-guessing process, arrives at the least fallible explanation. Its applicability to the present work is reinforced by Peirce's insistence that "a hypothesis [the object of testing] must always be considered a question" (ibid.:22). This is echoed by the linguist William Labov who, in his lectures when he taught at Columbia University in the 1970s, always insisted that a well-formulated question for investigation inevitably harbors a hypothesis.

The question-answer-question chain upon which the structure of this paper is based mimics in a small way Peirce's guessing-testing-guessing chain for a similar purpose—the advancement of knowledge and understanding. But this paper places the process mostly in historical perspective and is, for the most part, retrodictive. At different points in time, the questions and the answers accommodate historical events and their power to inject fresh nuances to what appear to be the same questions. In the process, the significance of both the question and the answer are transformed.

4. According to Kolstee (1982:1), Boas and Stumpf had heard the same Bella Coola Indians in 1885—Boas in Berlin and Stumpf in Halle. Boas gave Stumpf his (Boas's) transcription of two songs to add to Stumpf's study.

References

Adler, Guido. 1885. "Umfang, Methode und Ziel der Musikwissenschaft." *Vergleichende Musikwissenschaft* 1:5–20.

Blacking, John. 1973. *How Musical is Man?* Seattle: University of Washington Press.

Dyson, Freeman. 1995. "The Scientist as Rebel." *New York Review of Books.* 25 May, 31–33.

Ellis, Alexander J. 1885. "On the Musical Scales of Various Nations." In *Journal of the Society of Arts* 33:485–527.

Erikson, Erik H. 1974. *Dimensions of a New Identity. The 1973 Jefferson Lectures in the Humanities.* New York: W. W. Norton.

Foner, Eric. 2002. *Who Owns History?* New York: Hill & Wang.

Geertz, Clifford. 1983. *Local Knowledge. Further Essays in Interpretive Anthropology.* New York: Basic Books.

———. 2000. *Available Light. Anthropological Reflections on Philosophical Topics.* Princeton, N.J.: Princeton University Press.

Gould, Stephen Jay. 1989. *Wonderful Life: The Burgess Shale and the Nature of History.* New York: W. W. Norton.

———. 1995. "Left Snails and Right Minds." *Natural History.* April, 18.

Gray, John. 2006. "The Moving Target." *New York Review of Books.* 5 October, 22–24.

Hofstadter, Douglas R. 1997. "Semantics in C Major." Review of *Musical Languages,* by Joseph P. Swain. *New York Review of Books.* 12 October, 28.

Hornbostel, Erich von. [1905] 1975. "Die Probleme der vergleichende Musikwissenschaft [The Problems of Comparative Musicology]." In *Hornbostel Opera Omnia,* Vol. 1. Klaus Wachsmann, Dieter Christensen, and Hans-Peter Reinecke, eds., 247–70. The Hague: Martinus Nijhoff.

Jakobson, Roman. 1978. *Six Lectures on Sound and Meaning.* Cambridge, Mass.: MIT Press.

Kayzer, Wim. 1994. *'A Glorious Accident': Understanding Our Place in the Cosmic Puzzle.* New York: W. H. Freeman and Co.

Kolstee, Anton F. 1982. *Bella Coola Indian Music: A Study of the Interaction Between Northwest Coast Indian Structures and their Functional Context.* National Museum of Man Mercury Series. Canadian Ethnology Service Paper No. 83. Ottawa: National Museums of Canada.

Kuhn, Thomas S. 1996. *The Structure of Scientific Revolutions.* 3d ed. Chicago: University of Chicago Press.

McAllester, David. 1980. Review of *Music in Culture,* by Marcia Herndon and Norma McLeod. *Ethnomusicology* 24(2):305–7.

McGinn, Colin. 2008. "The Musical Mystery." Review of *Musicophilia,* by Oliver Sacks. *New York Review of Books.* 6 March, 33–35.

Merriam, Alan P. 1964. *The Anthropology of Music.* Bloomington: Indiana University Press.

———. 1969. "Ethnomusicology Revisited." *Ethnomusicology* 13(2):213–229.

———. 1977. "Definitions of 'Comparative Musicology' and 'Ethnomusicology': An Historical-Theoretical Perspective." *Ethnomusicology* 21(2):189–204.

Nettl, Bruno. 1983. *The Study of Ethnomusicology. Twenty-Nine Issues and Concepts.* Urbana: University of Illinois Press.

———. 2006. "We're on the Map. Reflections on SEM in 1955 and 2005." *Ethnomusicology* 50(2):179–89.

New York Times. 2007. "News Summary." 25 November, A2

Rhodes, Richard. 1992. Review of *Niels Bohr's Times. In Physics, Philosophy, and Polity*, by Abraham Pais. *New York Times Book Review*, 26 January.

Rhodes, Willard. 1956. "Toward a Definition of Ethnomusicology." In *American Anthropologist* 58(3):457–63.

Sacks, Oliver. 2007. *Musicophilia. Tales of Music and the Brain.* New York: Alfred A. Knopf.

Sebeok, Thomas A., and Jean Umiker Sebeok. 1982. "'You Know My Method': A Juxtaposition of Charles S. Peirce and Sherlock Holmes." In *The Sign of Three: Dupin, Holmes, Peirce*, edited by Umberto Eco and Thomas A. Sebeok, 11–54. Bloomington: Indiana University Press.

Seeger, Anthony. 2006. "Lost Lineages and Neglected Peers. Ethnomusicologists Outside Academia." In *Ethnomusicology* 50(2):214–35.

Stumpf, Carl. 1885. "Lieder der Bellakula Indianer." In *Vierteljahrschrift für Musikwissenschaft* 2:405–26.

Wade, Bonnie. 2006. "Fifty Years of SEM in the United States: A Retrospective." In *Ethnomusicology* 50(2):190–98.

PART III

In Honor of Our Principal Teachers

Bruno Nettl

L et me begin by saying that I feel very honored to have been invited to deliver the Seeger lecture this year. With the honor goes a rather formidable task, for the previous lecturers in this distinguished series have found it possible to survey long careers of research and to synthesize in a number of ways their views of the field and their contributions. I don't believe I'm far enough along to try to do this in a lecture. But if there are some things I have learned, I think the most appropriate way for me to use the time you have kindly put at my disposal is to pay homage to some of the people from whom I learned them. My title may make you suspect that I wish to honor the professors with whom I studied, or perhaps artists who gave me music lessons, or again perhaps the authors of books which I found particularly influential. Each of these would no doubt be an appropriate thing for me to do, as it might be for the member of any field of study. But, more than members of other humanistic fields and social sciences, excepting perhaps only anthropology and folkloristics, we in ethnomusicology are distinguished by the fact that we continue, after our formal studies, and throughout our work, to depend for our findings upon teachers. Most of what we learn, most of our contributions to knowledge, come about from close association with individuals who represent, but who also personify, the musical cultures of the world. We may refer to them as informants, or perhaps consultants, and they interact with us in many ways. They give us formal lessons, they answer questions in interviews, or they provide long, informal lectures over tea and cookies or spicy dinners. They allow us to record their performances, and they can be persuaded to criticize constructively our own explanations of their musical systems. In fact, they are teachers of ethnomusicologists as individuals, but they are also the teachers, the sources, of the field. Intensive work over long periods with such individuals distinguishes ours from other kinds of music

From *Ethnomusicology,* Vol. 28, No. 2 (May 1984), pp. 173–85 research. The quality of the work that has been produced rests to a large extent on such things as the ways in which we have selected our teachers, the degree to which they took us seriously, their conceptions of their own cultures, their veracity and their representativeness, and the quality of our interpretation of what they have taught us. I would like, therefore, to speak to you briefly about four men whom I consider in this particular respect to have been my principal teachers of ethnomusicology and to give an account of a few important points that they made to me regarding the nature of music and musical culture. It is a gesture of honor that I wish to make for myself, but also on behalf of all of us, colleagues and students.

Dramatic insights of the past quickly become everyday conventions of the present. And so we must remind ourselves that this hallmark of ethnomusicology, the gathering of data from people in the field, was not so very long ago viewed as a rather uncomplicated affair. Mainly, it was believed, one just recorded music and wrote down the musicians' answers to simple questions. Today of course we are wary of the notion that there is ever only one right way to comprehend a culture or a music. But to a graduate student in 1950, the suggestion that a culture is only what it seems to be in the view of its own participants or in that of an outside observer was quite a novel idea. And so, when I had the first opportunity to do something that approached the making of field recordings, I came to it with courage but naivete.

The time was the summer of 1951, and the scene, the (then) Archives of Folk and Primitive Music at Indiana University, an institution which was about to host a linguistic institute to which a number of people from American Indian reservations were to be brought to serve as informants. I had worked with some recordings of Arapaho songs and was therefore looking forward to the arrival of a member of that tribal group, hoping that he would be willing to record some songs along with his work as a language consultant. I had never, as a matter of fact, met an American Indian, and looked forward to the encounter with a good deal of boyish anticipation. One day I went to the workroom and was told by the secretary, tongue obviously in her cheek, that William Shakespear had arrived. "Who's being kidded," I thought, but opened the door to find a thin, balding, slightly stooped man in bluejeans and white shirt, smiling but pensive, sitting at the table. What does one say to one's first informant? A good question, I should think, for an ethnomusicological parlor game. I guess I came out with something like, "Is your name really Shakespear?" to which he replied affirmatively, with light accent, adding, "You can call me Bill."

We became friends, Bill assuming a rather avuncular role. I found that he was a man of great intellectual capacities and intellectual hunger. He wished to teach us, any of us who associated with him, faculty and students, about the language and culture of his people; but he also wished to learn more himself, began to read books by such authors as Kroeber and Mooney in the University library, and eventually, still dissatisfied, went on to request interlibrary loans. As you can imagine, this eroded for me the traditional conception of anthropology as the study of discrete and isolated cultures. I was nevertheless able to hold on to a corner of that notion in my recording of Bill Shakespear's songs, for he did not read music and had no access to recordings. But in the realm of ideas, the insight most memorable to me was the conception that musical cultures and systems are comprised of units of musical thought different in magnitude and nature.

It happened quite innocently. I had been wondering how collectors such as Frances Densmore and my own teacher George Herzog had persuaded a member of an American Indian society to sing many songs for cylinder recorders in short periods. To be sat in front of a machine and simply asked to sing songs might well, I should think, be a frightening experience. For Bill Shakespear it evidently was not. In our recording sessions, he would think for a minute, then sing, sometimes breaking into a burst of four or five songs; and then pause and repeat this procedure. The order of songs did not follow ceremonial prescription or social sequence. Only later did it occur to me to see why the singing of one particular song would stimulate him to sing certain other ones. In many cases I'll never know the answer; but occasionally his announcements helped. Thus, sometimes he sang songs whose tunes sounded to me related, and he also might identify them as such. But he was not always predictable. Once, after a song, he announced, "Now the same song, although very little difference in tone," but then he proceeded to sing something that sounded quite different to me. I queried; but he could not explain, only assert that he had meant what he said.

In my attempt to record as many songs as possible, I found that Bill sometimes ran out of steam, and it occurred to me that the question of song variants might be attacked, and his musical memory stimulated at the same time, if he were to hear some Arapaho songs previously recorded and sung by someone else. I played some from a collection, asking, after each song, whether he also would sing it. In most cases he claimed knowledge and, turning to my other wire recorder, sang his version. Some of the tunes sounded quite unlike what he had just heard, yet in other cases he might announce a fresh song which sounded to me just like something he had just sung. To be sure, in assessing his analysis, I had to be wary of being taken for a ride. Elderly informants often tire of young students and their naivete. But Bill Shakespear, clearly serious, eager to learn all he could about Arapaho culture even from white authors, wished also, by the same token, to be sure that we whites got things straight. And so he used this tune relationship question to illustrate an important though now obvious point, that songs that sounded or looked alike to an investigator might well be distinct units of musical thought in their own musical culture, while others that sounded quite different could be variants of one. The world's societies have many conceptions of their units of music, many criteria for determining relationships among the sounds that make up their musical universe. In the repertories of some, each performance is a distinct unit; in others, the total number of units may be small. There are pieces, tune families, modes, genres. Bill's conceptualization also formed for me part of a lesson later generally accepted in ethnomusicology, that one must study a music with the use of two sides of a coin: that of the investigator trusting his or her own observation of the way the system appears, and that of the culture itself, as articulated by knowledgeable informants, consultants, teachers. The two sides, once incongruously called emic and etic, may be quite different, and the difference itself of great import. Somehow, the courses in anthropology I had been taking had not made this as clear, although perhaps the professors had tried to impress it on me. Bill, as it were, made the relationship come alive.

Bill also disabused me of a long-held impression that ethnomusicological field work consisted of an active investigator and an essentially passive informant who simply answered questions and performed tasks, and showed instead the active and creative role that the informant may play in solving problems shared by him and the foreigner. Working under Carl Voegelin and Henry Lee Smith, and with Zdenek Salzmann, Bill and I were asked to look into the possibility of a tone system in the Arapaho language. For better or worse, Carl thought that my musical training along with my ignorance of linguistics was just what was needed to test his hunch that Arapaho had phonemic tone. It was Bill Shakespear who suggested that I try to write down his utterances on the staff, as he had seen me do for songs, and he then patiently spoke and had me repeat words and sentences until he was satisfied. The analysis of Arapaho as having high and low tone, each with three allotones, was later discarded by Salzmann in his definitive grammar, but Bill's enthusiasm and his interest in finding the answer, and in the technicalities of the subject itself, provided an unexpected vision of the intellectual person in what was then still called a primitive society.

Bill had much more of a general nature to teach. His view of his own culture, for example, suggested that interaction among societies was not simply pollution, and that one therefore should not spend all of one's time looking only for the pure and unadulterated, but rather that cultural mix was probably the norm. And for that summer, Bill had a distinct role on campus, taking interest in what was happening in Bloomington, but yet staying a bit aloof, smiling shyly and bestowing on all around him an aura of peace and quiet good feeling. Amusement about his name he accepted with dignity but with a twinkle in his eye. It turned out that this summer was a watershed not only in my life but also in his, for he returned to Wyoming, so I was later told, with a determination to hold on to cultural tradition, to learn it better and to teach it, and, according to the anthropologist Loretta Fowler, he went on to become, along with others in his family, a great leader of his people. Bill didn't think of himself as particularly musical, but he made it clear that you could not be a proper member of the Arapaho tribe without having its songs.

———

Speaking of the two sides of the coin leads me to the observation that ethnomusicologists seem always to be engaged in the resolution of tensions between pairs of principles. Thus, there has always seemed to me to be a disparity between our desire to study the entire musical society, to understand the musical life and everyman, and our tendency to look for outstanding musicians who define concensus and norm. Further, we distinguish synchronic and diachronic approaches to study, inevitably combining them in the end. Another of my American Indian associates effectively shed light on these relationships.

We are now with the Blackfoot people in Montana in the late 1960s. The people had tired of the never-ending parade of anthropologists and had of course never stopped being tired of the intrusions and domination of white people. But having become, in effect, members of the white economic and social systems, they tried to find ways in which their cultural tradition could be of use to them for the preservation of their ethnic identity. In this respect, they could be divided, and divided themselves, into at least three groups. One of these had completely westernized, another was trying to hold on to older traditions but was frustrated by poverty, and a third tried to steer a middle course, symbolizing it by use of a modern, partly pan-Indian, repertory of music and dance. In seeking consultants from each of these three groups I found some who did not fit easily, but had in the course of their lives moved from one to another. One way of gaining some insight into the role of music in Blackfoot life and into the interface between the synchronic and diachronic might be to find someone willing to tell me, in as much detail as he could remember, the course of his musical life, and to sing for me, as well as he could remember, all of the songs that he had learned.

The person willing to work with me, and from whom I eventually learned more about Blackfoot culture than anyone else, was Calvin Boy. It turned out that I got quite a different sense of the place of music in life from an autobiographical account than from conventional ethnography. In the course of Calvin's life, the first music was a mixed bag of traditional songs surreptitiously learned, of modern Indian songs acquired by sitting in with singing groups, and of Western music learned by playing French horn in a school band and going to Catholic church. Later, as a young man, Calvin began to associate with the modernized sector of society and became a member of singing groups accompanying social dances at intertribal and pan-Indian powwows. Eventually, as he grew older he took a greater interest in the more traditional and ceremonial music of his people, but by then it was late; much was no longer available. Thus, the three groups of Blackfoot mentioned above were also periods in Calvin's life. After the age of 40, he began to have drinking problems, had difficulty holding jobs, but found occasional sympathetic employment in the Museum of the Plains Indian, a government institution administered by John Ewers and later, Claude Schaeffer. There he could satisfy his interest in getting involved with traditional culture. And so, like Bill Shakespear, but from a position of much less authority, Calvin became an occasional student and an occasional teacher.

In some ways, I found the course of Calvin's musical life reflected that of others in the community. The old songs were property mainly of older men and women. This even reflected an earlier cultural tradition. After all, a Blackfoot man would expand his repertory throughout his life by moving through a series of age-grade societies, and a medicine man would continue learning songs throughout his life, having visions and perfecting his ceremonial and musical control of his medicine bundle. It might be an old man who would learn the most important and powerful songs. Calvin, though living in a modernized social milieu, was following this same path, even if to an outsider he might appear as a down-and-out derelict.

But Calvin also had something besides tribal tradition to guide the course of his life. It was the image of his stepfather, a great tribal leader who had urged his people early in the twentieth century to combine economic Westernization with the maintenance of tribal identity through ceremony and music. This man, Theodore Laststar, inspired Calvin but was also the focus of resentment because the stepson felt unable to live up to expectations. When Laststar urged on him the study of old ceremonies, Calvin resisted by singing pan-Indian songs. But once the stepfather had passed away, Calvin began to follow in his footsteps, taking a greater interest in the old. Even so, he still continued feeling resentful at his own much less exalted place in the community and tried in various ways to elevate himself, one of these being a desire to teach white people like myself. And so, if Calvin was representative of the homogeneous side of Blackfoot culture, he also had a unique story to tell.

When it came time for Calvin to sing his repertory for me, I was curious about the way in which he might set about to present it and about the degree of its internal consistency. On the first day, he sang about twenty songs, ran out of steam, and promised to continue, completing what he claimed to be his extant repertory, some seventy songs, by the end of the week. He was proud of the repertory, realized that he had something valuable, and indeed that it was, while not especially large, then surely unique. While he was willing to mow a lawn for a dollar, for "Indian work," as he put it, he wanted, though he didn't always get, $5 for a song.

Well, in the course of a week, I had heard Calvin's repertory, and of course I learned much from the way in which he grouped the songs, from observing the number of songs he could recall without long pauses, the order in which they appeared, and the points at which he needed prompting from his wife, Mary Boy, who helped him—as much from all these things as from the nature and style of the repertory itself. And while most members of the community looked down on him, praising instead his famed stepfather, Calvin had much to teach about what it meant to be, musically, a Blackfoot Indian, more perhaps than others more expert at singing and ceremony. I think back with pleasure to hours spent with him in his one-room house in the rural slum of Moccasin Flats in Browning, or in my little motel room, and in my car, for he periodically cajoled me into giving him rides to towns forty miles away on the gravel roads crisscrossing the grassy, domed-shaped foothills of the Rockies. I would say that Calvin was the Blackfoot everyman, his personal problems rather typical of those of the Blackfoot people, but like each everyman, a personality in which the components of culture produced an individual configuration. Unlike Bill Shakespear, who died highly honored by his people, Calvin passed away with little notice. His contribution to my education was great.

———

The third of my principal teachers whom I would like to honor is the only one still living, and he is perhaps known to a good many of you. Dr. S. Ramanathan has spent time teaching in the United States and has been closely associated with a number of ethnomusicologists. For myself, he was the person who introduced South Indian music, dispelled a good many preconceptions, and recently, for a few months in Madras, acted as a kind of guide to the musical culture. I tried to learn from him some of the kinds of things that those of you who have studied Carnatic music have learned much more thoroughly from many of its masters. But one thing that Dr. Ramanathan had to teach was an appreciation of the way in which the individual musician can make a unique niche for himself in a complex musical society. After all, rather like anthropologists dealing with culture, we, in ethnomusicology, usually study a music as a system, concentrating on those characteristics and values which are shared by all members of the population. The literature of ethnomusicology overstresses the homogeneity of the world's musics. But of course, even seemingly homogeneous societies are comprised of individuals, each contributing something essential to the whole. While Dr. Ramanathan is surely one of the more distinguished performers in Madras, he has succeeded in ways that differ from those of the majority of musicians, combining the activity of Carnatic music with a highly intellectual approach to all music, and with a special interest in pedagogy.

In a particular way, Dr. Ramanathan combines two important values in his tradition, conservatism and innovation. He has been determined to do what he could to keep the tradition intact, to perform and teach what he considers to be truly Carnatic music. But in doing this, unlike many of his colleagues, he turned in part to generally forgotten ways of the past. Thus, he collected folk songs in villages and tried to integrate them into the theoretical framework of the classical music, and he tried to revive what he calls an old practice, the singing of folk songs at final points in concerts. In Tamil-speaking Madras, he has worked on the revival of Tamil songs in what is largely a repertory of Telugu and Sanskrit texts.

At the same time, he tried to absorb influences from other cultures. A man of the broadest curiosity, he learned, when in the United States, all he could about Western teaching methods, visiting kindergartens, art schools, churches, about Gregorian chant and Hebrew cantillation. He studied Middle Eastern and Hindustani music. I believe that all this activity has played a role in the musical modernization of Madras, as Dr. Ramanathan, like his many colleagues, has helped to preserve Carnatic music by channelling change in its sound in conservative directions while at the same time Westernizing the social context.

In all this, Dr. Ramanathan learned and in turn had much to teach about the place of music in a modernizing culture. Contrary to musicians in certain other societies, he believes for Carnatic music that it is not who you are that determines your access to the music, but more your willingness to work and study. He is proud, therefore, of the many Americans he has taught. The point is that Carnatic music has become an international system which accepts students from other cultures, and recognizes their ability to perform if they learn its technical aspects. A bit more on this issue of the culture-specific nature of music later. But in attempting to learn something of the influences of Western culture on Carnatic music, I found Dr. Ramanathan to be a person who looked both backward and forward in promoting its growth, and who also looked beyond it for musical and intellectual inspiration.

Speaking of inspiration, I must say that Dr. Ramanathan had a personal lesson to impart as well, a lesson in how to grow older and younger at the same time. When I first knew Dr. Ramanathan, he was in his early fifties and seemed to be gradually heading for a peaceful life of retirement. Later, in Madras, then in his middle sixties, he struck me as a changed person, a man with prodigious energy who had many things to do, many ambitions, many demands on his time all of which he tried to satisfy, a man always on the go, obviously loving this busy life style. In 1982, he was awarded the highest honors of musicianship, happily surrounded by some of his American disciples, and he performed throughout India, slept on trains between concerts, grabbed forty winks between lessons, taught, lectured, published, attended concerts of young and old, never admitting fatigue. One had the impression that this man, after a long and distinguished career as a musician and scholar, felt that he was just now really getting started, and that the way to grow old (or not to grow old) was to give yourself many things to do, to serve your chosen field, and not to spare yourself.

―――――

The last in this group of principal teachers whom I wish to honor here played an important role in the twentieth-century music history of his country. Dr. Nour-Ali Boroumand was one of a small number of people who revived the classical music of Iran, reconciling it with the realities of twentieth-century industrial urban culture. Tehran, in the 1960s, was a very rapidly growing and modernizing city, its musical life really more Western than traditional, and few Tehranis knew anything about Persian classical music, a system pressed between the conservative Muslims and their disapproval of secular music and the modern technocrats and their belief that the traditional music does not fit modern conditions and should be discarded. Dr. Boroumand was the successor of legendary figures from the period around 1900: of Mirza Abdollah, who is thought to have created the modern radif, the basic repertory of Persian music; of his own teacher, Darvish Khan, who helped to develop modern concert life; of Ali Naqi Vaziri, the man who tried to introduce notation and Western harmony, developed teaching institutions, and encouraged women to enter the ranks of instrumentalists; of Musa M'aroufi, who standardized the radif and thus made his own version into the authoritative canon. Member of a wealthy family, Boroumand studied music as a boy but did so, characteristically, in order to become a competent amateur. To develop a profession, he was sent to Germany to complete high school and then to study medicine, and along with this he learned to play piano and to love the concerts of the Berlin Philharmonic. While still a student, he had the misfortune of losing his eyesight, so he returned to Iran. The doctoral title used by his friends was informal and honorary, but in his later middle age he still enjoyed giving medical advice to family and students. He then resumed his study of Persian music, applying his great intellectual energy to the idea of developing a definitive radif from those of his several teachers. But also, in line with the low esteem of the musical professional, he continued for decades to prize his amateur status as a musician. He had a great love for the German language, which he went on to teach, but in music he took very few students and steadfastly refused to perform in public. Only in his fifties, feeling ready to retire, was he persuaded, really more as a patriotic duty than anything else, to join the newly founded program of Iranian music at the University of Tehran, and he began to teach the radif to classes of a dozen students.

Of course I learned most of what I know about Persian music from him, but I would like to share with you some of Dr. Boroumand's teachings which seem to me more generally applicable.

He had a strong belief in the close association of music and other domains of culture. Dr. Boroumand's opinions would readily have found a home at a meeting of SEM. Iranian music, he said, could only be understood in a context of Sufism, Persian poetry, Islam, and perhaps it could not properly be performed abroad at all. Thus, he had important things to impart about the culture-specific conception of music. He seemed torn between a belief in music as something that belonged so much to its culture that no outsider could understand it properly, and its opposite, that Iranian music could compete with Western music only if it were learned by foreigners and understood throughout the world. I have often quoted his rather shocking statement to me, made after months of study on my part, to the effect that I would never understand this music, with the afterthought that I might well learn its structure, how it worked technically, but that I would never learn to react to it as did any Iranian on the street. And yet, on another occasion, he insisted that what he was teaching me must be promulgated, that his foreign students should write books and articles, so that people in Europe and America would understand. Between his teaching and that of Dr. Ramana-than, it becomes clear that in certain cultures, music, perhaps like religion, is considered to be something intelligible only to a member of its society, that it is not only the lessons and the practicing that determine whether you can learn a music, but also who you are. In other societies, the music is regarded to be potentially accessible to anyone. Boroumand was, I think, trying in his mind to resolve this question for Persian music, and while I surely have no answer, there is no doubt that this is a major issue for any society, and of great importance for the study of processes such as change, modernization and Westernization.

Dr. Boroumand was not considered a great performer, but, rather like Bill Shakespear and Calvin Boy, made his contributions to music in the realm of mind. He believed firmly that in order to learn a musical system, one must approach it in part through the thought behind it, as articulated by musical intellectuals. This is of course what music historians have always done in the study of theoretical treatises and verbal sources. But having the living treatise and the living performance in the same person may clarify the interaction of the two, and also the degree to which one cannot trust the one to give you the other.

For example, Dr. Boroumand asserted that while one can in fact learn to produce the sound of music in many ways, through many modes of teaching, all of which might produce the same audible effect, it may be essential for the maintenance of a music to have it taught in a particular way. When he taught the radif, or the hour of music attached to each dastgah, or the two or three minutes of melody which represented each gusheh, he insisted on his procedure. He would play only a short bit in each class or lesson, repeat, ask students to repeat, requiring precise reproduction of ornaments, and of rhythm despite the lack of metric cycle, and then tell the students quickly to go home and practice it. He discouraged their tendency to transcribe the music on the spot, but wanted them to learn from the sound. He refused to hurry the process, explaining that one must contemplate each section thoroughly, one did not learn the music properly without this contemplation. Of course, he admitted, one could go to a published radif and play the music from the notes, as he had once done with Haydn sonatas. But while you might end up producing the right notes, you would not have come to them properly. The preservation of a musical culture involves more than just the sound; the way it is learned, the attitudes held towards it, the ideas one had about it also had to be preserved, were part of the music. Dr. Boroumand would have chuckled at the thought that he was a kind of anthropologist; but what he presented to me was not really very different from Alan Merriam's model of music, the interaction of concept, behavior, and sound.

Like us, Dr. Boroumand grappled with the differential role of insider and outsider in the study of a music and realized that an outsider might need special concepts for explanation. Thus, on the one hand, he said in effect, if you want to study Persian music, you must learn it the way we teach it. But, on the other, spending a month as a visiting professor at the University of Illinois, he also went further. On the first day of a mini-course on Persian music, which he had organized in great detail with much thought, he began by saying, "In order to understand Persian music, you must first understand the song of the nightingale. I hear you do not have this bird in America, and so I've brought you a recording." And then, after playing about ten minutes of nightingale song recorded in his own garden in a traditional district of South Tehran for this group of rather baffled students in Urbana, he pronounced: "The nightingale never repeats itself and the most important thing in Persian music is never to repeat yourself exactly." Now, of course, nightingales and Persian musicians do repeat, but he had used this device to articulate a major theoretical principle and also to show with a powerful symbol why we, in America, might indeed never really understand this music.

Dr. Boroumand was a man confident of his own authority, a person of no false modesty, who understood the important role he was occupying in the contemporary history of his art, and he was a man of conservative attitudes who wished to prevent undesirable change in Persian music, particularly in the radif. Indeed, it was the radif that was his great love, and he would say, "it is really something extraordinary and fine, something quite unique, this radif that we have created in Iran. There is always more and more to be learned about it." And to be sure, if one studies the radif from recordings and notations, one is bound to agree that this repertory of some ten hours is an incredible complex of short units united by common motifs, a universe of ideas in which more and more of interest can always be found. We may think of Iran today as a nation of religious fundamentalists who avoid the arts, but Boroumand represented a totally different side of the tradition, that of the miniatures, the carpets, gardens, mosques, palaces, the lyrics of Hafez and Ferdowsi's grand epic, and the intricacies of avaz, the side of the culture that revels in the complex work of art, in the multiple interrelationship of many separate parts, to be appreciated through microscopic examination. Dr. Boroumand was sure that no one was quite as good at this approach to creating art and music as were the Iranians. As his disciple, I am inclined to agree. In any event, in a more general sense, Dr. Boroumand's approach to teaching underscored the benefits of looking at, restudying, contemplating even a small bit of apparently simple music, and finding within its confines a formidable network of connections. Perhaps by extension, one could learn from him an appreciation of the degree to which a culture with oral tradition can use severely limited materials to produce a great expanse of musical variety.

But if he wished to keep the tradition, he was himself also willing to learn and to change his mind. He was very impressed by the tendency of his American students in Illinois to think for themselves and to come up with insights, and wanted to train his Iranian students in the same way. I think he finally came to believe that Americans and Europeans could indeed learn Persian music, if not like the Persians, then in their own equally valuable way.

I am grateful for this opportunity to honor four individuals from among the many who are properly considered the principal teachers of our field. Like all of us, I owe a great debt to these musicians and scholars; without people like them, there would be no ethnomusicology. But as I think of the men whom I have here briefly sketched, coming from a group of diverse cultures, men with greatly varying degrees of formal musical or general education, I feel that what they have in common and what strikes me most is their essentially intellectual approach to music. They did not simply sing or play, but they thought about what they were doing, and in discussion they appreciated the conceptual questions that inevitably opened up. They laid stress on music as a system of ideas as much as a system of sound. Perhaps unconsciously, they were aware of the complexity of musical cultures and realized that the particular ways in which they might choose to present them made a difference.

It seems to me also that all of these men demonstrated a fundamental tenet of the anthropology of music, the need for studying music as sound and music as culture in tandem. Their instruction has confirmed to me this point of view; and I therefore continue to believe that there should not be, as it is sometimes articulated, one group of ethnomusicologists who adhere to the cultural side, and another, to the musical, but rather that each individual in our field, not at every moment of his or her life, but as a matter of general principle, should concentrate on the unity of the two.

And finally, the four teachers seemed to me to share a view of intercultural studies. They were aware of a fundamental issue in ethnomusicology, the problematic nature of interpreting a culture to which one is an outsider, and they surely had some ambivalence about people such as us. But in the end, I am glad to say that all believed that some important cause would be served by an outsider's study of their music.

Music, the Public Interest, and the Practice of Ethnomusicology

JEFF TODD TITON / Brown University

In *Ethnomusicology*, volume 35, no. 1, I named several special topics and invited articles on them for future issues of the Journal. This is the first: Music and the Public Interest. The authors asked me to attempt a unifying introduction. From where I stand, the theme of these articles is practice; and in this forum, under discussion is practice-informed theory. Public sector, applied, active, and practice ethnomusicology are the names that the authors in this issue give to what ethnomusicologists do in the public interest. What they have in common is work whose immediate end is not research and the flow of knowledge inside intellectual communities but, rather, practical action in the world outside of archives and universities. This work involves and empowers music-makers and music-cultures in collaborative projects that present, represent, and affect the cultural flow of music throughout the world. In the final analysis, of course, public ethnomusicology does result in knowledge as well as action.

Ethnomusicologists aren't the only ones who work in the field of music and the public interest. The field includes, for example, music therapists, managers of symphony orchestras, rock critics—anyone who mediates directly between music and the general public. But ethnomusicologists have a particular stake here, especially now when, in many societies, multiculturalism is an affirmative action policy issue in public programming. Multiculturalism in music means recognizing the integrity of the musical expressions of all peoples. Ethnomusicologists who present themselves as experts in this area can affect public policy.

In the United States, the movement to implement musical multiculturalism has been led by the Folk Arts Program of the National Endowment for the Arts, and therefore we begin this issue with an article by Daniel Sheehy, Folk Arts' current director, who holds the Ph.D. in ethnomusicology from U.C.L.A. For the past fifteen years Folk Arts has been in the forefront of public ethnomusicology.

From *Ethnomusicology*, Vol. 36, No. 3 (Fall 1992), pp. 315–22

As a granting agency, they facilitate high-quality public outreach programs such as festivals, artists-in-the-schools, apprenticeships, workshops, radio and television programs, and so forth, meant to honor and promote traditional family- and community-rooted music and other arts. In this connection I recall a 1981 Folk Arts Panel meeting when we were trying to determine whether to fund a particular proposal. One first-time panelist from the academic world furrowed his brow and sputtered, "But if we fund this we'll be interfering!," to which Bess Lomax Hawes, then Folk Arts director, said, "That's right, we're meddlers." Her point was that many forces are always at work in music-cultures, some by Folk Arts lights good, some not so good. Folk Arts is an action agency; of course it intervenes, and it has its reasons, many of which are brought up in this collection of articles.

The issue isn't whether intervention is an option; like it or not, ethnomusicologists intervene. Cardinal Newman's lofty idea of the university as a place where knowledge is accumulated for its own sake is self-serving for academics and misleading for everyone else. Universities are no different from other institutions in that they have a stake in maintaining their priesthoods of power and expertise and their places as guardians and arbiters of culture. Universities intervene; folk arts agencies intervene; museums intervene; research archives that do salvage ethnomusicology intervene. The issue, as Sheehy puts it, is not intervention but whether its purpose and effect is "worthy." His notion of worthy purpose is oriented towards practice: "to see opportunities for a better life for others through the use of musical knowledge, and then immediately to begin devising cultural strategies to achieve those ends."

Sheehy's review of the careers of forerunners John Lomax, Benjamin Botkin, and others reminds us that there is a history of applied folklore and ethnomusicology in the United States, as elsewhere, but that it has been omitted from the official histories of ethnomusicology. To his list of reasons for neglect I would add the pervasive belief that what we do, or ought to do, is science. For a discipline like ours with a history of worshiping at the altar of science, history itself must seem incidental to scientific progress, even a bit irrelevant. Moreover, applied work must seem too thoroughly bound to ideology, and therefore not disinterested in the way that science is supposed to be. But, again, science is scarcely disinterested, unless we equate disinterest with innocence or a failure of responsibility: consider, for example, the horrific consequences of taking particle physics (rather than, say, friendship) as the paradigm for the act of knowing. And, as Sheehy recognizes, the history of applied ethnomusicology in the United States includes many academics who may not think of themselves as working directly in the public interest but who have, at one time or another, "gone out of [their] way to act for the benefit of an informant or a community they have studied."

Sheehy describes four strategic aims of applied ethnomusicology: developing new performance frames, feeding back musical models to the communities that created them, empowering community members to become musical activists, and developing broad structural solutions. Bess Lomax Hawes's article details how a Folk Arts-sponsored event catalyzed a musical renewal among unaccompanied, African-American gospel quartets in the Birmingham, Alabama, region. The gospel concert offered a new performance frame in that the accompanying historical booklet became a bureaucratic currency and legitimized performances in other venues such as schools; it fed back to the singers and their families the musical model of the gospel reunion, and it reunited some groups that had ceased performing; and the concert and booklet "[empowered] the community studied, allowing the development of legitimate pride." Hawes points out that, in active ethnomusicology, it is always necessary to take the next action before the results of the previous action can be known, and she reminds us that we observe this principle in daily life anyway, pragmatically "trying out what [seems] logical and what might work, based on parallel observations and one's own reading of history." Here, "parallel observations" and "history" let us know that public ethnomusicology is always a collaborative effort, and quite the opposite of the lone ethnomusicologist in the library, thinking the world of music. Hawes' case study reveals the impact of a single event, one that did not seem too promising when it occurred. Multiply that by thousands of similar events in the past twenty-five years and one begins to sense the impact of public ethnomusicology.

Anthony Seeger's article moves into another arena of public ethnomusicology: music law. His concern is copyright, a thorny issue that, as he points out, many ethnomusicologists would like to wish away. After all, if music is a priceless gift, shouldn't it be free? U.S. copyright law states that music is property: as Seeger points out, Woody Guthrie's "This Land Is Your Land" remains property of the Guthrie estate. And if the laws regarding intellectual and artistic property conflict with ideals, the situation is compounded when ethnomusicologists subject to one set of national laws work with peoples in other nations, or with peoples who in their dealings with others operate on the basis of local custom rather than national jurisprudence. In this journal, to take a practical example, we require authors of articles to hold us harmless against claims brought about by the publication of copyrighted material in their articles. This is standard procedure for publishers; but to the author it says, in effect, Don't bring us your problems.

Seeger reminds us, as Henry Kingsbury did in an earlier article in the Journal (1991), that we would do well to consider interpretive discourse in the arena where it has the most obvious practical consequence: the law. Copyright is but one of several places that law impacts ethnomusicologists. Because law always involves rights and obligations, thinking about music and the public interest in terms of law requires probing the legal as well as ethical basis of our work. Who and what grants ethnomusicologists the right, as well as the authority, to study, reveal, and represent themselves and others in their works? Who grants Folk Arts the right to award money to certain groups and not others? The answers to these questions are embedded in the power relations and economic and political legitimation of publicly accountable institutions such as universities, record companies, museums, and arts institutions, not in some abstract realm where knowledge is supposedly pursued for its own sake. Seeger knows this because music law has taught it to him, and he recognizes reflexively that he has various and not entirely consistent interests resulting from his involvement with music from different vantage points.

Unlike the others, Martha Ellen Davis writes from a position inside rather than outside the academy, although I will note that all of these authors have been employed by universities at one time or another; and she reminds us that it is both possible and desirable for academics to pursue public ethnomusicology. In her wide-ranging article, she urges ethnomusicologists to consider the rewards of public work and to think of employment outside the academy and the research archives not as a less-desirable alternative to university work but as a worthy vocation in itself. She points out that the field of ethnomusicology can look to folklore as a public work role model, yet she would agree that because ethnomusicologists are not simply folklorists whose subject is world music, ethnomusicology as a profession ought not follow that model blindly or uncritically. She offers two case-studies of her public work, one from the Dominican Republic, the other from the Canary Islands. Her work exemplifies all four of Sheehy's strategic aims; perhaps most telling is that in the Canary Islands the work is being carried on without her, by the locals whom she has helped empower, Carmen Nieves Luis Garda and Isidro Ortiz Mendoza.

Davis's reference to American Pragmatism as a basis for public ethnomusicology links these articles to recent developments in philosophy, sociology, and cultural studies. In the 1980s an anti-theoretical movement emerged from within the great interdisciplinary hue and cry that came eventually to be known simply as Theory. I am not referring here to those who merely resisted Theory and mistakenly hoped that it would become interred with the tarnished reputation of Paul de Man. I mean, instead, a position that elevates practice over theory, a belief that theory is empty unless derived from practice, a feeling that, as Richard Rorty dramatically and influentially announced, philosophy as traditionally conceived was dead (1979). Rorty meant that the philosophical project of trying to find Truth, something upon which to ground Knowledge, was doomed. Rorty was but one of several thinkers (Michel Foucault, Edward Said, Hayden White, Roland Barthes, Susan Stewart, Stanley Fish—the list could go on and on) who fought the "essentialism" of those who claimed truth was something eternal, "out there" (or "in here") to be "found." In his view, and in the view of most Theorists, truth is shifting, situational, and humanly (if not socially and culturally) constructed. What Rorty called pragmatism (with a small *p*) emphasized practice and devalued theory. Theory was doomed to pursue Truth; practice would construct truths. In my view, the most far-reaching attack on scientific and philosophical essentialism is being carried out by feminist epistemologists (see, for example, Code 1991 and Harding 1986, 1991), but it is apparent throughout the (paradoxically theoretical) work of many others involved with issues of race, class, gender, and sexuality.

Pierre Bourdieu's emphasis on practice is well known to readers of this journal. In a recent statement, he suggests that practice is virtually incomprehensible from the standpoint of the academy. "The scholastic vision destroys its object every time it is applied to practices that are the product of the practical view and which, consequently, are very difficult to think of, or are even practically unthinkable for science" (1990:382). That scholastic vision Bourdieu has in mind springs, of course, from Newman's idea of the university where the scholar has time and freedom from necessity, "retiring from the world and from action in the world in order to think that action" (ibid.). This is not the vision of the authors in this special issue. As Bau Graves writes, "The discipline of ethnomusicology exists very much within the parameters of the academic world. Its internal politics, procedures of legitimization and means of communication are all received from the academic tradition [and] certainly a part of the university's mystique rests upon its separation from the world at large" (1992:5). I myself would prefer to see a reflexive theorizing of practice that is aware of the consequences of situating ethnomusicology both inside the academy and outside of it, one that, in the words of Habermas, "investigates the constitutive historical complex of the constellation of self-interests to which the theory still belongs across and beyond its acts of insight," yet one that "studies the historical interconnectedness of action, in which the theory, as action-oriented, can intervene" (1974:2).

When I think of music's contribution to theorizing practice, I am reminded that I view my being in the world musically as nontrivially different from my non-musical ways of being. Although we may not all be highly skilled performers, I am sure we have experienced a manual, or practical, side of musical being when we sing, dance, compose, or play an instrument: the relationship among sound, time, our bodies, and our consciousness, on the one hand, and the bonding among music-makers in a group on the other. Certain types of these practical, musical relationships have served ethnomusicologists as an ideal for human relationships generally (see, for example, Lomax 1968).

Public ethnomusicology and folklore is, of course, not without its critics. Some writers (for example, Harker 1985, Middleton 1990, Shepherd 1991, Keil 1978, and Whisnant 1983) have recycled the colonialist charges leveled at cultural anthropology and in one way or another aimed them at folklore and ethno-musicology, academic and public. The cultural studies critique, directed most forcefully at British folklorist Cecil Sharp and his intellectual offspring but also to the history of folklore and ethnomusicology in the United States, includes charges of elitist condescension, romantic nationalism, and an agenda of racial and ethnic segregation and purity hidden beneath the calls for cultural equity, cultural conservation, and multiculturalism.

Defenders of public ethnomusicology often feel that these charges are unfair, that they are directed against an older generation of scholars and activists, and that contemporary practice is well aware of, and does its best to guard against, colonialist tendencies in what is conceived as just the opposite of colonization: an affirmative action program for minority music cultures (in the United States, those outside the Western classical tradition). No one would claim perfection; action is risky, and sometimes one makes mistakes; but consider the alternative, non-action. Although Charles Keil has argued passionately against the term "folk," for example, he does important public ethnomusicology on behalf of youth in the Buffalo, New York parks and schools. Moreover, public ethnomusicologists testify to an enormous number of successful interventions, public projects that worked, and for which the world is better off as a result. More recent work in cultural studies takes the point of view that fears of homogenization among music-cultures are misplaced; that all music-cultures, even supposedly endangered ones, are always engaged in appropriation; and that "popular" music ought to be viewed neither as a threatened voice of the folk nor as an irredeem-ably corrupt and manipulated commodity, but rather as a site of conflict, where hegemony is always resisted by popular guerilla movements and subversion, with or without the intervention of public ethnomusicologists (Middleton 1990; Lipsitz 1990).

My own view is to welcome this dialogue and think that it has much to contribute to our understanding of music, culture, and ourselves, but as another participant in it I am prepared to defend fieldwork and public ethnomusicology as a way of knowing and doing. Although that defense is out of bounds in this introduction, I hope I will be permitted to sketch out one direction it might take. People working in cultural studies tend to disparage fieldwork as, not to put too fine a point on it, the politics of surveillance. But I think that those who would condemn it shut themselves off from a valuable way of knowing that is constitutive of those disciplines (ethnomusicology, cultural anthropol-ogy, folklore) that employ it. As a way of knowing and doing, fieldwork at its best is based on a model of friendship between people rather than on a model involving antagonism, surveillance, the observation of physical objects, or the contemplation of abstract ideas. Fieldwork, after all, is another name for a prin-cipal constituent in public ethnomusicology, work in the field rather than the laboratory; and although historically it is the biological metaphor that underlies the term, I construct a horticultural, nurturing metaphor there, and I prefer it to the bristling profusion of military metaphors in cultural studies. From a practical point of view I think nurturance better leads us to what Sheehy calls, and the other authors would agree are, worthy purposes and strategies in the world of action. With apologies to Milton, they do not serve who also stand and wait, theorizing.

References

Bourdieu, Pierre
    1990   "The Scholastic Point of View." *Cultural Anthropology* 5 (1990):382–391.
Code, Lorraine
    1991   *What Can She Know? Feminist Theory and Construction of Knowledge.* Ithaca, NY: Cornell University Press.
Graves, James Bau
    1992   "Ethics and Ethnics: Public Sector Ethnomusicology and the Mediation of Culture." M.A. thesis, Tufts University, Medford, MA.
Habermas, Jürgen
    1974   *Theory and Practice.* Translated by John Viertel. Boston: Beacon Press.
Harding, Sandra
    1986   *The Science Question in Feminism.* Ithaca, NY: Cornell University Press.
    1991   *Whose Science? Whose Knowledge? Thinking from Women's Lives.* Ithaca, NY: Cornell University Press.
Harker, Dave
    1985   *Fakesong: The Manufacture of British 'Folksong,' 1700 to the Present Day.* Milton Keynes: Open University Press.
Keil, Charles
    1978   "Who Needs the Folk?" *Journal of the Folklore Institute* 15:263–265.
Kingsbury, Henry
    1991   "Sociological Factors in Musicological Poetics." *Ethnomusicology* 35/2:195–219.
Lipsitz, George
    1990   *Time Passages: Collective Memory and American Popular Culture.* Minneapolis: University of Minnesota Press.
Lomax, Alan
    1968   *Folk Song Style and Culture.* Washington: American Association for the Advancement of Science.
Middleton, Richard
    1990   *Studying Popular Music.* Milton Keynes: Open University Press.
Rorty, Richard
    1979   *Philosophy and the Mirror of Nature.* Princeton, NJ: Princeton University Press.
Shepherd, John
    1991   *Music as Social Text.* Cambridge (U.K.): Polity Press.
Whisnant, David
    1983   *All That Is Native and Fine: The Politics of Culture in an American Region.* Chapel Hill: University of North Carolina Press.

Toward an Ethnomusicology of the Early Music Movement: Thoughts on Bridging Disciplines and Musical Worlds

KAY KAUFMAN SHELEMAY / Harvard University

Ethnomusicology has long occupied what might be termed a "liminal" space among the disciplines. Triangulating between the arts, humanities, and the social sciences, ethnomusicology has long held the ambiguous, middle ground between historical musicology and anthropology. If anthropology provided the methodological tools for musical ethnography, a heterogeneous world of musical performance contributed the sounds, settings, and significances that ethnomusicologists have sought to document and understand. Yet while ethnomusicology absorbed theories from across the disciplines, ethnomusicologists in North America have continued to find their most secure institutional homes not within departments of anthropology, linguistics, cultural studies, or as area specialists, but within schools of music and music departments. Finally, while questioning power inequities within the societies they study and interrogating their discipline's colonial roots, ethnomusicologists have continued to pursue studies of "other" musics—musical traditions that in some way stand outside the world of the Euro-American classical tradition, whether these boundaries are defined by geographical origins, transmission patterns and technologies, or socio-economic positions. In the following essay, I would like to offer a preliminary ethnography of the early music movement, drawing from it what I hope are useful insights into the collapsing musical boundaries in our changing world and the new agendas that might unite musical scholarship through a shared pedagogy and practice of musical ethnography. To this end, I will preface my case study with a brief disciplinary overview and return to this broader perspective in the conclusion.[1]

I. Ethnomusicology, Ethnographic Method, and "Non-Western" Music

In an introduction to a special issue of the *Journal of the American Musicological Society* (*JAMS*) published in 1995, Regula Qureshi discussed the relationship between anthropology, history, and a broader musicology that includes ethnomusicology. Qureshi characterizes the "anthropologizing of music history," the primary and most productive relationship to date of anthropology and historical musicology, as beginning with "a recasting of the musical product into the realm of experience" (Qureshi 1995:335). The four essays that follow Qureshi's introduction interrogate music in culture through highlighting the notions of "dialogue, de-essentializing, and difference" (Qureshi 1995:339). Indeed, the special *JAMS* issue builds on historical musicology's growing engagement with a range of anthropological theories that have served to enliven and enrich the musicological palette, forecast earlier in writings by Tomlinson (1984) and Treitler (1989).

Ethnomusicologists, of course, have drawn freely on anthropology; indeed, they have spent much of the second half of the twentieth century trying to remake their own discipline in its image. To note just a few milestones, one might cite Merriam's *Anthropology of Music* (1964), Alan Lomax's *Cantometrics* (1976), Timothy Rice's remodeling of ethnomusicological theory (1987) based on readings of Clifford Geertz, and Mark Slobin's schema for transnational musics (1993) which draws upon Arjun Appardurai's notion of "ethnoscapes" (Appadurai 1990). Ethnomusicological research and writing have further interacted closely with a number of different streams of anthropological thought, ranging from structuralism, to symbolic, linguistic, and reflexive anthropology. While none of these efforts has resulted in a new theory that moves beyond its anthropological model, there have been, particularly recently, a number of increasingly nuanced case studies.

Yet there is one area allied to anthropology in which ethnomusicologists alone have innovated. I have earlier suggested (Shelemay 1996b) that the domain of ethnographic method is where ethnomusicologists have most successfully and creatively occupied a disciplinary space midway between anthropology and musical scholarship. One is tempted to dub this a true "anthromusicology." But since terminology is already so problematic, I will draw instead on a distinction made over a decade ago by Anthony Seeger (1987). While historical musicologists are now beginning to participate actively in an "anthropology of music," bringing the "concepts, methods, and concerns of anthropology" to studies of music history, ethnomusicologists have in the meantime moved much more aggressively toward what Seeger has termed a "musical anthropology," exploring the way[s] "musical performances create many aspects of culture and social life"

(1987:xiii). I believe that the ethnomusicological adaptation and transformation of the ethnographic method to the study and experience of musical act and sound provide the key to explore these formative processes set into motion through musical invention and performance. Here ethnomusicologists have carved out a special relationship to anthropological theory and method from which historical musicologists could potentially benefit. This is a juncture where a partnership between ethnomusicology and historical musicology could prove fruitful, yet neither side has yet capitalized on its possibilities.

The *JAMS* issue on music anthropologies and music histories also suggests future possibilities that bridge disciplinary boundaries. All four grapple substantively or indirectly with ethnographic dilemmas: One raises questions highlighted during the fieldwork process (Monson), a second critiques ethnography and resulting interpretations of others (Agawu), and the two final contributions (Tomlinson, Feldman) seek to re-imagine insiders' perspectives, through lenses of poststructuralist and ritual theory respectively, of the distant worlds of Aztec song and opera seria. While Monson and Agawu, both of whom have done fieldwork in the traditions they discussed, explicitly address the ethnographic process, Tomlinson's and Feldman's essays move more directly to anthropological theory, side-stepping exploration of the ethnographic encounter. This is unfortunate, if one agrees that not only does "fieldwork constitute ethnomusicology," but that the ethnographic experience can be viewed as a pathway to experiencing and understanding music, as well as to ask what it is like for a person to make and to know music as lived experience (Titon 1997:87).

If disciplinary boundaries between anthropology, ethnomusicology, and musicology overlap, these boundaries are nevertheless maintained by a longtime divide between musics studied. However, the ethnographic challenge of distinguishing musical boundaries between the West and the Rest raises a number of possibilities for new, shared fields of inquiry. I will address this issue as it arises with regard to the early music movement below, but here would offer a few broader comments on the conceptualization of "non-Western music" vs. "Western music" and the manner in which I believe this opposition must be collapsed if we are to traverse successfully the divide between historical musicology and ethnomusicology and make more fruitful the relationship of both to anthropology.

Anthropology's and ethnomusicology's longtime historical engagement primarily with materials and musics from outside of Europe and North America has led to a close association of both of these disciplines with the unfamiliar, conceptualized within a framework of difference, and often characterized as exotic. This perspective has been further exacerbated by a tendency to assume isomorphism between space, place, and culture (Gupta and Ferguson 1992).

The recent rethinking of totalizing and bounded notions of culture has fallen on sympathetic ears in ethnomusicology none too soon, coinciding with the movement away from foreign fieldsites to the study of a variety of musics "at home" as well as the increasing investigation of popular and transnational styles. Yet the longstanding binary division of music into categories of "Western" and "World Music" has not really been challenged head-on and will not be dismantled by a simple change of field venues. That ethnomusicologists have largely remained silent on this issue can be attributed perhaps to their desire to preserve clear boundaries between their own pursuits and identity in the face of an overwhelming presence, at least in most American academic institutions, of "Western" musical traditions traditionally performed and studied.

On the ground, wherever scholars actually practice a musical ethnography, it is becoming increasingly difficult to discern where boundaries conceptualized and named geographically can in fact be drawn (Shelemay 1996a). This is true of virtually all musical traditions, whatever their historical provenance, locale, human networks, class associations, economic settings, or transmission patterns. That most "Western" of musics, the twentieth-century Euro/American orchestral tradition, has long been influenced by multiple musical traditions, practiced by an international array of performers and composers, and appreciated by aficionados stretching from Boston to Tokyo. Similarly, popular musics largely dispersed through the media of recordings, radio, and concert tour have crossed so many musical and social boundaries that they can no longer be partitioned. Witness the transformations of Sufi *qawwali*, which exists variously as devotional song and secular concert genre in Pakistan while constituting a popular, commercial genre abroad (Sakata 1994:89). Even what have been termed "subcultural musical sounds" (Slobin 1993) attached to particular local or ethnic communities are in actuality both heterogenous and international. Here I would cite the repertory of paraliturgical hymns transmitted, performed, and still actively composed Syrian Jews from New York to Buenos Aires, who set sacred Hebrew texts to melodies variously borrowed from mass-distributed Arabic films and recordings, North American popular songs, and the compositions of Beethoven and Rachmaninoff. (Shelemay 1998) The categories of "Western-music" and "non-Western music" have disintegrated, if indeed these rubrics ever had the integrity with which they were invested by scholars. The complex of musical activities, traditions, and musicians I will discuss (termed "early music" by both its practitioners and a wider community internationally), is among those commonly categorized as a subset of Western music. That this categorization once again poses problems is not surprising and will enter in important ways into the discussion below.

The acknowledgment of the "other" in anthropology (usually discussed in musical scholarship in reference to "non-Western" musical traditions) has recently been extended to characterize unfamiliar aspects of the past in a variety of historical disciplines (such as Lowenthal 1985). Thus Gary Tomlinson has written that

> I began my study of Renaissance musical magic, then, with a keen sense of its distance, its unfamiliarity, its otherness. This sense linked the project from the first with anthropological thought. (Tomlinson 1993:4)

Yet the idea of otherness, which has attracted some historical musicologists and which has led them to explore creatively the anthropological literature, has served only to erect barriers to a true discourse with ethnomusicologists, who in the past applied their ethnographic techniques primarily to musics outside the West and only on rare occasion discussed the "Western" art music tradition. A true musical anthropology would seem to hold great potential for the study of "Western music" as well, yet this venture has been less actively contested than trivialized or ignored. Bruno Nettl has summarized the range of responses to his own efforts to carry out an ethnography of classical music culture in American Schools of Music (Nettl 1995:xi–xii), noting that Western classical music is the "last bastion of unstudied musical culture." His work, along with that of Henry Kingsbury (1988), Philip Bohlman (1989), and Ruth Finnegan (1989), provide fine examples of ethnographies of music schools and conservatories, chamber music as ethnic music, and music of an English urban area. However, the growing musicological literature informed by anthropology generally omits any reference to this type of ethnomusicological activity. Yet fewer historical musicologists have themselves experimented with ethnographic method or have drawn upon its data in the context of their own research designs.[2]

Here we arrive at a juncture where both ethnomusicology and historical musicology are missing a grand anthromusicological opportunity. It is the possibility and potential of the convergence of historical musicology and anthropology, with the experience of ethnomusicology as mediator in the realm of ethnographic method, that leads me to explore this prospect through discussion of a recent ethnography of the early music movement in Boston. My purpose in the next section of the paper is to provide enough basic information about both the ethnographic process and the materials it gathered to explore some of the potentials and pitfalls of ethnomusicologies of "Western music" and the role that ethnomusicologists could play in moving musical scholarship further in these directions.

II. In Search of "The Lost World"

> "Things ain't what they used to be and they never were."
> (Joel Cohen, 1 October 1996)[3]

In early June of 1997, Steven Spielberg's blockbuster movie "The Lost World" opened in Boston and the public was treated to visions of a dinosaur running amok in Los Angeles. A few days later, on June 10, 1997, the ninth Boston

Early Music Festival (BEMF) began, a week-long, biennial gathering where thousands of practitioners and afficionados of the early music world swarmed over the Boston landscape, attending hundreds of virtually round-the-clock concerts throughout the metropolitan area, viewing displays and demonstrations of period instruments of all types, and frequenting a commercial exhibit featuring everything from the latest recordings and editions to custom-made theorbo cases. I draw the analogy between "The Lost World" and the BEMF not because either seeks to resurrect a lost past, but because of the manner in which both of these endeavors construct and transform the past in the present, whether bringing rampaging, maternal dinosaurs to the screen or mounting a very postmodern production of a seventeenth-century opera (Luigi Rossi's "L'Orfeo"). If both are ostensibly in search of "lost worlds," they are also very active agents in that search, constituting cultural productions that have substantial symbolic and economic force, sophisticated aesthetic agendas, and an impact well beyond their respective "worlds" of cinema and music.

During the 1996–1997 academic year, I collaborated in a team research project centered at Harvard on early music in Boston. The ethnographic process actually began a full half-year before, as I, with my partners in this venture, historical musicologist Thomas Forrest Kelly and ethnomusicologist Carol Babiracki, planned the project, negotiating with each other and individuals active in the early music movement to establish a fieldwork plan for the coming fall. Our goal was to begin to chart the boundaries, workings, and participants of the early music world as constituted in the late 1990s in Boston, which has long served as the primary American center for such activities. We envisioned the 1996–1997 iteration as the first stage in a longer-term research effort. In collaboration with a group of eighteen graduate and undergraduate students,[4] we carried out ethnographic research within the context of an intensive fall 1996 seminar, supplemented by a year-long "workshop" attended by class members, additional graduate students, and others in the Harvard community interested in early music. We worked primarily with four ensembles considered by themselves and others to be active in the early music movement. The groups were 1) Tapestry (a vocal ensemble of four women who sing primarily medieval selections); 2) The Voice of the Turtle (a four-person instrumental/vocal ensemble which performs mainly a Sephardic song repertory with its historical roots in the Renaissance); 3) The Boston Museum Trio (a Baroque instrumental trio); and 4) The King's Noyse (a Renaissance string consort). Each of these four groups participated in class presentations and interviews, a process followed up (except with the King's Noyse because of scheduling problems) by more focused ethnographic inquiry undertaken by a small team of students. The teams, each supervised by one faculty member, carried out further individual and group interviews, attended rehearsals and concerts, administered audience surveys, and gathered additional primary and secondary materials ranging from old programs to published recordings. I would note that our efforts also included a survey of and attendance at a cross-section of early music concerts in Boston during fall 1996,[5] and, throughout the entire 1996–1997 academic year under the auspices of the workshop, a series of presentations by and interviews/discussions with a number of other individuals active in the early music movement, including prominent instrument makers and instrumentalists, leaders of major ensembles, and a number of musical professionals and amateurs. In drawing on these materials for this essay, I acknowledge the collaborative efforts of my faculty and student colleagues as well as the cooperation and knowledge of so many members of the early music community in Boston.[6] I would mention here that many of the quotations included below are taken from informal, spoken discourse and reflect the impromptu and informal venue in which they were made.[7]

It should also be noted that, due to the involvement of members of the research team as performers and scholars of early music, and the academic backgrounds and current affiliations of many in the early music movement, the distinction between ethnographer and research associate was more often than not blurred. Indeed, exploring and coming to terms with the overlapping professional and personal networks as well as shared life venues and values proved to be one of the most challenging aspects of this project. It deserves much more careful attention and analysis and is the subject of some further discussion below. One member of our faculty team, medievalist Thomas Kelly, has been a generative figure in the early music movement, directing period ensembles and productions, involved in numerous early music organizations, and producing editions. Among the student members of the team were several musicians who performed professionally in Boston and elsewhere, and others who were active in studying and editing repertories relevant to the early music movement. Of our colleagues who directed or participated in the ensembles with which we worked, several are faculty members at our own and other Boston educational institutions. The close and symbiotic relationship between those active in the early music movement and the scholars who were ostensibly studying the scene provided a challenging venture in "insider" ethnography as well as an unusual opportunity to critique the relationship of scholarship to the "real world" of music. While ethnographers have been criticized in the past for constructing "the Other" in terms of spatial and temporal distance (Fabian 1983:xi), such a separation would not have been likely to arise in a study such as our own. Rather an opposite problem arose, traces of which can be found throughout the interview transcripts and in fieldnotes: Here ethnographers and practitioners shared time, place, and institutional lives to the extent that the borders between the identity of researcher and subject in the early music study can only be described as blurred. Interviews sometimes slipped into conversations or even into spirited debates as members of the research team became at once musicians, audience members, or occasionally, critics. Early music practitioners, speaking from their own experiences, referred often to the scholarly literature and critical editions, which they know intimately and on which they draw in preparing detailed notes for concert programs and published recordings. One day members of the research team welcomed figures from the early music world into our classroom as expert informants. The next, they interacted with these same individuals over coffee, by telephone, or e-mail, alternately soliciting further advice or exchanging information on issues of performance practice or repertory. If the ethnographer is inevitably implicated in "making" his or her subject, the study of the early music movement provides an unparalleled opportunity to critique not just the workings of a remarkable musical subculture, but much of the course of the scholarly enterprise so heavily implicated in its making.

What is "Early Music"?

What is early music and what are its boundaries? In an unpublished summary of a survey of the early music movement sponsored by the membership organization Early Music America, Thomas Kelly wrote that "the field would seem to comprise three related elements: a body of music, those who perform it, and the way(s) in which the performers approach the music" (Kelly 1989:2). Yet, as Kelly notes, "as the early music revival continues apace, however, definitions and boundaries of all types change, become indistinct, or fall away altogether" (ibid.). There is a substantial background to the present-day movement dating back to the nineteenth century that I cannot address in detail here, but which was explicated in an article by Howard Mayer Brown, whose lead I will follow in glossing "early music" as "an interest and involvement with the music of the past" (1988:30).

But what type of involvement do we find with music of the past? And which pasts? Our project intended to incorporate inquiry into aspects of musical performance, but to also move beyond it to explore more deeply the social and cultural factors that have rendered "early music" a living tradition in the twentieth century. If there is a widespread assumption that the basis of early music activity is a search for "historical faithfulness to the past" (Kenyon 1988:6), both the literature and ethnographic inquiry present strong challenges to that view. Ethnographic research tends to support perspectives such as that of scholar/performer Laurence Dreyfus, who has written that early music is a late twentieth-century ensemble of social practices, signifying "first of all people and only secondarily things" (Dreyfus 1983:298). Musicologist Richard Taruskin, himself a longtime performer of the Renaissance repertories, has perhaps most clearly set forth a view that contextualizes the complex relationship of the early music movement to the past, to a contested world of historically-informed performance practice, and to the values of the late twentieth century:

> I am convinced that "historical" performance today is not really historical; that a thin veneer of historicism clothes a performance style that is completely of our own time, and is in fact the most modern style around; and that the historical hardware has won its wide acceptance and above all its commercial viability precisely by virtue of its novelty, not its antiquity. (Taruskin 1988:152)

This perspective is echoed by individuals active in Boston early music circles. Joel Cohen, the director of the Boston Camerata, noted in an interview that

> I would rather not use the word "early music" now. I think it's more a question of how you approach performance and I try, when I perform . . . to place it in a historical context. You know . . . to find out what the surrounding values are. And in that sense, it's—as Taruskin correctly points out,[8] it's a . . . modernist approach, 'cause nobody ever did that before—[they] just played . . . I'm not so sure there's a movement, but there's still early music going on . . . I think a lot of people went into it . . . because they could make it theirs . . . I wanted to do something which would leave me some space. (Joel Cohen, 1 October 1996)

Thus the early music movement, while drawing on music of the historical past, is powerfully informed by the creative impulses of its practitioners and the aesthetics of the present. Yet the "otherness" of the past remains ever-present, both a motivating force and strong drawing card for some practitioners and many in the audience (as well as critics in the media), who revel in productions of works "you read about in the history books but never hear" (Tommasini 1997:17). However, this "otherness" is inevitably and sometimes dramatically inflected by a late twentieth century sensibility, with difference articulated by many as a central value of the movement at large.

Present-day creativity thus joins with historical awareness and operates actively in all domains of program planning and performance practice. For example, violinist Daniel Stepner noted the creative role of members of the Boston Museum Trio, consisting of himself, gambist Laura Jeppesen, and keyboardist John Gibbons, in such basic and little discussed processes as selecting and formulating their own repertory:

> There's lots of music that's appropriate for us to play together, but very little, relatively little music that was written specifically for these instruments. (Daniel Stepner, 22 October 1996)

Furthermore, each performance of a composition is an innately creative act:

> Laura and I were playing the two lines that Bach wrote, and John was filling in the harmonies, but he was also inventing a third voice a lot of the time, particularly in the slow movement, and to me that's in a way one of the exciting things about this music is that there's a lot of room for improvisation. . . . I did a few little decorative

improvisations but there was some real invention going on in the keyboard playing which doesn't get noticed, and talked about much. (ibid.)

While their performances are certainly "historically informed," the Boston Museum Trio is at the same time "re-inventing" music of the past, a process acknowledged as an imaginative and exciting one:

> I think the beauty and attraction of early music is that we don't ultimately know, despite all the notation . . . [how] it sounded. We have to recreate it. And through the filter of our imaginations and personalities. And that's what's so challenging and exciting about music that hasn't been recorded yet or music for [which] there are no recordings by the composer. (Daniel Stepner, 29 October 1996)

Musicians in all of the ensembles with which we worked testified to the central-ity of creative activity in their conceptualization and performance of musical repertory. For example, the founder of the King's Noyse, a Renaissance string band active since 1987, noted that

> I could just say this is a twentieth-century phenomenon. In many ways I do. This is a twentieth-century thing. What I enjoy doing the most is repertoire from the sixteenth century and I enjoy the parameters of sixteenth-century reaction, and I try to *stick* to those, but I think of it as being a music of now. And I've often thought about doing violin band arrangements of modern tunes . . . you want to just do the Beatles and put out a Christmas album and finally make some money. You know, it would *still* be a Renaissance violin band and would draw from popular music genres and make it a twentieth-century event. (David Douglas, 5 November 1996)

What is the Early Music Movement?

From an ethnographic perspective, the early music movement can be seen less as a bounded stream of musical discourse than a multi-faceted world of musi-cal and cultural experience. In terms of conventional parameters of time and space, one finds a virtually unlimited array of musics and musical practices from a full range of accessible historical styles primarily emerging from Europe and America, but infused both in the past and present with many cross cur-rents. Here Joel Cohen's invocation of the metaphor of the blind man and the elephant serves nicely to summarize the challenge of providing an overview of this complex phenomenon:

> I'm sure we've got pieces of the elephant . . . somebody's touching the elephant's tusk, somebody's got his tail, nobody's got the whole elephant, you know. So . . . we're sharing elephantology with these guys. (Joel Cohen, 1 October 1996)

In a presentation to the Harvard early music seminar, Cohen set forth a series of rubrics that help to "map" the early music movement, at least from the perspective of its participants from the 1960s forward in the northeastern United States. I will draw here on Cohen's categories, with some reorderings and with added discussion of musical instruments, musical values, and socio-economic domains. I am interested to establish a concise framework for theoretical and methodological remarks as well as to provide a backdrop, however sketchy and incomplete, against which my conclusions can be evaluated. An "elephantology" of the early music movement can usefully begin with the following eight points, each of which was present in the materials and observations of our fieldwork; deeper historical perspectives and further documentation can be gained from writings of Dreyfus 1983, Haskell 1988, Kenyon 1988, and Taruskin 1995.

1. Amateurism and Professionalism

Several of our research associates noted that the Boston early music movement had its root in the world of musical amateurs, with a "push toward professionalism" beginning only in the 1960s. The arrival of "outsiders" such as Arnold Dolmetsch from Europe (in 1905) to participate in the manufacture of harpsichords served as a catalyst for Boston-based early music activities, as did the later presence of others who helped found organizations such as the Cambridge Society for Early Music (Friedrich Von Huene, 24 September 1996).[9] The Boston Chapter of the American Recorder Society, founded in early 1956, encouraged amateur musical performance, and its concerts accommodated a wide range of both historical and modern repertory. Indeed, in order to gain wider recognition for the recorder, the Recorder Society commissioned recorder works from contemporary composers. Amateur musical groups proliferated, such as an ensemble for recorders, voice, lap harp, viol, lute, and guitar, called "The Cantabrigians," a clever appropriation of the name by which Cambridge residents are known (Arthur Loeb, Oral History prepared for Archive of Viola da Gamba Society, typescript). By the 1970s, however, the movement took a turn toward professionalism and increasing specialization.

2. Specialist Performers

Boston provided a congenial location for professional musicians, many of whom found homes at area educational institutions or with firms of instrument makers. Outstanding early music musicians who made Boston home included harpsichord virtuoso Ralph Kirkpatrick, organist E. Power Biggs, and numerous others.[10] Many musicians gravitated to Boston after graduating from music schools elsewhere and studying in Europe; the plethora of musicians and possibility of a variety of work opportunities in the early music domain were important attractions (Dan Stepner, Laura Jeppesen, 29 October, 1996).

Most of the professional musicians with whom we worked, despite a close association with a primary ensemble, also performed with several other groups. While a few specialize in the music of a particular period, most participate in a range of repertories, shifting playing techniques and even instruments as appropriate. For example, violinist Daniel Stepner is a founding member of the Boston Museum Trio and performs with the Boston Baroque. Yet he also plays with the Lydian String Quartet, a classical quartet in residence at Brandeis University, and for Boston Music Viva, a contemporary music group. Stepner's activities bring to life Laura Jeppesen's remark that

> Our trio repertory is not everything to us. We each have a life that is—or a musical life—that is completely apart from the trio. . . . We all are autonomous. (Laura Jeppesen, 21 October 1996)

3. Instruments

Although there are some ensembles that are almost exclusively vocal (such as Tapestry), central to the early music movement are musical instruments, particularly the period reproductions made by an impressive number of instrument makers. Many of our associates provided considerable detail about their instruments, conveying not just extraordinary technical knowledge, but the instrument's history and social significance with great elegance. Laura Jeppesen began her own detailed narrative about her career by first introducing her "designer gamba," about which she acknowledged wishing she could see "lined up" with all the people who have played it (Laura Jeppesen, 22 October 1996). Jeppesen proceeded to give a long discourse on the history of the viola da gamba and its repertory, which I cite in part here:

> When you talk about the history of the instrument it's interesting that its heyday was in a different country at a different time. So in the sixteenth century . . . we would look at Italy . . . and then Italian gambists went to England. Seventeenth century England is very interesting for the gamba—where the gamba was a . . . social instrument. It was owned by landed gentry. . . . The French used the gamba in different ways. Louis (XIV), who was the great connoisseur . . . who had fine, discerning taste, surrounded him(self) with the best musicians, artists of his time. . . . Germans came to the French court to listen and study. . . . So the gamba stayed really within the confines of the eighteenth century until its revival. (ibid.)

In this context, it is notable that David Douglas of the King's Noyse defines his group not so much by its repertory, but by its musical style and distinctive instrumental composition of a "Renaissance violin band, meaning a consort of the violin family":

> Another important difference about the King's Noyse besides how we play is literally the instruments that we play. The instruments in the sixteenth century were most ideally made as one consort. . . . The violin family was best heard as a consort designed to sound and blend with one another. . . . But you want the instruments, the sound of each of the instruments to lock in together so that it really sounds like

one sound from top to bottom. These instruments are copies of instruments that exist in a couple of different places, primarily the Shrine to Music in Vermilion, South Dakota, . . . a great collection of instruments in the middle of nowhere. And they are copies of instruments made for Charles IX, in France, in Paris, in the 1570s and 1580s. (David Douglas, 5 November 1996)

Many individuals came to early music through an initial involvement with instruments and instrument collections. Laura Jeppesen was exposed to the viola da gamba at Yale when she worked as a research assistant on a project with gambas in the musical instrument collection. Many ensembles have emerged from association with collections, such as the Boston Camerata, which was founded in conjunction with the musical instrument collection at the Boston Museum of Fine Arts. Today the Museum remains patron to an annual concert series by an ensemble that carries its name, the Boston Museum Trio.

There is an important material culture aspect to the early music movement that revolves around musical instruments, their construction, and performance practices. Not surprisingly, many of our interview sessions incorporated substantial discussion of tunings, bridge positions, and details such as the presence and/or absence of end pins on viola da gambas. Yet these conversations cannot be characterized simply as discussions of technical issues; rather they provided detailed exegeses that connected grounded musical practice (which individuals usually demonstrated) directly to the musical experience itself as well as to other cultural domains. For instance, Ellen Hargis of the King's Noyse discussed at length the content of period paintings, which in revealing to twentieth-century musicians that bridges were placed lower on seventeenth century violins, transformed present-day performance and perception of the music from that era (Ellen Hargis, 5 November 1996).

4. Specialist and Non-specialist Ensembles

Testimony by a number of research associates sketched a divide between specialist and non-specialist ensembles. Ensembles established earlier on, in the first wave of professional groups in the 1960s, such as New York's Waverly Consort, continue to perform diverse repertories. Joel Cohen, whose Boston Camerata performs and records a wide range of traditions from medieval Christian and Jewish repertories ("The Sacred Bridge," 1990) to American Shaker music ("Simple Gifts," 1995), credits the increasing specialization by early music ensembles largely to the influence of the late Thomas Binkley, who had a distinguished teaching career in Europe and the United States.[11] The four ensembles with which we worked during fall 1996 can all be classified as specialist ensembles; it is noteworthy that Laurie Monahan, the founder and director of Tapestry, studied with Binkley at Indiana University.

5. Musical Values and Performance Practices

That musicians discuss performance practices in detail is no surprise, but the manner in which they were able to articulate details of musical practice as well as values behind them was one of the richest outcomes of the ethnographic process. For instance, while testimony about musical instruments is perhaps more easily rendered because of the easy availability of the instruments themselves, we found that singers also provided nuanced discussions of vocal production as well speculated on the difficult philosophical issues surrounding the voice and textual articulation. Ellen Hargis, who performs with the King's Noyse, and who realized the role of Orfeo in the BEMF revival of the Rossi opera that served as the centerpiece of the 1997 Boston Early Music Festival's musical offerings, provided extensive commentary on philosophical issues related to textual articulation and dialects:

> I sort of take a philosophy that despite the conflicting evidence, I have to be a single singer. I have one voice. Even if I were projecting myself back and saying, OK, I'm at some court in the seventeenth century and I'm singing this pile of songs, I probably wouldn't have at that time tried to be five different people from five different districts, but would have made a reasonable approximation and sung in my own voice and my own pronunciation. So that's what I sort of try to do now is to come up with a system for whatever repertoire we're doing that works for that language, that work for most of the texts, and of course, we choose texts that go together. I'm not forced to sing wildly different things . . . I will make compromises, for instance. I was once faced with singing an Old French word that was the equivalent of the modern "seul," alone, and the old pronunciation was "sool," which means drunk. . . . I thought this will make people giggle, they'll get distracted from the song, it's really not worth being historically accurate in this case 'cause it'll be so distracting to people. So I compromised on that one, I probably sang somewhere in between. (Ellen Hargis, 5 November 1996)

6. Local Roots and National/International Networks

If Boston has served as the American center for early music movement during the second half of the twentieth century and is the permanent home of the BEMF, it also has close ties to other places and is an important node in an international early music network. The BEMF itself, in addition to its international biennial festival, presents a year-round concert series mainly featuring ensembles from outside Boston and often from abroad. There is a general acknowledgment of a close and symbiotic relationship between "in town" and "out of town" activity, the latter incorporating touring and recording activities, along with more prestige (Joel Cohen, 1 October 1996).

Many individuals discussed studying in Europe, which in the past carried considerable cultural capital and offered otherwise unavailable training:

> When I decided to study the viola da gamba, I knew I had to go to Europe. . . . In those days, you just had to. There were some gamba players here, but the major activity was happening there. (Laura Jeppesen, 29 October 1996)

Jeppesen went on to note that she was the only American student in a broadly international group during her gamba studies in Belgium in the early 1970s, a period when her future Boston Museum Trio colleagues Daniel Stepner and John Gibbons also studied and worked as apprentice performers in Europe. The centrality of the Netherlands to Baroque music performance practice was stressed by Naʿama Lion, a Baroque flute player from Israel who spent three years studying in Holland before settling in Boston (Naʿama Lion, 26 November 1996).

Indeed, it may well be that Boston's old and continuing historical ties to European culture has both engendered and sustained its connection to early music, a relationship characterized by Joel Cohen as "co-dependent." Boston is still viewed by some as "more European feeling than New York" and continues to attract an international array of musicians who come together to comprise local ensembles. One such example is Tapestry, one of whose four members was from Belgrade, a second from Puerto Rico. In summary, Boston is "a place where you can make a living as a musician, freelancer . . ." (John Gibbons, 11 November 1996).

7. Institutions

Early music life is tightly organized and both individuals and many groups have close ties to Boston institutions. As noted above, some ensembles began in conjunction with instrument collections, notably the Boston Camerata, and later, the Boston Museum Trio, at the Boston Museum of Fine Arts. Several Boston-area institutions have at different times past and present offered early music degree or certificate programs, including the New England Conservatory, Boston University, the Longy School of Music, and Harvard University. Many individuals prominent in the early music scene teach at these institutions, leading to outcomes such as the establishment of the ensemble Tapestry, which emerged in 1994 from the longtime working relationship of Longy faculty member Laurie Monahan with three of her students. Early music activity is also supported as part of extracurricular life on university campuses; a notable example is the early music program in residence since 1976 at Harvard University's Mather House (Elfrieda Hiebert and Naʿama Lion, 26 November 1996).

In addition to the American Recorder Society and Viola da Gamba Society already mentioned above, many other professional associations have active chapters in Boston; these range from the Lute Society of America, to the American Guild of Organists, and other even more specialized groups such as the Intergalactic Double Reed Society.

Several historical Boston churches provide institutional settings for on-going early music activity, notably the choir of the Church of the Advent (est. 1844) and the weekly performance of Bach Cantatas at Emmanuel Church (est. 1860) (Noel Bisson and Andrew Shenton, 24 February 1997). The First Congregational Church in Cambridge designated Tapestry as its ensemble in residence. Finally, several of the largest Boston music ensembles can be said to constitute institutions in themselves, such as the Handel and Haydn Society, established in 1815.

8. Social and Economic Factors

Ethnographic inquiry into the early music movement reveals a complex community, with multiple pathways and networks. The social dimensions and rehearsal processes of different groups can be highly personal and idiosyncratic, as noted in the discussion of the Quadrivium and Voice of the Turtle below.

A provocative, but largely unexplored finding of our preliminary study, is that professional associations in the early music community have given rise to real familial and biological relationships. We were surprised at the number of references to musical transmission from parents to children beginning with the example of Dolmetsch himself (Friedrich Von Huene, 24 September 1996)[12] to that of the children of Mather House early music program founder Elfrieda Hiebert (26 November 1996). The prospects for familial transmission of early music in the future are further enhanced by the marriages of musicians who perform together, including the presence of couples in two of the four groups with which we worked, the Boston Museum Trio and the King's Noyse. One member of the Boston Museum Trio noted, "I think that our trio has the attributes of a good marriage. . . . Well, we have a marriage in it" (Laura Jeppesen, 22 October 1996).

In the economic arena, our research associates were quite outspoken about the challenges to both individuals and ensembles in the late twentieth century music economy. Several commented at length on the existence of extensive governmental and municipal support of early music in Europe and contrasted it to the dearth of official patronage in the United States. Virtually all participants in our study noted that early music audiences were smaller and that revenues from concerts were lower than they had been in earlier decades. However, the decline in early music activity was characterized as applying mainly to small groups, while audiences were thought possibly to have grown among more "mainstream" groups (Na'ama Lion, 26 November 1996).

We heard a great deal of the testimony about economic and practical aspects of surviving in the early music world, learning that virtually all ensembles are burdened with administrative tasks and paperwork and must devote a great deal of their time to such practical matters. Virtually everyone spoke to the challenges of trying to make a living amid intense competition in a specialist market. The economic constraints on all groups also served to provoke occasional sharp comments about the few early music groups that have attained a modicum of commercial success. The fact that most musicians play in multiple groups or hold other (often academic) positions can be attributed in large part to economic necessity. Most groups and their individual musicians are also forced to tour in order to schedule the critical mass of concerts necessary to make even a modest living. Events such as BEMF must be considered not just as cultural and social events, but as critical to the economic life of the early music community in Boston and beyond.

The economic network supporting and interacting with the early music groups, individual performers, and institutions includes management agencies, instrument makers, music publishers, and recording companies. In particular, the availability of a current recording can spell the difference in a group's ability to obtain engagements and maintain an active relationship with their audience between live concerts. Recordings play a particularly crucial role in early music circles by both circulating performances and providing detailed documentation of repertory, texts and translations, performance practices, and the group's statement of purpose. The investment of time and resources necessary to produce a commercial recording is mentioned as a barrier for all but the largest and most well established ensembles.

Is "Early Music" "Western Music"?

On the surface, early music seems to be the quintessential "Western" musical experience, a living monument to the past of the Euro-American art music tradition. Yet a closer look raises many questions. Take the instrument exhibit at the heart of the BEMF which in 1997 occupied several dozen rooms on a full floor of the Park Plaza Hotel, and in 1999 spilled over into the Radisson Hotel as well. While dominated by keyboard, string consorts, and wind instruments of European origin, one could also find Celtic harps, penny whistles, Native American nose flutes, and ocarinas. One instrument maker (Kelischek Workshop of Brasstown, North Carolina)[13] noted that "folk and traditional instruments are early instruments, too" (S. Larson 1997:16). Perhaps most strikingly, the theme of the 1999 BEMF was "Music of the Mediterranean," with a program that included a range of Spanish and Ottoman musics.

Many early music professionals are interested in aspects of world music and incorporate it into their world view and performance practice. Joel Cohen has noted that

> I think that that's what's unfair about early music, because Indian music is early music—we don't call it early music. Chinese music is early music, Arabic music

is. . . . I'm interested in other cultures besides European, but the only ones in which I'm personally happy performing is where I can feel like there's something that I share with the other culture. (Joel Cohen, 1 October 1996)

Cohen has in recent years moved to collaborate with Middle Eastern musicians as well. Beyond an explicit involvement with the cross-cultural, one finds a concept of early music performance as collapsing time and space, transcend-ing arbitrary boundaries, and providing a new context in which old musical relationships can be re-evaluated. When discussing a performance of a Baroque suite, Daniel Stepner noted that

> The last was, I think, a relatively neat evocation of a rustic dance. And there's a lot of . . . time and space travel in this music. I think a baroque suite is often a way of evoking other cultures, other countries, other climes . . . and this is in a part of that tradition. As in . . . coaching the Dumky Trio, Dvorak piano trio [1892] and I always thought the Dumky was a Czechoslovakian dance. In fact it's a Ukrainian dance, which the Czechs imported and . . . Dvorak was ready because it would become popular in Czechoslovakia in his time. There's a lot of this. There's a lot of . . . multi-cultural awareness despite the political boundaries. Ah . . . one, two, three hundred years ago. And this is a testament to that. (Daniel Stepner, 22 October 1996)

If many aspects of the early music repertory are seen as in connection with a variety of other musics, there is also an appreciation that many of the period ensembles and repertories crossed what are in twentieth-century scholarship perceived as clear boundaries. There is also a strong appreciation for the diversity of European musics of the past:

> Fortunately, in the sixteenth and seventeenth [centuries] there's a wealth of different kinds of music to explore, and depending on where you're at, Germany, England, Italy, France. We've done a couple of English projects based on ballad tunes, which is what "The Queen's Delight" is, and "The King's Delight," containing both original polyphony from the period that we play and also arrangements of monophonic material. And we've done two Italian projects . . . and a couple of German programs. And there's so many different kinds and styles of repertories . . . affected by this whole approach of really much more freedom, of not just trying to interpret what's there, but to try and do it as though a professional dance musicians and dance band were performing it. (David Douglas, 5 November 1996)

In the case of the King's Noyse, it is explicitly acknowledged that

> the violin consort from the Renaissance, the sixteenth century was a professional ensemble almost entirely. You made your living playing violin for people to dance to and as an entertainment instrument. It was a lot like the role of jazz in our society now. Although there was a lot more because there wasn't a well-defined art music in the sixteenth century—the popular and the art music were sort of one, were more or less connected, and so a lot of the popular music drew from . . . what we might consider to be art music formats. And there was just more cross-over than there is now. (ibid.)

One of the most interesting conjunctions of the cross-cultural with the early music movement can be found in the genesis and performance practice of The Voice of the Turtle. This ensemble, formally established in 1978, had its start as part of the Quadrivium Consort, a group founded in 1967 by a most original and eclectic transplant to Cambridge, Marleen Montgomery.[14] The Quadrivium's activities included group instruction and musical performance at Marleen's home, with all-night sessions involving close listening drawing upon techniques of yoga and meditation as well as eating, drinking, and socializing. Public performances by Quadrivium were infused with ritual, heavily choreographed, and fully exploited the performance space. The musical repertories explored and performed by the Quadrivium were quite varied, ranging from all types of Medieval and Renaissance music to Sacred Harp and other folk musics of American and European provenance. While working on Spanish cantigas during 1973–1974, one member of the Quadrivium came across published editions of Sephardic songs, which later became the central repertory of Voice of the Turtle. Ensemble member Derek Burrows mentioned in an interview that the group first experimented with one or two Sephardic songs, which were so well received by their audience that the ensemble slowly moved to a focus on Sephardic music.

Over the last decade, Voice of the Turtle has carved out a distinctive space, describing themselves in their promotional literature as "a non-profit, tax-exempt organization promoting the study and performance of Sephardic, Medieval, and Renaissance music," with album notes referring to their repertory as "folk music passed down by oral tradition." Voice of the Turtle artistic director Judith Wachs compiles the group's repertory through primary research in sound archives in North America and Israel, through use of major published editions of Sephardic song, and through selective use of newly composed songs by living exponents of the tradition. Wachs has also done fieldwork among elderly Sephardic Jews in the United States and Israel, and often plays tapes of original field recordings for the ensemble at rehearsals as they begin to create their own versions of the individual songs. Voice of the Turtle uses a variety of musical instruments to accompany the songs, ranging from a reproduction of a medieval Spanish bagpipe, to a variety of Middle Eastern drums and chordophones. Similarly, the group attempts to keep vocal and instrumental style, as well as harmonic textures, within a range they feel is congruent with a Mediterranean style.

I have gone into considerable detail on the background and activities of the Voice of the Turtle because their inclusion in our study, due to their strong connection with "world music," was a matter of some concern to members of the research team. At the beginning, there was the suspicion that they represented an anomaly in the early music landscape. Yet, ethnographic data demonstrate that this group, still comprised of four of its five original members, in fact shares with many others an interest in, appreciation of, and affinity for connections with the repertories and processes of many other musical traditions.[15] Somewhat ironically, the Voice of the Turtle also proved to have particularly deep early music roots in Boston, stemming from their genesis in the Quadrivium. The Voice of the Turtle's involvement with world music therefore can be seen as bringing together several streams of tradition they share with others in the Boston early music world: As the legacy of a creative and eclectic leader, Maureen Montgomery; as an outgrowth of the impact of the 1960s counter culture of the period and place in which they were formed, a broader cultural trend that has not been adequately acknowledged as a generative element in the broader early music movement; as the outcome of a creative process giving rise to distinctive group identity, repertoire, and performance practice; and as a pragmatic response to the enthusiastic following they began to build among a growing sector of the audience interested in Sephardic music.

While I have stressed the overt connections with and manifestations of world music in early music circles, there is yet another important aspect of early music performance practice that serves to render even performance of familiar historical repertory "other" or "exotic." Laurence Dreyfus has termed this process "defamiliarization," pointing to tendency of early music performances to depart from expected norms of performance practice, at once upsetting conventional expectations and displacing attention from the interpreter on to the composition. Hotly contested performances (some subsequently canonized and distributed in recordings) such as Joshua Rifkin's Bach B Minor Mass (1981) serve not just to "exoticize" Western music, but also to unsettle a classical music establishment heavily vested in "authentic performance."[16]

A Comment on "Authenticity"

Perhaps no single issue has had as lengthy an exposition among scholars concerned with early music than the notion of "authenticity." Here, too, the ethnographic encounter provides a striking counterpoint to the musicological conversation. David Douglas noted that while the early music community is very concerned about whether something is right or wrong, they have a "love-hate relationship" with the word authenticity and shun it (5 November 1996). Joel Cohen dismisses the entire conversation with an anecdote:

> I had this argument with Tom Binkley once. I said, "What do you mean by authenticity?" He says, "What's an authentic troubadour song? The first time it was done." I said, "Suppose [the singer] had a tummy-ache that day. He may have sung like a pig. It may have sounded much better the next night, you know." (Joel Cohen, 1 October 1996)

While some knowledgeable amateurs do mention "authentic reconstructions" as a mode of performance that "helps to make it more like it might have been" (Arthur Loeb, 26 November 1996), others refer to the expression as "a loaded word," adding that "it is what we don't know that is fun" (Na'ama Lion, 26 November 1996). Laurence Dreyfus was again quite close to the mark when he suggested that here emerges an intense struggle for values, since preferring one interpretation over another "amounts to a manifesto *pro* or *contra* authenticity" (Dreyfus 1983:306–8). In this manner, an ethnography of the early music movement provides insight into not just the unsettling of repertories and performance practices, but into what Richard Taruskin has summarized as music historians' sensitivities about "some enduring Dolmetsch-inspired mythology, the belated intervention of positivist musicology, and the ideology of our museum culture" (Taruskin 1988:198).

"Early Music" as "New Music"

A final ethnographic datum brings the discussion of a modern aesthetic of otherness full circle. As we attended a cross-section of concerts during the fall of 1996, the research team noted with interest (not to mention some surprise) that many early music concerts feature newly composed or commissioned works. Particularly prominent were the compositions of Patricia Van Ness, whom we invited to speak to our early music workshop the following spring. On that occasion, Van Ness explained that her association with the early music movement began in 1990 and grew out of her own attraction to medieval music as recreated in the twentieth century and its congruence with her own personal sound aesthetic:

> In the Boston area, it has been my fortune to find a wealth of early music musicians whose work seems to exemplify and embody my notions of beauty. They are expert at pureness of tone, focus, the limited use of vibrato, and the delivery of sensuous lines requiring intensity and concentration. (Patricia Van Ness, 12 May 1997)

Van Ness sets to original music her own sacred poems, which she composes in English and has translated into Latin. She explains that Latin honors the medieval tradition, works better than English, "because the use of a translation seems to shroud the immediacy of the text—it becomes a sort of veil . . . adding mystery and remove." Thus in the work and commentary of Van Ness that we once again encounter an aesthetic of otherness, a present-day value deeply embedded in the early music movement at large.

III. Ethnomusicologies of "Western Musics"

> I think early music was a window into history that the standard conservatory training didn't give us. Not only music history, but general history. There's a lot of tangents which have been very exciting, I think, just reading about the history parallel to the music we play. Not musical history necessarily, political history and so on, cultural history, primarily.
> (Daniel Stepner, 29 October 1996)

If historical musicologists wish to recast music history into the realm of experience, there is no better way to gain understanding than to explore such processes as constituted in the present. To make music is to participate not just in symbolic behavior, but in actions shaped by the exigencies of a given time and place. Ethnography lays bare the multiplicity of factors that shape musical discourse—and the manner in which music itself can shape behaviors and outcomes in other domains. Ethnographic inquiry constantly brings pragmatic, grounded issues into focus:

> If you're a professional musician, the bottom line is you have to sell the goods. I mean, people have to really want to be able to dance, and so you have to come up with a way of doing that that accomplishes your goal so you'll be hired back. (David Douglas, 5 November 1996)

Ethnography militates against assumptions about the way things were and, to paraphrase Peter Jeffery, can help us "re-envision the past" differently. It informs the fieldworker about the vagaries of individual initiative, underscoring the reality of divergent perspectives even in the face of seeming unanimity. As an example, take the following exchange between longtime Boston Museum Trio colleagues Laura Jeppesen and John Gibbons (22 October 1996) following their performance of a composition by Marais:

> LJ: I think of this music as being the music that you find when you get to the exterior of Versailles—the big chateau. And you go in past the rooms where the great ambassadors were welcomed and you go further in. You get to the rooms where the women are sitting [in] their chambers, writing letters. You go in further . . . You come to the innermost place where the King sits with his favorite musician—Marais, and maybe Robert de Bizet, theorbo player—and then you enter Louis' heart . . . Forgive me, I get very sentimental about him. . . .
>
> JG: I never think about that. I never think about such things as people or buildings or anything like that. The music is just too . . . distracting.

Ethnographies of living traditions thus provide a rich opportunity to enhance understanding of musical life traditionally viewed only through the lens of written historical sources; as such, they can help guide the music historian, bringing into focus transmission processes and musical meanings as situated among real people in real time. Ethnographies of "Western musics" may serve to collapse both disciplinary and musical boundaries. For historical musicologists, they could provide a venue in which the assumptions of scholarship can be tested and disputed. For ethnomusicologists, ethnographies of "Western music" provide a lively field in which power relations are largely symmetrical, putting to rest ethical issues of longstanding concern. Such research agendas can only be mounted through negotiation, with the ethnographer subject to many of the same pressures and constraints as the "subjects" of any study. For both music historians and ethnomusicologists, many if not most of whom grew up performing historical European repertories, ethnographies of "Western music" render the fieldwork process intensely reflexive. Bringing "Western music" into the picture renders ethnographic training a necessary rite of passage not just for ethnomusicologists, but for music historians as well.

I am not suggesting that historical musicologists carry out fieldwork to uncover some imagined residue of the historical past, nor that they need impose "presentist understandings" of artworks (Tomlinson 1984:358).[17] However, eth-nographic study of living traditions could both enhance the historical musicolo-gist's appreciation of the workings of a fully contextualized music culture and expose the interaction between musics and musicians. Here music historians would do well to draw upon ethnomusicologists' experience in studying complex urban musical traditions, transnational musical movements, and the manner in which music and musicians actively construct their own social, political, and economic worlds. Finally, an engagement with ethnomusicological observation and interviewing would provide historical musicologists with a new lens on anthropological theory, placing current theoretical speculation within a meth-odological framework through which those propositions can be tested

Ethnographic research could test and illuminate several subjects of current interest, for instance, the role of the body in musical performance and percep-tion. An ethnographic approach to live instrumental performance on period instruments enables one to move quickly beyond surface details of construction and performance practice to testimony about aspects of physical sensation and affect. When David Douglas demonstrated a seventeenth-century technique for holding the violin lower on the arm, which he testifies results in a "freer bow arm," he went on to comment that it provided "the same kind of physical freedom that can be associated with the freedom of dancing" (5 November 1996). Douglas' exegesis provided insights into musical performance as a bodily practice that both connects with and shapes human interaction, as well as impinges upon issues of spatial and social control. While paintings and other visual records of musical performance have often been interrogated for insights into the musical construction of social meanings (see, for example, Richard Leppert's *The Sight of Sound* [1993]), the almost exclusive restriction of historical inquiry to the eye (whether in reading paintings or texts) neglects a rich venue for potential insights. Ethnographic interviews can change our perception of music as a way of life, such as encountering testimony that Arnold Dolmetsch, doyen of musical authenticity, had early musical instruments carved into the balustrade of the central staircase in his Cambridge home (Friedrich Von Huene, 24 September, 1996).

A Postscript and Proposals

I therefore offer two related proposals: first, that training in broader musicology should necessarily involve ethnographic experience with living musical traditions; and second, that these fieldwork ventures should necessarily include a good measure of research on those very "Western repertories" not often enough the object of ethnographic attention. In realizing both of these goals, I submit that historical musicologists would be well advised to draw upon decades of ethnomusicological experience with musical ethnography and their growing interest in ethnomusicologies of "Western music." I'd also offer a none-too-gentle hint that ethnomusicologists need to emerge from behind a veil of cross-cultural difference and participate in joint ethnographic ventures.

Certainly our nascent study of the world of early music paid rich dividends, stimulating the music historians, ethnomusicologists, and performers alike. Occasionally there were frustrations, such as moments when several members of our team expressed concern that the flood of social and cultural data was threatening to overwhelm the "musical" issues. There were memorable moments for the experienced ethnographers among us, such as when colleagues from an ensemble with which we worked desired (indeed demanded!) a critical response to one of their performances, not ethnographic "neutrality." Yet all, I think it can be said, experienced a good measure of wonder and excitement at encountering living traditions so actively performed and willingly shared, situated within a richly documented history, discussed in such a thoughtful, even poetic, manner, and pursued with extraordinary creativity. David Douglas may have inadvertently spoken for everyone when he reflected that:

> I think there are certain things that early music offers to us that involves elements of investigation and discovery. It seems very much like a journey where I don't really know what is going to happen next, it's not well laid out in front of me. And I never know what I'm going to learn that'll inspire . . . open some door of perception that will allow a new feeling about something I've never had before. (David Douglas, 5 November 1996)

Notes

1. This paper was drafted for and presented at an invitational conference held at Washington University in St. Louis titled "The Sound of Culture: Anthropological Theory and Ethnographic Methods in the Study of Western Music," September 20–21, 1997, sponsored by the Program in Social Thought and Analysis and the Department of Music. I am grateful to Richard G. Fox, Ingrid Monson, Regula Qureshi, Bruno Nettl, Veit Erlmann, Gary Tomlinson, and Robert Kendrick for helpful comments on the draft presented there.

2. Qureshi (1995:337) has noted that Peter Jeffery's *Re-envisioning Past Musical Cultures* (1992), with its unusual call for an ethnomusicological approach to music of the past, is a notable exception and was conceived during the years Jeffery collaborated with an ethnomusicologist—myself—on

a project that in fact worked from ethnographic materials backwards into manuscripts (Shelemay and Jeffery 1993–1997).

3. Here Cohen cites the title of Duke Ellington's "signoff song," performed at his first Carnegie Hall Concert in 1943 (M. Tucker 1993:210).

4. Student members of the research team included: Michael Barrett, Wesley Chin, Judah Cohen, Caprice Corona, John Driscoll, Aaron Einbond, Alex Fisher, Hubert Ho, Tiwill Huval, April James, Peter Kalmus, David Lyczkowski, Jennifer Morales, Michael Olbash, Judith Quiñones, Julie Rohwein, Charles Starrett, and Andrew Talle. I thank and acknowledge each of these individuals for their special contributions to this project.

5. In preparation for this process, historical musicology graduate student Jen-Yen Chen, who served as assistant for both the seminar and year-long workshop on early music, compiled a listing of early music concerts in Boston from September 20, 1996 to January 19, 1997. Some sixty-four different musical events are included in his list, a number of which were repeated multiple times or extended over a period of several days. I am grateful to Jen-Yen Chen for his assistance in compiling and archiving the materials from our project and to Harvard College and the Harvard Graduate School of Arts and Sciences for the funding that supported this work.

6. However, interpretations and conclusions drawn from these materials and suggestions made for future research are my own unless otherwise attributed.

7. Interviews cited are listed in the bibliography. I am grateful to Joel Cohen, David Douglas, John Gibbons, Ellen Hargis, Laura Jeppesen, Daniel Stepner, Patricia Van Ness, and Judith Wachs for permission to quote from presentations or interview transcripts.

8. See Taruskin (1988:197), where he suggests "that in modern performances, including those modernistic ones I call authentistic, modern audiences have been discovering a Bach they can call their own—or, in other words, that Bach has at last been adapted with unprecedented success to modern taste."

9. Dolmetsch, who was affiliated with Chickering & Sons, remained in Boston until 1911, when he returned to Europe. See Campbell 1980.

10. Thomas Kelly provided an outline summary of early music in Boston for our first class session which I have drawn on in part here.

11. In 1959, Thomas Binkley, an American, organized the Studio der frühen Musik in Munich, which took "an ethno-musicological approach to performance practice, rather than relying solely on written documentation form medieval Europe" (Brown 1988:49–50). Binkley borrowed practices and instruments from North African and Middle Eastern musicians, resulting in what has been termed "a Mediterranean style" (Taruskin 1988:142). Binkley later returned to the United States, joining the faculty at Indiana University.

12. See Campbell 1980:530, for details of the activities of Arnold Dolmetsch's children in founding organizations such as the Society of Recorder Players (son Carl, in 1937) and Viola da Gamba Society (daughter Natalie, in 1948); children of Carl Dolmetsch have remained active in the early music movement as well.

13. According to the Boston Early Music Festival and Exhibition Program Book (1997:60), Kelischek Workshop imports and exports worldwide a range of instruments from krumhorns to pennywhistles; its associated Susato Press specializes in native American music.

14. This discussion draws in part on "An Ethnography of Voice of the Turtle," submitted as a final project in January, 1997, by a team consisting of Judah Cohen, Caprice Corona, Hubert Ho, David Lyczkowski, and Judith Quiñones for which I served as faculty advisor. I acknowledge them and also thank Judith Wachs of the Voice of the Turtle for permission to quote the original interviews and materials they provided.

15. Voice of the Turtle is also not the only early music group to use ethnographic techniques in search of new repertory and performance techniques. Joel Cohen and the Boston Camerata worked closely with the Shakers of Sabbathday Lake in preparing the compact disc "Simple Gifts: Shaker Chants and Spirituals."

16. A striking example of defamiliarization was witnessed by this ethnographer at the BEMF 13 June 1997 concert of Capriccio Stravagante, a Paris-based ensemble that performs French Baroque Chamber music. The ensemble, citing the precedent of eighteenth-century French sources, seeks to engage the listener "by leading the ear and detouring it with surprises" (Skip Sempé, Program notes for 13 June 1997, in *Boston Early Music Festival and Exhibition Program Book* 1997:220–221). That the intent was also to unsettle the musical establishment is made clear in the notes as well: "The idea of "non-interpretation" developed by certain specialists of the last few decades is a particularly debased tradition. It is the unwillingness either to unite or separate profanity from profundity that has caused the grave misunderstanding and subsequent misinterpretation of certain earlier repertories" (ibid.:221).

17. There have been a number of studies where ethnography of present-day practice in fact makes possible historical inquiry and stands in a direct relationship to past practices. See Shelemay and Jeffery for one such example.

Sources Cited

Bibliography

Agawu, Kofi. 1995. "The Invention of "African Rhythm." *Journal of the American Musicological Society* 48:380–95.

Appadurai, Arjun. 1986. "Introduction." In *The Social Life of Things: Commodities in Cultural Perspective,* edited by Arjun Appadurai, 3–63. Cambridge: Cambridge University Press.

———. 1990. "Disjuncture and Difference in the Global Cultural Economy." *Public Culture* 2(2):1–24.

Bellman, Jonathan. 1998. *The Exotic in Western Music.* Boston: Northeastern University Press.

Bohlman, Philip V. 1989. *"The Land Where Two Streams Flow": Music in the German-Jewish Community in Israel.* Urbana: University of Illinois Press.

Boston Early Music Festival and Exhibition Program Book, 10–15 June, 1997. 1997. Cambridge, MA: Boston Early Music Festival Inc.

Boston Early Music Festival Exhibition, 8–13 June, 1999. Music of the Mediterranean. Cambridge, MA: Boston Early Music Festival, Inc., 1999.

Brown, Howard Mayer. 1988. "Pedantry or Liberation? A Sketch of the Historical Performance Movement." In *Authenticity and Early Music,* edited by Nicholas Kenyon, 27–56. Oxford: Oxford University Press.

Campbell, Margaret. 1980. "Dolmetsch." In *The New Grove Dictionary of Music and Musicians,* edited by Stanley Sadie, Vol. 5, 528–31. London: Macmillan.

Chen, Bernice K. 1997. Welcome letter. *Boston Early Music Festival and Exhibition Program Book, 10–15 June 1997,* p. 7. Cambridge, MA: Boston Early Music Festival.

Dreyfus, Laurence. 1983. "Early Music Defended against its Devotees: A Theory of Historical Performance in the Twentieth Century." *The Musical Quarterly* 69:297–322.

Fabian, Johannes. 1983. *Time and the Other. How Anthropology Makes Its Object.* New York: Columbia University Press.

Feldman, Martha. 1995. "Magic Mirrors and the Seria Stage: Thoughts Toward a Ritual View." *Journal of the American Musicological Society* 48: 423–84.

Finnegan, Ruth. 1989. *The Hidden Musicians. Music-Making in an English Town.* Cambridge: Cambridge University Press.

Gupta, Akhil, and James Ferguson. 1992. "Beyond 'Culture': Space, Identity, and the Politics of Difference." *Cultural Anthropology* 7:6–23.

Haskell, Harry. 1988. *The Early Music Revival: A History.* London: Thames and Hudson.

Jeffery, Peter. 1992. *Re-Envisioning Past Musical Cultures. Ethnomusicology in the Study of Gregorian Chant.* Chicago: University of Chicago Press.

Kelly, Thomas Forrest. 1989. "Early Music in America. A Report on a survey conducted by Early Music America." New York: Early Music America (typescript).

Kenyon, Nicholas, ed. 1988. *Authenticity and Early Music.* Oxford: Oxford University Press.

Kingsbury, Henry. 1988. *Music, Talent, and Performance: A Conservatory Cultural System.* Philadelphia: Temple University Press.

Larson, Susan. "The world of early music." *The Boston Globe,* 13 June 1997: C13, C16.

Leppert, Richard. 1993. *The Sight of Sound. Music, Representation, and the History of the Body.* Berkeley: University of California Press.

Lomax, Alan. 1976. *Cantometrics: An Approach to the Anthropology of Music.* Berkeley: University of California Extension Media.

Lowenthal, David. 1985. *The Past is a Foreign Country.* Cambridge: Cambridge University Press.

Merriam, Alan. 1964. *The Anthropology of Music.* Evanston: Northwestern University Press.

Monson, Ingrid. 1995. "The Problem with White Hipness: Race, Gender, and Cultural Conceptions in Jazz Historical Discourse." *Journal of the American Musicological Society* 48:396–422.

Nettl, Bruno. 1995. *Heartland Excursions. Ethnomusicological Reflections on Schools of Music.* Urbana: University of Illinois.

Qureshi, Regula Burckhardt. 1995. "Music Anthropologies and Music Histories: A Preface and an Agenda." *Journal of the American Musicological Society* 48:331–42.

Rice, Timothy. 1987. "Toward the Remodeling of Ethnomusicology." *Ethnomusicology* 31:469–88.

Sakata, Hiromi Lorraine. 1994. "The Sacred and the Profane: Qawwali Represented in the Performances of Nusrat Fateh Ali Khan." *The World of Music* 36(3):86–99.

Seeger, Anthony. 1987. *Why Suya Sing. A Musical Anthropology of an Amazonian People.* Cambridge: Cambridge University Press.

Shelemay, Kay Kaufman. 1996a. "Crossing Boundaries in Music and Musical Scholarship: A Perspective from Ethnomusicology." *The Musical Quarterly* 7913–30.

———. 1996b. "The Ethnomusicologist and the Transmission of Tradition." *Journal of Musicology* 14:35–51.

———. 1998. *Let Jasmine Rain Down. Song and Remembrance Among Syrian Jews.* Chicago: University of Chicago Press.

Shelemay, Kay Kaufman, and Peter Jeffery. 1993–1997. *Ethiopian Christian Liturgical Chant. An Anthology.* 3 vols, with CD. Madison: A-R Editions.

Sherman, Bernard D. 1997. *Inside Early Music: Conversations with Performers.* New York and Oxford: Oxford University Press.

Slobin, Mark. 1993. *Subcultural Sounds: Micromusics of the West.* Hanover: Wesleyan University Press.

Taruskin, Richard.1988. "The Pastness of the Present and the Presence of the Past." In *Authenticity and Early Music,* edited by Nicholas Kenyon, 137–207. Oxford: Oxford University Press.

———. 1995. *Text and Act: Essays on Music and Performance.* Oxford: Oxford University Press.

Titon, Jeff Todd. 1997. "Knowing Fieldwork." In *Shadows in the Field. New Perspectives for Fieldwork in Ethnomusicology,* edited by Gregory F. Barz and Timothy J. Cooley, 87–100. New York: Oxford University Press.

Tomlinson, Gary. 1984. "The Web of Culture: A Context for Musicology." *19th-Century Music* 7:350–62.

———. 1993. *Music in Renaissance Magic. Toward a Historiography of Others.* Chicago: University of Chicago Press.

———. 1995. "Ideologies of Aztec Song." *Journal of the American Musicological Society* 48:343–79.

Tommasini, Anthony. 1997. "Even at Birth, Opera Wed the Stirring and the Silly." *The New York Times,* 14 June 1997: Arts 17.

Treitler, Leo. 1989. *Music and the Historical Imagination.* Cambridge: Harvard University Press.

Tucker, Mark, ed. 1993. *The Duke Ellington Reader.* Oxford: Oxford University Press.

Discography

The Boston Camerata. 1990. *The Sacred Bridge.* Erato.
———. 1995. *Simple Gifts. Shaker Chants and Spirituals.* Erato.
The Waverly Consort. 1992. *1492, Music from the Age of Discovery.* EMI Classics.
Anonymous 4. 1992. *An English Ladymass: Medieval Chant and Polyphony.* Harmonia Mundi.
The King's Noyse. 1993. *"The King's Delight." 17c Ballads for voice and violin band.* Harmonia Mundi.
The Voice of the Turtle. 1994. *Under Aegean Moons: Music of the Spanish Jews of Rhodes and Salonika* (Paths of Exile Quincentenary Series, Vol. IV). Titanic Records.

Interviews and Oral Histories

Friedrich Von Huene, 24 September 1996
Joel Cohen, 1 October 1996
Daniel Stepner, Laura Jeppesen, John Gibbons, 22 October 1996
Laura Jeppesen, Daniel Stepner, 29 October 1996
David Douglas and Ellen Hargis, 5 November 1996
John Gibbons, 11 November 1996
Arthur Loeb, Oral History prepared for Archive of Viola da Gamba Society, typescript, and 26 November 1996
Elfrieda Hiebert and Na'ama Lion, 26 November 1996
Noel Bisson and Andrew Shenton, 24 February 1997
Patricia Van Ness, 12 May 1997

Ethnomusicology and Difference

Deborah Wong / University of California, Riverside

M y generation of ethnomusicologists experienced two things: the arrival of multiculturalism in the academy, and the ascendance of cultural studies in the humanities. Many of us who finished our graduate work and began teaching in the 1990s did so in music departments struggling with the (often unasked-for) necessity of opening up to difference, and some of us explored new critical tools in an effort to explain what was needed and why.

I offer a snapshot of ethnomusicology and the culture wars of the 1990s. My understanding of that decade was shaped by own experiences, but I take a two-pronged approach to the bigger question of why many ethnomusicologists found themselves immersed in the effort to introduce difference into music departments at a historical moment when the American academy was in transition. First, I address the question of why ethnomusicologists have been somewhat reluctant to engage with various critical approaches to difference (feminist theory, minoritarian discourse, etc.) that are well-established in ethnic studies, women's studies, popular culture studies, and literary studies. Second, I deploy the method I know best—ethnography—to address the kinds of institutional conflicts that ethnomusicologists experienced during that decade. This essay is thus an effort to draw together several kinds of consideration: historical overview, close ethnographic work, and prolegomenon.

The Culture Wars

The 1990s were a tumultuous time for ethnomusicologists in the academy. I did graduate work at the University of Michigan from 1983–91 and started teaching full-time at Pomona College in 1991, when I was plunged headlong into an ideological environment for which I wasn't really prepared. This was no

From *Ethnomusicology*, Vol. 50, No. 2 (Spring/Summer 2006), pp. 259–79

one's fault: my scholarly training was outstanding but took place at a juncture before ethnomusicology caught up with the critical upheaval that had already taken place in the rest of the humanities and social sciences. In the early 1990s, the culture wars were at full tilt. Ethnic Studies curricula were well established and the canon had just been displaced in literature departments . . . but not, of course, in music departments. I was the first tenure-track ethnomusicologist in the Department of Music at Pomona College (a liberal arts college in southern California),[1] and that initial year of teaching (always a rite of passage) was challenging. I was ready to change, ready to think deeply about teaching, and ready to insert myself into the radical pedagogy of identity politics. Colleagues already addressing these matters quickly became friends and allies. The intersection of discipline, gender, and race in my own person was a pedagogical tool in some ways and a problem in others. My department had had only passing contact with ethnomusicology; it had only one other faculty member of color (then in a non-tenure-track position), and had never tenured a woman. Sharing resources and making room for ethnomusicology wasn't simple: a few colleagues were threatened, confrontational, and obstructive. Department meetings were sometimes fraught even when some colleagues tried to mediate, and a few were brilliantly strategic in levering change into the curriculum in ways that made ethnomusicology more than an afterthought.

Ethnomusicologists are well equipped to explore a variety of niches in any academic institution, and I gravitated toward Women's Studies and an emergent initiative in Asian American Studies. I wasn't yet working in those areas but was driven by an untheorized instinct that my gender and ethnicity had a bearing on how I might make a place for ethnomusicology at the institution—and more deeply, a place where I might explore my own need to situate ethnomusicology as a vehicle for thinking about difference. Colleagues in those disciplines led me to a world of scholarship that essentially redirected how I was thinking—or was *able* to think—and gave my research a totally new trajectory. My intellectual development was thus tied to my gendered, raced, and ethnomusicologically disciplined location within the academy.

It took some years to acquire the critical language to talk and write about this. The blunt vocabulary of identity politics wasn't unrelated to what I needed, but it was cultural studies that provided crucial ways to think and talk about how identity and subjectivity create particular terms of possibility. I wasn't a native anthropologist when I turned toward Asian American Studies as an Asian American ethnomusicologist; rather, I was a cultural worker with a situated knowledge base. As I have written elsewhere, the Los Angeles uprising took place at the end of my first year of teaching (Wong 2004:3); the need for a theorized politics of identity was simply self-evident, and compelling examples were all over the Ethnic Studies scholarship I had begun to explore.

Anthropologists George Marcus and Michael Fischer forecast my own experiences with the theory and praxis of identity. When I shifted from Southeast Asian Studies to (Asian) American Studies, I brought home the ethnographic methodologies I had learned abroad, and I wasn't alone in this. As Marcus and Fischer (1986; 1999:112–13) put it,

> There has always been a domestic interest in anthropology, especially in American anthropology where the exotic subjects were American Indians, immigrants, and urban migrants ... [I]ncreasingly, anthropologists whose first ethnographic projects are in foreign settings later develop serious research interests in some domestic topic. It is also the case that many students, while trained in the classics, are defining their initial projects within the cultural diversity of American society. However, we find the cases of those who have worked abroad and then at home most interesting: they define the situation with the greatest potential for the development of cultural critique intimately linked to projects elsewhere.

Ethnography thus became a critical tool for addressing difference in the U.S. Marcus and Fischer refer to this process as "repatriation," i.e., bringing anthropology home for the express purpose of thinking critically about the very terms of American culture (1986, 1999:113). I spent most of the 1980s learning as much about Thai culture as I could and then turned toward Asian American performance in the 1990s. During the 1990s, cultural relativism was reconfigured from an absolute value to something more contingent; at the same time, more and more graduate students in ethnomusicology turned toward American topics, often focused on popular music, which further shifted the preoccupation with relativism toward critique.

In the 1990s, cultural critique suddenly became central to the pedagogical function of ethnomusicology in American higher education. The culture wars made this unavoidable. Bruce Robbins notes that universities were "othered" by the conservative media when it became evident that the ferment of multicultural education was changing the very conception of public culture. He writes that the sudden enthusiasm for trashing academe in the early 1990s was meant "to reprovincialize American culture, [and] to tighten up the limits of who will be counted in its pertinent culture." Edward Rothstein's infamous column in *The New Republic* (1991),[2] titled "Roll Over Beethoven: The New Musical Correctness and Its Mistakes," marked the moment when ethnomusicologists were drawn into the fray and put in center ring. Rothstein's diatribe against "multiculturalists," as he called them, touched on the work of Anthony Seeger, Regula Qureshi, Bell Yung, Bruno Nettl, and Chris Waterman, singling them out as having demonstrated the pervasiveness and importance of high culture distinctions across the globe (though I would guess that these ethnomusicologists were perturbed to see the use to which their work was put). Rothstein described the ideological changes within higher education as "disintegration from within" (34) and singled out ethnomusicology as a disciplinary indication of how misguided scholarship was under multicultural directives. He described ethnomusicology as having "evolved" from collection and preservation to attempting "to become the Other" through bimusicality—a shift that he viewed as an abdication of the West's intellectual achievements because it required "a submission to the systems of judgment employed by the culture being studied." He called for a return to Western liberalism in no uncertain terms (1991:34):

> Multiculturalism is a twisted version of Western teachings, flourishing in the hothouse of a democracy that renders all distinctions suspect and all learning elitist . . . The multiculturalist is a universalist without universalism, an artist without a vision of art; a monster child of Western culture; a baleful, unwitting tribute to the tradition he hungers to depose.

By rendering ethnomusicology the work of "multiculturalists," Rothstein spelled out the place of the discipline in the culture wars. Ethnomusicologists were thus virtually forced to become part of the cultural critique project almost overnight.

Still, ethnomusicologists have been hesitant to bring scholarship and pedagogy into closer conversation.[3] I don't know of any ringing responses by ethnomusicologists to the Rothsteins of the culture wars. Many ethnomusicologists have effected sweeping change on the frontlines of the curricular debates yet are far more likely to be advocates in the classroom than in their scholarly work. Yet the curricular impact has sometimes been profound. At the University of California, Berkeley, for instance, ethnomusicologist Bonnie Wade was involved in the faculty-led effort that resulted in the campus-wide American Cultures requirement instituted in 1991—an institutional effort to make cultural critique part of the curriculum. As the general catalog explains,[4]

> Students who entered Berkeley in fall 1991 or there-after . . . must satisfy the American cultures breadth requirement in order to graduate . . . Faculty from many departments teach American cultures courses, but all courses have a common framework. The courses focus on themes or issues in United States history, society, or culture; address theoretical or analytical issues relevant to understanding race, culture, and ethnicity in our society; take substantial account of groups drawn from at least three of the following: African Americans, indigenous peoples of the United States, Asian Americans, Chicano/Latino Americans, and European Americans; and are integrative and comparative in that students study each group in the larger context of American society, history, or culture. The courses also provide students with the intellectual tools to understand better their own identity and the cultural identity of others in their own terms.

Wade created Music 26AC, "Music in American Culture," and submitted it in the first round of courses created to satisfy the requirement. It almost immediately became one of the largest courses in the Department of Music and has been a pedagogical training ground for many of its graduate students. The course is taught by an ethnomusicologist with the help of graduate teaching assistants.[5] In Fall 2005, Music 26AC, "Music in American Culture," had a maximum enrollment of 360, with 351 students actually enrolled. In sum, the Department of Music at Berkeley stepped up to the table and offered an ethnomusicology-driven course that has, after fourteen years, offered literally thousands of undergraduates music-centered skills for thinking about race and ethnicity in the U.S.

While the Berkeley example is especially noteworthy, it was strategically brilliant rather than utterly unique. Inserting world music courses into the requirements for music majors always implies a certain critique, though articulating it hasn't always been the strong point of our discipline. As a Society, we have been a bit doggedly apolitical (until very recently, as I will discuss below). We have tended to rely on cultural relativism in its most simplistic form, and in a way that is heavily reliant on liberal humanism. That is, we tend to resort to fairly basic relativist arguments about equal worth, when the strongest arguments focus on the political economies of uneven access to resources and the intervention of education (and performance) into those economies. At this level, we have fallen far behind; discussions around issues of canon formation and control have gone on in English departments for twenty years, often at a level of critical sophistication that music departments only gesture toward.

Ethnomusicology and Cultural Studies

Much of the critical edginess in those English departments was generated by cultural studies, which gained a lot of ground during the 1990s. I discovered cultural studies all at once, when I read the edited collection *Cultural Studies* (Grossberg, Nelson, and Treichler 1991) and encountered the work of bell hooks, Stuart Hall, Homi Bhabha, etc. These riotous and provoking writings converged around arguments that: power/hegemony can be addressed through interpretive work; resistance and agency can be made visible through new critical tools; scholarship can be socially engaged; Marxist theory is alive and well; and it is possible to move interpretively between high and low culture in ways that problematize both. This collection opened up a sphere of scholarship that already had its own genealogies and interstices. Cultural studies also provided a powerful critical language for thinking about music and music departments—it was like discovering guerilla warfare. There was no turning back once I understood that a lot of smart people were thinking about the death of the canon in terms that were immediately applicable and actionable.

Ethnomusicological scholarship in the 1990s became increasingly politicized and, in some cases, increasingly adventurous. More and more, our work addressed power and cultural movement. Yet an ethnographic base remained our touchstone even as it stretched and expanded. With no pretence at coverage (and apologies for worthy books not mentioned), I would like to point out certain books by ethnomusicologists that offered a new and commanding engagement with cultural theory and critical studies during the 1990s and changed our discipline by so doing. These included (but were certainly not limited to):

> Christopher Alan Waterman, *Jùjú: A Social History and Ethnography of an African Popular Music* (1990).
> Veit Erlmann, *African Stars: Studies in Black South African Performance* (1991).
> Katherine Bergeron and Philip V. Bohlman, *Disciplining Music: Musicology and Its Canons* (1992).
> Jocelyne Guilbault, *Zouk: World Music in the West Indies,* 1993.
> Martin Stokes, ed., *Ethnicity, Identity and Music: The Musical Construction of Place* (1994).
> Charles Keil and Steven Feld, *Music Grooves: Essays and Dialogues* (1994).
> Bernard Lortat-Jacob, *Sardinian Chronicles* (1995).
> Ingrid T. Monson, *Saying Something: Jazz Improvisation and Interaction* (1996).
> Veit Erlmann, *Nightsong: Performance, Power, and Practice in South Africa* (1996).
> Gage Averill, *A Day for the Hunter, A Day for the Prey: Popular Music and Power in Haiti* (1997).
> Timothy D. Taylor, *Global Pop: World Music, World Markets* (1997).
> Michelle Kisliuk, *Seize the Dance!: BaAka Musical Life and the Ethnography of Performance* (1998).
> Harris M. Berger, *Metal, Rock, and Jazz: Perception and the Phenomenology of Musical Experience* (1999).

These books represent ethnomusicologists' increasingly explicit emphasis on cultural theory. Ethnography remained our central methodology, and most single-authored books remained focused on particular places and peoples, but theoretical questions moved closer to the center than before.[6] Many of these books address cultural contact, exchange, and transitions from colonial to post-colonial contexts. Almost all focus on popular musics. The words "power" and "performance" appear in several of their titles. Some outlined a shift toward experimental, self-consciously "humanistic" ethnographic writing (e.g., *Music Grooves, Sardinian Chronicles,* and *Seize the Dance!* especially).

For me, the single most influential book of the decade was edited by two graduate students. *Shadows in the Field: New Perspectives for Fieldwork in Ethnomusicology* (1997) emerged out of several conference panels organized by Gregory F. Barz and Timothy J. Cooley and provided a sustained argument for how ethnomusicology might contribute to the shakeup that had already taken place in anthropology in the 1980s. Better late than never—*Shadows* provides a vivid picture of how issues of located position had trickled down to ethnomusicology, and it provided a model for how ethnomusicologists could participate in the reflexive undoing of traditional empirical ethnographic work.

The 1990s also featured a pronounced rise in the sheer number of ethnomusicological publications—perhaps one of the most important developments for our discipline during that decade. The University of Chicago Press was the first to step forward decisively for ethnomusicology. The majority of the books I listed above were published by the University of Chicago Press in the series "Chicago Studies in Ethnomusicology," headed by editor David Brent (an anthropologist) and series editors Philip Bohlman and Bruno Nettl. This publishing niche eked out a deeply influential footprint for the discipline.[7] Chicago was not alone, but it was, in my opinion, the only major university press to focus specifically on ethnomusicology as a discipline. Other presses offered important music-centered publications. Due largely to the dedicated work of Assistant Director Judith McCulloh, the University of Illinois Press has long published excellent books on music (particularly but not exclusively American musics) and created important publication possibilities for ethnomusicologists, but was less purposefully focused on creating a profile for the discipline than was the University of Chicago Press. The "Music/Culture" series published by Wesleyan University Press started releasing books in (I believe) 1993, and most of its books (including some in ethnomusicology) are engaged with cultural studies. This series represents a useful counterpoint to the Chicago series in its loose emphasis on certain critical approaches rather than disciplinary location. By the mid-1990s, Oxford University Press had started an ethnomusicology series, and Garland and Routledge also became important publishers for ethnomusicology. *The Garland Encyclopedia of World Music* (published 1997–2002) was a milestone for the discipline. Routledge's series titled "Current Research in Ethnomusicology" offers published versions of dissertations. Duke University Press doesn't have an ethnomusicology series, but Editor-in-Chief Ken Wissoker has consistently published work on music that is strongly theoretical, often with a base in anthropology. In short, an explosion (relatively speaking) of publishing possibilities in the 1990s granted ethnomusicology a new presence and focus.[8]

In short, the overall profile of ethnomusicological scholarship gradually became more experimental and more aligned with developments in the humanities at the same time that my generation of young educators was struggling in the foxholes of music departments. At the time of this writing, gender, sexuality, and race studies have yet to be taken up by ethnomusicologists in any widespread way; work focused on these key parameters of difference is still scattered.[9] Ethnomusicologists address gender more routinely than before, though often at the level of "showing" how gender construction occurs "through" music and frequently without the help of feminist theory.[10] Sadly, *Queering the Pitch: The New Gay and Lesbian Musicology* (Brett, Wood, and Thomas 1994) represents an important juncture in musicology, but there are no ethnomusicologists in that collection, and in many ways—eleven years later—most ethnomusicologists have still not engaged deeply with sexuality studies or queer theory despite the fact that music is often a key performative means for defining the terms for pleasure and desire. We have been even slower to explore critical race theory (even though quite a few ethnomusicologists now work on American popular music, which is inevitably 'about' race at some level).[11] In sum, ethnomusicologists have finally begun to define their research around questions of difference, but very cautiously—often with a conflicted avoidance of critique, evidenced by the avoidance of theoretical models focused on social justice issues.

The View from the Trenches: Ethnomusicologists Talk

And yet, difference defined our presence in the classroom and even in the hallways of our departments during the 1990s. We have been disastrously slow to acknowledge that our discipline is ideologically threatening to the very foundations of most music departments. Informally, we have long talked about these issues, but have regarded them as idiosyncratic to particular places and institutions rather than as systemic problems that could be addressed in coordinated ways; any individual ethnomusicologist is essentially on his or her own when certain predictable problems arise while trying to establish ethnomusicology within traditional music departments.

Ethnomusicologists talk with one another about the challenges of working in environments defined by specialists in Western European art music. These testimonials have a strong dramatic quality, fill a cathartic and empathetic purpose, and are a central means for maintaining an internal compass. I have been listening to ethnomusicologists' stories about themselves for almost twenty years, and I focus here on four ethnomusicologists' accounts of their experiences in music departments. I aim to relocate some of these stories from their informal, subterranean place in our own lived practices and to listen to them more purposefully. Certain cultures take first-person accounts very seriously indeed, e.g., the importance of the *testimonio* in Latino/a culture.[12] I focus here on ethnographic work I conducted with ethnomusicologists, and then consider the patterns evident in these experiences and the strategies we can take away from them.[13]

I conducted detailed oral interviews with four ethnomusicologists, exploring their experiences working and teaching in music departments. I began with a set of fixed questions which addressed different spheres of power and authority within music departments, relationships with colleagues, starting and teaching non-Western music ensembles, promotions, relationships to other departmental programs, the place of ethnomusicology in the curriculum, defeats and successes, moving into positions of authority such as department chair or administration, etc. My purpose was to gather first-hand information about experiences ethnomusicologists had while teaching in music departments in order to make visible the praxis of institutional change in the U.S.

There was a marked increase in American ethnomusicology positions in the 1990s. Two structural changes were behind this change. Multicultural ideologies of American education were one. Second, the National Association of Schools of Music (NASM) requirement that Schools of Music *must* offer such courses had a direct impact on hiring practices and curricula. Although many institutions and departments choose to cover world music courses by hiring part-time lecturers or by adding them to the course load of resident musicologists, there has certainly been a sea change in awareness leading to a (very relative) burgeoning of full-time positions for trained ethnomusicologists.

I was directly inspired by Victoria Lindsay Levine's study of world music survey courses in music departments and her strategy of interviewing ethnomusicologists. As she put it, the world music survey reflects "larger academic struggles surrounding multicultural and global education," and she regards these struggles as "a pedagogical cross-roads" that opens up much broader issues (Levine 2001:2). Ethnomusicologists tend to be keenly aware that they are engaged in a long-term process of political change, and it is therefore worth considering *how* they think about their local position in this much bigger endeavor, and how the challenges of such work can affect ethnomusicologists' thinking over the long-term. Ethnomusicologists think globally but act locally, and the modality of the local is my point of entry. If we think about music departments as microenvironments and as social systems in their own right, the lessons learned from American Ethnic Studies and Women's Studies can help us to understand how ethnomusicologists' practices are sometimes, if not often, shaped over the long-term by their social placement in relation to their colleagues and the curriculum in which they operate. Ethnomusicologists' social location is essentially ideological and political, yet the discipline has tended to resist an openly politicized reading of its institutional location, so I aim to productively defamiliarize our understandings of our disciplinary profile. Most effective activist responses begin locally, and the institutional work of ethnomusicologists is similar to the work of any politically progressive movement. In turning an ethnographic eye toward the ground-level responses of individual ethnomusicologists to this hands-on, often protracted, and frequently difficult work, I hope to offer a more strategic model—and a less accommodationist one—for the rising third generation of trained American ethnomusicologists in the academy. Ethnomusicology has become more established in American higher education, but we are still often held at arm's length—ideologically, personally, and structurally. I theorize our experiences as strategic responses to the foxhole politics of multiculturalism, wielding ethnography as our most ethical response to the real challenges of representing difference in music departments. I argue that the patterns emerging from their accounts are in many ways unique to the ideological environment of the 1990s in the U.S.

I spoke with certain kinds of ethnomusicologists for this study. First, I chose women, because I believe that the pattern of music departments hiring woman ethnomusicologists to fulfill two kinds of minoritarian positions at once (discipline and gender) is widespread. Second, I chose women who were mid-career or senior when I interviewed them in 2002, and thus had had some time to accumulate experience and to reflect on their situations. Third, I chose woman ethnomusicologists who would generally be considered successful if not eminent by other ethnomusicologists, i.e., they have published widely and are recognized as good educators. I do not reveal their names. Ours is a small community; there are far fewer than six degrees of separation between each of us—and between each of these women and the colleagues with whom they negotiate professional relationships. Fourth, all four began teaching full-time during the 1990s and had the experiences described below during that decade.

The women I interviewed taught in small liberal arts colleges, a state university, and a conservatory from anywhere between six and fourteen years. One of the schools had had a tenure-track position in ethnomusicology since 1970; another hired my interviewee due to NASM requirements. All are in long-term, full-time positions. One is a full professor with tenure; the other three are associate professors, one with tenure, two without. Two had strange and even confrontational experiences while on the job market in the early 1990s when interviewing in departments without full-time ethnomusicologists on the faculty. One was asked point-blank whether she was dedicated to the eradication of Western European art music (WEAM)[14] in higher education. Another noted that two schools where she interviewed for positions seemed "confused" about what they wanted; for instance, different faculty members in the same department asked her about radically different areas, e.g., one seemed to think she should focus on African musics and another on Asian musics.

All were proportionately outnumbered in their present departments. That is, each is the lone ethnomusicologist in her department, each of which has anywhere from five to eight other full-time tenured or tenure-track faculty positions in WEAM. All four women felt that ethnomusicology was viewed as necessary but marginal to the workings of their department. One said that her colleagues saw ethnomusicology as "a sideline, maybe even an evil influence." As another put it, her colleagues saw world music courses as "an important sideline." Their respective undergraduate majors were required to take from one to one and a half courses in ethnomusicology (the "half" being a required team-taught course); in one case, music majors were required to take one academic world music course and a world music ensemble (a total of two ethnomusicology courses). In another case, a single ethnomusicology course requirement was in place for one brief semester before students complained that it was too much of a burden. Two of the four women were able to establish more than one world music ensemble and apparently did so very successfully (two in one case and three in the other), though achieving standing budget lines for those ensembles was difficult. All thus taught music majors at certain points but mostly taught a large number of non-music majors. One in particular noted that music majors tended to take her courses "reluctantly" and to "sit it out" intellectually, whereas she had had quite a few non-majors take two, three, or even four of her courses voluntarily and enthusiastically. She wondered aloud "where these attitudes come from," that is, whether music majors' disinterest in anything except WEAM were formed long before they arrived in higher education, or were "indoctrinated," as she put it.

Colleagues' attitudes toward world music were noted by all. At best, some of the women felt that their area was simply not "taken seriously." At worst, their work was actively resisted and denigrated. Several pointed to the unacknowledged racism inherent in these attitudes. One noted a colleague who sometimes puts on "funny accents" when talking about ethnomusicology-related matters and who says things like, "The next thing you'll need is a room for the baton-twirlers!" One cited collegial disinterest as a means of holding her (and what she represents) at arms' length; when she came up for promotion, only one colleague actually looked at her book. One reported that a colleague flatly stated he "didn't want to know the music of inferior people." Several women said that ideological issues were consistently "personalized"—i.e., colleagues argued that "the problem," however defined, was located in the personality of their particular ethnomusicologist, seeing her as working for her own personal gain rather than in the service of an idea. In short, all had the ongoing sense that neither they nor indeed the musics of the non-Western world were regarded as important or even significant, and that these attitudes were acted out in sometimes spectacularly ethnocentric and racist ways.

All had had notable successes in their departments and were ready and willing to talk about them. Several were particularly proud to have established world music ensembles that had drawn considerable student and community interest. All pointed to the popularity and large enrollments (of non-majors) in their courses as an indication of success and felt that time and student interest was ultimately on their side. One said she felt the fact that her courses were not required meant that the students who took her courses were therefore all the more interested, dedicated, and receptive, and that this was a hidden success. One noted that she had doubled the number of world music courses offered in her department since the time she arrived: when first hired, she was required to teach WEAM appreciation, but she had managed to be released from all WEAM-related teaching and had thus been able to establish a total of eight world music courses which she teaches on a full-time rotating basis. All pointed to strong ties (both formal and informal) with other departments and programs as a deeply pleasurable success. Two cited successful infiltrations of the music major. In one case, music majors were required to take a course team-taught by the ethnomusicologist and a WEAM theorist; in the other case, the ethnomusicologist had successfully implemented a required course in "comparative music theory" that teaches ear-training skills and music analysis but, as she put it, teaches the students skills beyond the notes "by stealth," i.e., she also emphasizes issues of transmission, beliefs, values, etc., which they absorb while ostensibly focused on "the notes."

All had had notable defeats as well, almost entirely in two areas: the curriculum and access to resources. As one put it, the fact that she has been at her institution for a decade but only one of her courses is required is a defeat. Access to positions of authority is an especially pressing issue. Two of the four women were at points in their careers where they could (and indeed should) have been invited to serve as the chair of their departments but had not been. One noted that she would possibly never be asked to serve as chair, and if she were, it would likely be at the end of her career. As the first woman in her department ever to be promoted to full professor, she felt it very unlikely that her colleagues could imagine a woman *and* an ethnomusicologist representing the department as chair. Instead, she took a full-time temporary appointment outside her department to acquire administrative skills and experience (as the director of an interdisciplinary program at her institution). The other interviewee was put up for consideration as chair, resulting in a divided faculty vote and a bitter grievance procedure that ended in formal mediation (which she felt was effective, even though she still was not invited to serve as chair).

I asked each woman whether she had ever felt angry over the position of ethnomusicology in her department, and all said yes. In fact, one said, "Grrrr, yes," describing it as "long-term, constant, demoralizing." One said yes but that its specific nature was rooted in "frustration" at being "diverted" and "thwarted." She said that allowing anger to show simply wouldn't serve her purposes and that she shows her anger to only a few colleagues whom she "trusts," which on "a good day" is three or four people. Another cited both short-term and long-term constant anger. She said that she thinks she has a gendered response to anger that is reinforced by her colleagues, referring to "the large-scale gender politics of the department." She noted that she tends to "hide" her anger and to "hold it in," first explaining this as an ingrained, gendered approach to her own anger and then noting that this is systematically reinforced by her colleagues. She said she has been "bullied" by male colleagues—in mundane ways during faculty meetings and in more intimidating one-on-one confrontations. When she complained to the department chair, she was told that her colleagues' feelings were hurt and that it wasn't professional for her to show her own anger in response. She noted that her male colleagues were not similarly advised. Another reflected on the long-term debilitating effects of feeling "furious all the time," noting that she had swung between depression and feeling that her frustrations were somehow her own fault before coming to an awareness that these were "systemic problems." She said that her anger lay both in "feeling used" and in being continually "deflected away" from her work.

I asked what kind of single, sweeping change any of them might make in their departments, and one said that having more than one ethnomusicologist on the faculty would be a start. She said she needs "help making the decisions, to decide where the department should go." She said she gets tired—that being the "perpetual cheerleader," having to have "three times the enthusiasm," and expending so much necessary energy "flag-waving for ethnomusicology" take their toll. Another said that an equitable or proportionately equal departmental budget would be her wish. She felt that since one out of eight faculty members is an ethnomusicologist, access to one-eighth of the resources would be fair— whereas she has had to do considerable fund-raising (particularly for world music ensembles) outside the department.

All had specific advice and strategies for long-term effectiveness, immediately citing alliances with units outside music. Area studies, Women's Studies, race/ethnicity programs, etc., were all key ways to increase the visibility of ethnomusicology, especially by cross-listing courses. The collegial support offered through these contacts was essential to each woman's sense of purpose and possibility. One said that participating in the department's planning process was key: periodic outside evaluations (e.g., as required for reaccreditation) opened up moments of opportunity. She felt that she had effectively "used external evaluation processes to achieve change, by being aware of broader institutional initiatives." All pointed to the necessity of being in touch with other ethnomusicologists. One is in a notably unsupportive department but lives in a major urban area and is able to attend events and share resources with ethnomusicologists in three other local institutions. Another regards her activities with SEM as "a lifeline," which helps her maintain her "sense of self."

Lessons Learned

Broader points emerge from these conversations. Curriculum is probably *the* major source of frustration for ethnomusicologists. Access to material resources was the other dominant issue. A pervading sense of isolation was often part of ethnomusicologists' experiences within music departments in the 1990s, even when countered by reaching out into other corners of our institutions.

Most music majors require only one ethnomusicology course, and both this phenomenon *and* the reasoning behind it are constants in ethnomusicologists' talk amongst themselves. The reasoning for maintaining a majority of WEAM-focused courses is curious. The WEAM "tradition" (which of course is actually many traditions, threaded together from many times and places, though its constructed nature is rarely acknowledged) is implicitly understood as complex, demanding considerable time and effort in order to be properly understood. That this is certainly true for any music is not understood. The point is, WEAM *requires* this. Following this logic, it is therefore impossibly damaging to *take away* courses from the WEAM-centered music major because this would irreparably affect students' fundamental knowledge base. Therefore, there is no "room," no "space" in the music major for more than one course in ethnomusicology (if that). Qualifications quickly follow: that no judgment of other musics is implied but that this is rather a matter of practicality (and rationales of GREs and entrance to graduate programs are inevitably raised). So it is not a matter of elitism or indeed of ideology at all, in any way, but rather a matter of pragmatism: it is unfortunate but necessary that there is only limited "space" available to the ethnomusicologist in a music major.[15] Where no space is made, world music is an added requirement and thus a literal *and* metaphorical burden for music majors. Ethnomusicologists' pervasive sense that they were not taken seriously by their colleagues was thus a structural reality. Ethnomusicologists rub shoulders on a daily basis with colleagues who enforce basic contradictions in environment and ideology: they attest to their "respect" for the subject matter of ethnomusicology but regretfully cannot find anything more than limited "space" for it within the structure of the music major. Nor can the contradiction be acknowledged. Like all core cultural values (anywhere), its nature is implicit—a matter of understanding, not of discussion. Calling for an explicit discussion and examination of these values is seen as aggressive and even threatening and can prompt extreme responses. Add the parameters of gender (and possibly ethnicity, sexual orientation, class, etc.) to this and the environment is suddenly quite charged.

I also interrogate a usually unspoken dimension of ethnomusicologists' lives in music departments—their emotional lives, which are not separate from issues of power and authority. Isolation, hopelessness, resignation, despair, and anger were personal *and* political responses. Anger is a modality especially worthy of ethnographic attention, and black feminists in particular have argued that anger is a necessary and even enabling political response. Being told that it is not "professional" to express anger or trying to parse the relationship between anger and "frustration" is also a politicized response.

Studies of woman faculty members' experiences in departments and universities with "chilly climates" have suggested that the consequences of these minoritarian positions are far-reaching. Beyond the toll taken on individuals, the effects of isolation and obstruction are played out through research never undertaken, curricula that never change, and students whose curricular options remain limited. In her examination of the fighting words debate, Patricia Hill Collins observes that "the effect of dehumanizing language is often flight rather than fight" (1998:85):

> When confronted with their own inferiority, Black women and other groups that have been historically marginalized within academia often demonstrate similar reactions to those who encounter hate speech. In the face of subtle yet pervasive insults of contemporary racially coded academic discourse, some targets may remain silent. By their silence, they may appear to demonstrate tacit agreement with the dominant discourse. Others simply leave the academy by dropping out of classes, remaining A.B.D.'s . . . in perpetuity, or, in the case of a woman of color serving on my dissertation committee, one day simply tack a sign to the office door that says, "I can't work here any more. I'm not coming back."

Perhaps my shift from writing about ethnomusicology to writing about hate speech and racism seems abrupt, but the parallels are apt and useful—indeed, I think they are not parallels as much as closely related matters. A significant percentage of North American ethnomusicologists are women or scholars of color—or both—so it is important to take seriously the impact of the doubled or tripled minoritarian position in the music department lived by some ethnomusicologists. Furthermore, the rhetorical and discursive environments in which we live establish and maintain the critical terms through which we can do what we do and think what we think. The debates around hate speech and fighting words offer some useful handles. In *Excitable Speech,* Judith Butler argues that (1997:4)

> To be injured by speech is to suffer a loss of context, that is, not to know where you are . . . Exposed at the moment of such shattering is precisely the volatility of one's "place" within the community of speakers; one can be "put in one's place" by such speech, but such a place may be no place.

The models we have for strategizing about ethnomusicologists' locations in departments of WEAM are terribly limited. We need to think outside the mode, outside the meter, beyond the binary. We are strongly encouraged, implicitly and by example, to make the best of it, to complain only in private, and to try to work the system as it exists. We learn to avoid confrontations or to use them only as a last resort. We learn to hope for very little, glad to have a seat at the table but knowing enough not to ask for seconds. Ethnomusicologists often experience the kinds of institutional discrimination and isolation similar to those experienced by ethnic minorities and women because we metonymically represent the Other. Rather than struggle to "fit in" to a conversation already established outside the terms of ethnomusicology, we might consider the strategies that have effected social and political change for minority communities. More than one of the ethnomusicologists I interviewed offered the following tactics:

(1) Expect trouble—you won't have to go looking for it. You will almost certainly have to argue repeatedly and over the long-term for access to resources.

(2) Get involved in the life of your institution beyond your department, e.g., in area studies programs and other interdisciplinary programs. These relationships may be formal or informal, but they provide access to resources (both material and informational) and can form an essential network of colleagues who can help in any number of ways.

(3) Stay on top of broader institutional initiatives and make yourself part of them. Reaccreditation procedures and periodic outside evaluations are important moments for possible change (curricular and beyond).

(4) When things go wrong, seek help immediately. Don't wait until you are isolated or immobilized.

(5) Find mentors both inside and outside your department.

(6) Regard colleagues' disinterest as a route toward certain freedoms.

A few ground-breaking ethnographies of music institutions have showed how the social structures defining the practices within them are always "about" much more than music, and are always about the terms of authority (Nettl 1995, Kingsbury 1988, Born 1995). Henry A. Giroux has argued that any critical consideration of education entails thinking about pedagogy as a broader political and cultural project (1994). "Teaching" and "education" are part of (but not the exclusive sites for) learning the means to generate interventions into history and society—leading to the broader category of "critical pedagogy," which emerges from higher education as well as many other sites. Giroux's abundant writings reconceptualize the relationship between pedagogy and civic engagement, and between the university and the public sphere. He writes that the "most important task" of the university should be its role in "creating a public sphere of citizens who are able to exercise power over their own lives and especially over the conditions of knowledge acquisition" (1995:302).[16] Ethnomusicologists know that they teach more than just the music but have been mightily distracted by (neocapitalist) arguments of relative "worth" (music A is just as important as music B), which draw them away from the more pressing project of showing how music is part of a public sphere that can be redefined at any moment.

Since we were reluctant to publicly acknowledge that our discipline is ideologically threatening to the very foundations of most music departments, we were also slow to establish bodies within SEM that could strategize about these issues.

We are making up for lost time.[17] In 1996, Elizabeth Tolbert and I co-founded the Section on the Status of Women; since then, the Gender and Sexualities Task Force, the Crossroads Project, and the Committee on Careers and Professional Development (among others) have become places where ethnomusicologists can gather to talk story, identify patterns, link research and teaching, and problem-solve. This turn toward thinking about ethnomusicology as a politicized project is *the* most important change I have seen since I joined SEM in 1985. Thinking about ethnomusicology as a career that often carries the burden of nested differences (what we teach and, often, who we are) is a very productive change made necessary by the 1990s. Rather than assume that accommodation is required, more of us are reaching out to colleagues and other corners of campus in an effort to locate ethnomusicology within critical discourses that arc across the humanities and social sciences. Ethnomusicology has always been interdisciplinary, but the stakes were different in the 1990s: it was then suddenly possible to argue that part of your authority was your experiential life base in your gender, ethnicity, sexual orientation, etc., and that your subjectivity as an ethnomusicologist was part of what made your perspective valuable. But turning toward situated knowledge also created significant vulnerabilities when difference was hypercentralized in both the person and the activity of ethnomusicology in many music departments.

The imprint of these broader critical and political forces is all over our discipline, and the question remains whether we will be able to make our work relevant to these same discussions in other areas of the humanities and social sciences. The challenges of the early twenty-first century include the conservative backlash against difference and new forms of cultural imperialism that make it necessary for intellectuals to speak, teach, and organize. Our work, whether research or teaching, is inherently progressive but only as proactive as we insist that it be.

Acknowledgments

A version of this essay was presented at the 50th annual meeting of the Society for Ethnomusicology in Atlanta for the Commemorative Roundtable, "Perspectives from Five Decades: Members of SEM who have joined between 1955 and 2000 contribute their thoughts on the history of SEM." I thank Bruno Nettl for organizing the roundtable. The section of this essay drawn from interviews was first presented in the panel "What is Ethnomusicology Doing in Music Departments?" at the 47th annual meeting of the Society for Ethnomusicology, Estes Park Center, Colorado, October 23–27, 2002. Bonnie Wade, Philip Bohlman, Anthony Seeger, and Katherine Hagedorn generously provided information about their institutions and more. Elizabeth Tolbert and I have been talking about these issues for more than a decade and I thank her for feedback and inspiration. I especially thank the four unnamed ethnomusicologists who allowed me to interview them and to include their comments here. Email: deborah.wong@ucr.edu.

Notes

1. Anthony Seeger taught in the Department of Anthropology at Pomona College from 1974–75. He did not teach any ethnomusicology courses (but had a strong impact on then-undergraduate Marina Roseman)(p.c.).

2. Edward Rothstein was formerly the chief music critic for *The New York Times* and music critic for *The New Republic*. He is now a cultural critic for *The New York Times*.

3. See Wong 1998a for more on this.

4. Online at http://www.berkeley.edu/catalog/undergrad/requirements.html#amcult (accessed on 12 December, 2005).

5. Wade created and taught the course with the help of Marisol Berríos-Miranda and Anthony Brown, then graduate students. She relates that she "wanted music to be in the vanguard" of helping to make the American Cultures requirement a reality, and she also saw the need for a course that could give graduate students in ethnomusicology a chance to teach something related to their own work. Ethnomusicologists Jocelyne Guilbault and Ben Brinner currently alternate teaching the course. Approximately one hundred and fifty undergraduates are turned away from the course every semester (Wade, p.c.).

6. I do not mean to imply that previous work in ethnomusicology was radically different in this regard. But the 1980s produced far fewer ethnomusicological monographs; for example, throughout the 1980s, the majority of the books reviewed in this Journal were written (risking a generalization) by non-ethnomusicologists. Steven Feld's *Sound and Sentiment* (1982) was unusual for its emphasis on broad theoretical questions.

7. I thank Phil Bohlman for sharing the history and development of "Chicago Studies in Ethnomusicology."

8. One could say that the cart was driving the horse because the publication boom was partly motivated by increasingly product-driven professional standards within the academy. Like other humanists, ethnomusicologists were expected to "produce" one if not two books for tenure, so the university press market expanded to meet the demand.

9. See Koskoff 2005 for an astute examination of this problem.

10. Some of the best recent work on gender by ethnomusicologists is in Moisala and Diamond 2000 and Magrini 2003 (and both collections are informed by the groundbreaking collection, Koskoff 1987). Sugarman 1997 remains a model of its kind.

11. The marked exception is *Music and the Racial Imagination* (Bohlman and Radano 2001), which lays out a cross-cultural view of musical racialization. The massive introduction to the volume offers an erudite and pointed critique of how and why music scholarship has denied race for so long.

12. For example, *I, Rigoberta Menchú: An Indian Woman in Guatemala*, by Rigoberta Menchú, with Elisabeth Burgos-Debray (introduction) and Ann Wright (translator) (Verso 1987).

13. Anthropologist Donald Brenneis's participatory research on NSF grant panels and meta-scholarship (1994) is an example of the kind of reflexive critical response I aspire to here.

14. I thank Eric Martin Usner for his formulation of "WEAM" as an acronym meant to reveal the ideological foundation that supports and maintains the authority of this repertoire.

15. An aside is necessary here. One of my interviewees teaches in a conservatory, and some of her WEAM-based colleagues made no bones about the global hierarchy of musics. Many of the non-Western musics that she taught or promoted through concerts were described by her colleagues as "inferior," performed by "inferior" musicians. Her efforts to invite amateur musicians from refugee communities to perform on campus created a minor furor, ending in her dean's insistence that she only invite "quality" performers to participate in their concert series. In short, even the gesture of "understood" equality is not yet universal.

16. For a particularly trenchant example, see Giroux's recent essay in which he revisits Adorno's effort to reimagine education after Auschwitz and links it to a critical pedagogy that might enable interventionist readings of the photographs from Abu Ghraib (infamously depicting the torture and

degradation of Iraqi prisoners by U.S. soldiers in 2003–04). He suggests that politics and pedagogy are in fact intimately related (2004:11):

> Public pedagogy not only defines cultural objects of interpretation, it also offers the possibility for engaging modes of literacy that are not just about competency but also about the possibility of interpretation as an intervention in the world . . . Making the political more pedagogical in this instance connects what we know to the conditions that make learning possible in the first place.

17. The College Music Society, the American Musicological Society, and the Society for Music Theory preceded SEM, for example, in establishing Committees on the Status of Women and Committees on Diversity.

References

Averill, Gage. 1997. *A Day for the Hunter, A Day for the Prey: Popular Music and Power in Haiti.* Chicago: University of Chicago Press.

Barz, Gregory F., and Timothy J. Cooley, eds. 1997. *Shadows in the Field: New Perspectives for Fieldwork in Ethnomusicology.* New York and Oxford: Oxford University Press.

Benokraitis, Nijole V. 1997. *Subtle Sexism: Current Practice and Prospects for Change.* Thousand Oaks, CA: Sage Publications.

Berger, Harris M. 1999. *Metal, Rock, and Jazz: Perception and the Phenomenology of Musical Experience.* Hanover, NH: University Press of New England.

Bergeron, Katherine. 1992. "Prologue: Disciplining Music." In *Disciplining Music: Musicology and Its Canons,* edited by Katherine Bergeron and Philip V. Bohlman, 1–9. Chicago: University of Chicago Press.

———, and Philip V. Bohlman, eds. 1992. *Disciplining Music: Musicology and Its Canons.* Chicago: University of Chicago Press.

Berman, Paul, ed. 1992. *Debating P.C.: The Controversy over Political Correctness on College Campuses.* New York: Laurel.

Bohlman, Philip V. 1992. "Ethnomusicology's Challenge to the Canon: The Canon's Challenge to Ethnomusicology" and "Epilogue: Musics and Canons." In *Disciplining Music: Musicology and Its Canons,* edited by Katherine Bergeron and Philip V. Bohlman, 116–136 and 197–210. Chicago: University of Chicago Press.

———, and Ronald Radano, eds. 2001. *Music and the Racial Imagination.* Chicago: University of Chicago Press.

Born, Georgina. 1995. *Rationalizing Culture: IRCAM, Boulez, and the Institutionalization of the Musical Avant-garde.* Berkeley: University of California Press.

Brenneis, Donald. 1994. "Discourse and Discipline at the National; Research Council: A Bildungsroman." *Cultural Anthropology* 9(1):23–36.

Brett, Philip, Elizabeth Wood, Gary C. Thomas, eds. 1994. *Queering the Pitch: The New Gay and Lesbian Musicology.* New York and London: Routledge.

Butler, Judith. 1997. *Excitable Speech: A Politics of the Performative.* New York and London: Routledge.

Collins, Patricia Hill. 1998. *Fighting Words: Black Women and the Search for Justice.* Minneapolis: University of Minnesota Press.

Erlmann, Veit. 1991. *African Stars: Studies in Black South African Performance.* Chicago: University of Chicago Press.

———. 1996. *Nightsong: Performance, Power, and Practice in South Africa.* Chicago: University of Chicago Press.

Giroux, Henry A. 1994. "Doing Cultural Studies: Youth and the Challenge of Pedagogy." *Harvard Educational Review* 64(3):278–308. http://www.henryagiroux.com/online_articles/doing_cultural.htm (Accessed 7 December, 2005).

———. 1995. "Academics as Public Intellectuals: Rethinking Classroom Politics." In *PC Wars: Politics and Theory in the Academy,* edited by Jeffrey Williams, 294–307. New York and London: Routledge.

———. 2004. "What Might Education Mean after Abu Ghraib: Revisiting Adorno's Politics of Education." *Comparative Studies of South Asia, Africa and the Middle East* 24(1):5–24.

Grossberg, Lawrence, Cary Nelson, Paula A. Treichler, eds. 1991. *Cultural Studies.* New York and London: Routledge.

Guilbault, Jocelyne. 1993. *Zouk: World Music in the West Indies.* Chicago: University of Chicago Press.

Keil, Charles, and Steve Feld. 1994. *Music Grooves: Essays and Dialogues.* Chicago: University of Chicago Press.

Kingsbury, Henry. 1988. *Music, Talent and Performance: A Conservatory Cultural System.* Philadelphia: Temple University Press.

Kisliuk, Michelle. 1998. *Seize the Dance! BaAka Musical Life and the Ethnography of Performance.* New York: Oxford University Press.

Koskoff, Ellen, ed. 1987. *Women and Music in Cross-Cultural Perspective.* New York: Greenwood Press.

———. 2005. "(Left Out in) Left (the Field) The Effects of Post-Postmodern Scholarship on Feminist and Gender Studies in Musicology and Ethnomusicology, 1990–2000." *Women and Music* 9:90–98.

Landrine, Hope, and Elizabeth A. Klonoff. 1997. *Discrimination Against Women: Prevalence, Consequences, Remedies.* Thousand Oaks, CA: Sage Publications.

Levine, Victoria Lindsay. 2001. "The World Music Survey in the Twenty-First Century." Paper presented at the College Music Society International Conference, Limerick, Ireland.

Lortat-Jacob, Bernard. 1995. *Sardinian Chronicles.* Chicago: University of Chicago Press.

Magrini, Tullia, ed. 2003. *Music and Gender: Perspectives from the Mediterranean.* Chicago: University of Chicago Press.

Marcus, George E., and Michael M. J. Fischer. 1986, 1999. *Anthropology as Cultural Critique: An Experimental Moment in the Human Sciences,* 2d ed. Chicago: University of Chicago Press.

Moisala, Pirkko, and Beverley Diamond, eds. 2000. *Music and Gender.* Urbana and Chicago: University of Illinois Press.

Monson, Ingrid. 1996. *Saying Something: Jazz Improvisation and Interaction.* Chicago: University of Chicago Press.

Nettl, Bruno. 1995. *Heartland Excursions: Ethnomusicological Reflections on Schools of Music.* Urbana and Chicago: University of Illinois Press.

Robbins, Bruce. 1995. "Othering the Academy: Professionalism and Multiculturalism." In *PC Wars: Politics and Theory in the Academy,* edited by Jeffrey Williams, 279–93. New York and London: Routledge.

Rothstein, Edward. 1991. "Roll Over Beethoven: The New Musical Correctness and Its Mistakes." *The New Republic,* 4 February, 29–34.

Stokes, Martin, ed. 1994. *Ethnicity, Identity and Music: The Musical Construction of Place.* Oxford, UK and Providence, RI: Berg Publishers.

Sugarman, Jane C. 1997. *Engendering Song: Singing and Subjectivity at Prespa Albanian Weddings.* Chicago: University of Chicago Press.

Waterman, Christopher. 1990. *Jùjú: A Social History and Ethnography of an African Popular Music.* Chicago: University of Chicago Press.

Wong, Deborah. 1998a. "Ethnomusicology and Critical Pedagogy as Cultural Work: Reflections on Teaching and Fieldwork." *College Music Symposium* 38:80–100.

———. 1998b. Review of *Shadows in the Field,* edited by Gregory F. Barz and Timothy J. Cooley. *the world of music* 40(2):181–85.

———. 2004. *Speak It Louder: Asian Americans Making Music.* New York and London: Routledge.

Thoughts on an Interdiscipline: Music Theory, Analysis, and Social Theory in Ethnomusicology

GABRIEL SOLIS / University of Illinois, Champaign-Urbana

In an analytical and hortatory article in the *Yearbook for Traditional Music* about theory in ethnomusicology, and on the nature of ethnomusicological theory, Timothy Rice manifests a telling contradiction regarding music theory as a part of the discipline (2010b).[1] The article is quite useful in providing systematic ways of thinking about social theory and its role in ethnomusicology as well as the autochthonous modes of theorizing—about society, about culture, about the world—that we do in our discipline; but where it comes to theorizing about musical sound, Rice is unclear in a way that is at least unhelpful to his argument in the article, and potentially deleterious to our practice as a discipline as we move into the future.[2] On the one hand, he draws on a host of examples of the most significant work in the field in which theorizing about and closely analyzing musical sound plays a central role, but on the other, when he discusses music theory (by which I believe he means the production of generalizations about musical structure in the abstract) he does so in a way that diminishes its currency and importance to ethnomusicology. In this essay, I take the position that we need a metatheoretical perspective on the discipline that recognizes the ongoing significance of close analysis of musical sound in a range of studies and the production of music theory by ethnomusicologists over the past thirty years. This work, I argue, is not separate from the "interpretive turn," as Rice calls the growing importance of social theory in ethnomusicology since the 1980s, but, rather, interconnected with it. As Martin Stokes says in his portion of the entry on "Ethnomusicology" in the *New Grove Dictionary*, the opposition between "texts and contexts" can be seen as a false one (Pegg et al. n.d.).

As will become clear throughout this article, my use of the term "music theory" is intentionally somewhat vague here. I take it, in the first instance

From *Ethnomusicology*, Vol. 56, No. 3 (Fall 2012), pp. 530–54

(seemingly in much the same way as Rice), as referring to the kinds of investigation of musical sound that are commonly taught in music theory and analysis courses or published in music theory journals in America—generalizations about structures of pitch, rhythm, and form—but I also intend a shift of sorts in thinking, to make the case that many of the ways ethnomusicologists have engaged with musical sound are themselves reasonably thought of as music theory, even if they look quite different from the more conventional model. I do not intend this article to offer a unified music theory (though I will suggest some lines of theoretical investigation that I find useful and interesting) but rather to offer a perspective on disciplinary practice. My aim, and the thing that I believe makes this article a useful addition to the extensive tradition of disciplinary reflection in ethnomusicology, is to highlight the extent to which we produce theory about musical sound and structure, and the ways that our music-theoretical activity can be productive within ethnomusicology, as the field contributes to musicology writ large, and, beyond this, to the humanities and social sciences.[3]

While this article is not only a response to Rice, his prominent metatheoretical writing substantially motivates it, and as such a more detailed look at his piece in *The Yearbook* is useful. The article is organized around a list of seven domains in which ethnomusicologists theorize, with the aim of "understanding more clearly the theorizing we already do and, in the process, help[ing] us develop a more robust theoretical tradition" (Rice 2010b:103). Rice's theoretical domains make sense, inasmuch as they have some logical cohesion and represent areas in which ethnomusicologists have produced not just isolated studies, but bodies of work over time. At least two of his seven domains—"General theories about the nature of music" and "Interlocal theory about musical processes in related communities and their contribution to community and area studies"—and perhaps a third—"Cross-cultural theories about music in relation to the many themes of interest to ethnomusicologists and their contribution beyond the discipline to general studies of those themes"—ought reasonably to incorporate, or in fact to *be* music theory. Indeed, his description of ethnomusicological theory begins essentially with what I would call music theory: "Ethnomusicological theory involves the writing of descriptions, classifications, comparisons, interpretations, and generalizations about music . . . in general" (ibid.:105) Yet throughout his discussion of these various areas of ethnomusicological theory, he seldom metadiscursively acknowledges the ways that ethnomusicologists engage in theory about musical sound as such (though a number of his examples, including his own study of Bulgarian multi-part singing, could certainly be thought of in that way).

Instead, Rice focuses on theory about social process. For instance, in his discussion of our "general theories about the nature of music," Rice avoids any mention of theories about musical structure, highlighting instead theories such as "music is a social behavior," "music is a nonverbal practice that can, outside verbal discourse, create gendered individuals and other socially constructed subjectivities," or "music's particular form and effects depend on its means of production" (ibid.:111). Likewise, in the discussion of "interlocal theory about musical processes in related cultures," Rice focuses not so much on formal aspects of musical structure interculturally as on social processes between groups: "comparing musical processes in related communities should yield ethnomusicological theory about, for example, the cultural work different musical genres do: within a geographically bounded culture; in a particular ethnic, racial, religious or kinship group; in nations within a particular area of the world; or in a set of historically or socially related institutions" (ibid.:120).

It might be reasonable to argue that all of these (and further) general theories rest on analysis of musical sound and structure, but Rice goes out of his way to preface his entire study with an off-hand dismissal of music theory as an exogenous and currently marginal practice to the discipline. Having laid out the social-theoretical areas of most interest to contemporary ethnomusicology, he performs a surprising conflation of music theory and science: "Perhaps most striking by its absence from my list of types of theory is scientific theory; this is because I believe most ethnomusicologists no longer employ it" (ibid.:103). He goes on to say, "Since the 1970s . . . these forms of theory have been supplanted by social theory, although to be sure, both scientific theory and music theory continue to have their advocates" (ibid.:104). Rice is not alone in focusing his metatheoretical study on social theory to the exclusion of music theory; but he is unusual, if not unique, in so explicitly diminishing the importance of music theory and analysis in the process.[4]

The implication that music theory is categorically and historically similar to scientific theory in ethnomusicology might be correct if by music theory we imagine Alexander John Ellis and the measurement of pitch intervals in various musical systems (1885). If, however, we see music theory more expansively—as, for instance, does Michael Tenzer, whom Rice includes as one of two ethnomusicologists still defending a place for music theory in the discipline, and as I intend to do in this article—then the obviousness of the connection dwindles. Indeed, Tenzer specifically objects to the implication that music theory and analysis—whose interrelation I will take up below—is somehow scientific. In the introduction to *Analytical Studies in World Music*, Tenzer says, "Music analysis must be rigorous but it is essentially creative, with only tangential claims to being scientific" (2006:6).

In ethnomusicology, to distinguish "music theory" from "social theory"— both of which I believe are often produced from within the discipline, as well as borrowed from other disciplines—I would rely on a distinction between aspects of music that can be understood as sonic features and aspects that are beyond the strictly sonic.[5] Thus, music theory at its most basic might be the production of generalizations about musical sound based on its observation and in order to better understand further instances of it. There are many sources of generalization and many ways to use these theories to understand other works, performances, and events; but it should be clear that theory and analysis are interpretive endeavors that move well beyond the statistical description that was common in comparative musicology. Such music theory, I would argue, should be—and, indeed, is—neither of limited value to questions about music as social practice, nor marginal to the discipline of ethnomusicology at large, but rather of central importance in practice and in principle to both.

I do not intend to argue for a return to an ethnomusicology before what Rice calls the "interpretive" turn (2010b:104), nor for an ethnomusicology like the one advocated by Mervyn MacLean that is not "awash in social theory" (2006:337), nor for a pre-new-musicology without serious considerations of the power dynamics in representations that Gary Tomlinson, Susan McClary, and others so cogently made a part of music history in the 1990s (McClary [1991] 2002; Subotnik 1991; Tomlinson 1993; Brett, Wood, and Thomas [1994] 2006). Rather than offer a *revanchist* argument simply for a focus on "the music itself," or on music in the abstract, I argue here that in fact theorizing about musical sound gives ethnomusicologists useful tools for undertaking interpretive studies, and for reaching a full understanding of the domains affected by the power dynamics that characterize any instance of music-making. Debates over the value of "close reading" conducted in musicology in the 1990s (Tomlinson 1993; Krims 1998) are germane here. I am not as confident as Michael Tenzer when he answers his own question about doing musical analysis in the affirmative (2006:9); but I believe quite strongly that musical sounds are primary among the aspects of music making that we study (along with associated imagery, costume, embodied performance, and so on), and that while our methods for investigating sound must be held up to critique, a turn away from close consideration of those sounds (I prefer thinking about "close listening" and "close playing" to "close reading") impoverishes our work as a discipline.

I should note that I write here mainly about ethnomusicology as it is practiced in institutions in the United States, England, and Australia, the disciplinary communities with which I am most familiar. I cannot hope to address the practice in Continental Europe, Africa, Asia, or Latin America, though such a perspective would undoubtedly provide valuable insight. I suggest, based on work originally written in French and German and translated into English, and work written in English by Continental and French Canadian scholars, that the disavowal of music theory and analysis that I see as endemic to ethnomusicology in the United States, and to some extent the United Kingdom and Australia, is not part of other traditions.

I begin this article as practically as possible, focusing on what I think the place of music theory and analysis actually is in ethnomusicology today. In part, this amounts to a survey of recent work, in order to establish some sense of the relative volume of theoretically and analytically inclined work; more importantly, in this section I set out a typology of music theory and analysis in recent ethnomusicological work. In order to come to a better picture of how recent work fits in the history of the discipline, I then briefly look at a few representative approaches to music theory and analysis in older ethnomusicology—before the "interpretive turn." I then return to metatheory of the discipline, to put my thoughts on music theory and analysis in ethnomusicology in perspective. While I believe that a number of recent metatheoretical studies have not adequately accounted for music theory, mine is not the only one to recognize its importance. Finally, I draw on two of my own recent areas of research to suggest reasons for a more explicit valuation of music theory and analysis in ethnomusicology.

Music Theorization in Ethnomusicology
After the "Interpretive Turn"

It is ironic that Rice would lump music theory in with scientific theory at this moment, as one of the "pre-interpretive turn" paradigms, inasmuch as, if nothing else, 2011 marked the first issue of the online journal *Analytical Approaches to World Music* (http://aawmjournal.com), with articles by a number of leading scholars on theoretical aspects of particular musical systems from Africa and Asia, and at least one synthetic article offering a cross-cultural theory of temporal elements of music. This journal, and Michael Tenzer's edited volume that inspired it (2006), might actually be taken to mark the estrangement of music theory from ethnomusicology, were they the only examples of music theory being derived from and used in ethnomusicological study. Indeed, the editors, Lawrence Shuster and Rob Schultz, reported in the introduction to the first issue that the new journal follows on the initial International Conference on Analytical Approaches to World Music (AAWM) (Shuster and Schultz 2011). The next step in such a trajectory might well be the establishment of a new academic society; and while societies, journals, and conferences do not constitute disciplines in and of themselves, they are their apparatuses.[6]

That said, most of the contributors to *AAWM* are self-identifying ethnomusicologists, and, moreover, the journal is by no means the limit of recent music theoretical activity in the discipline. For instance, 2010 saw the publication of a special issue of *Music Theory Online* (16/4, November 2010) dedicated to the analytical and theoretical study of rhythm in African music, including both music theorists and ethnomusicologists. In any case, I suggest, while music theoretical and analytical approaches may not be the main point of the majority of work in the field in the past twenty years, they hold a significant place. A review of the major journals in ethnomusicology shows a minority, but consistent, presence for such work. Over the past decade, the flagship British journal *Ethnomusicology Forum* (including volumes issued under its former title *British Journal of Ethnomusicology*) has roughly thirty percent of its articles engaging in substantial, theoretically informed analysis of musical sound and/ or in the production of music theory. Within that range there is no discernable trend, either in terms of numbers of articles inclined in this way or in terms of particular kinds of theory or uses of analysis. A survey of the preeminent American journal, *Ethnomusicology*, shows a similar result. A rigorous survey of recent books and conference papers in ethnomusicology would be a bigger undertaking, but it is my informal impression that most books in the discipline turn to musical analysis, if not theory, at some point, and that many conference presentations are more oriented towards such work than are articles in the primary journals.

A number of distinct approaches to theory and analysis are clearly part of our discipline, as seen in the articles published in ethnomusicology journals, books in the discipline, conference papers, and other, less canonical formats for academic publication. It will be worthwhile to take a moment at this point to explain the distinction I make between theory and analysis, and suggest why it is a useful distinction in understanding the place(s) of music theory in ethnomusicology as a discipline. By and large I follow Michael Tenzer in thinking that "a description of the immanent, underlying principles uniting diverse musics (however delineated) is best thought of as a theory; analysis is the application of theory to reveal individuality within and between levels of structure" (2006:6). I might add that in the process of revealing individuality, analysis can often reveal commonality as well. An important point to add is that the hierarchies Tenzer refers to in the act of analysis—in "the encounter between the hierarchy-seeking mind and the music-sound event"—may be found at various levels, and theories that act as generalizations at one level may not be generalizable to higher levels (ibid.). Finally, it should be noted that analysis often generates theory.

Much recent ethnomusicology that works in a significant way with musical analysis does not necessarily do so in order to arrive at new theories of musical form or structure. The authors may arrive there incidentally, but more commonly they achieve a synthesis of the musicological and anthropological goals of the "interdiscipline," arriving at theory about the effects of music in a larger sense through considered, sensitive analysis of specific works and performances. Much of the material that Rice discusses that I see as engaged with music theory and analysis is of this sort. Marc Perlman's study of *pathet* and gender in *gendèr* parts in Central Javanese gamelan performance is particularly cogent in this regard, inasmuch as he argues that "the more detailed our technical analyses, the more opportunities we will have to show how sounds and context are subtly intertwined" (1998:68).

Rice describes this as a case of "adding some social theory into the music-theory [*sic*] mix" (2010b:119), but I would look for a more holistic description of Perlman's approach here, in order to fully grasp the ways in which musical analysis, itself driven by a body of theoretical thought, is the basis of, and a necessary driving force for, other theoretical findings. Similar structures of argument can be found to one degree or another in, for instance, David McDonald's article "Geographies of the Body: Music, Violence and Manhood in Palestine" (2010) or Frederick Moehn's "A Carioca Blade Runner, or How Percussionst Marcos Suzano Turned the Brazilian Tambourine into a Drum Kit, and Other Matters of (Politically) Correct Music Making" (2009). McDonald's study of "the relationship between violence, performance and the attainment and enactment of masculinity among Palestinian male youths in Jordan and the West Bank" does not propose any new theory of musical form or structure in Arabic music, but looks at the ways song types originally used in one context have been redeployed in another to mark masculinity in social space (McDonald 2010:191). Unearthing the musical production of masculinity in affective terms requires McDonald to listen structurally, in the first instance.

Moehn's article works through a similar structure of argument, tracing the meanings embedded in otherwise non-musical discourse in interviews with Brazilian percussionist Marcos Suzano through a close examination of his music, to explore the ways the musical and the political can be discursively interactive in one artist's career. Suzano becomes the locus for an ethnomusicology here that looks at the "auditory entanglements" (Guilbault 2005) that make a study of one musician's musical creativity also a study of larger Brazilian politics (Moehn 2009:302). The article draws on analysis of sound—timbre, texture, digital effects—more than traditional domains like melody or rhythm, and thus does not draw extensively on music theories from outside ethnomusicology. Ultimately, this material points toward the development of new music theory, articulating generalizations about the ways these domains structure the experience of sound.

That said, significant new music theory can, and often does, come out of studies that are not explicitly intended to be music theoretical. In fact, Rice's own study of Bulgarian two-voiced singing (*dvuglasno peene*) fits this description well. His struggle to understand why the "two-voicedness" of two-voiced singing was confounded by the apparent presence of a third voice in one village eventually led him not to a new cross-cultural theory of the basic elements of music, but it did lead him "into a theoretical conversation with Bulgarian scholars who had studied this tradition" (2010b:115). Rice ultimately does venture a theoretical position—one many of us have found in our field work—that local normative descriptions are theories that may not hold true in all instances. I would go further, however, to say that he does, at least implicitly, offer a musical theory (which he derives from the practice of cognitive anthropology) when he says, "this performance was clearly not a haphazard, accidental variation on a norm, but a fully conscious, well-understood practice" (ibid.:115). Theories such as this do not necessarily look like what we have come to think of and expect music theory to be, particularly because of the extent to which it is provisional and limited in its claims, but they are precisely the kind of generalizations about musical structures and their relation to cognitive processes that could be engaged with by others and used in further study of the same tradition.

In this sense, ethnomusicological music theory may be much closer to much of the newer work in the discipline of music theory than it once was. While music theory and analysis is often seen in relation to the materials taught in undergraduate theory and analysis courses, recent research in the discipline has moved strongly in the direction of studying cognition. David Temperley's *The Cognition of Basic Musical Structures*, for instance, or Justin London's *Hearing in Time*, as well as much of the work published in the journal *Music Perception*, follows lines of thought that can be seen as complementary to the cognitive turn in ethnomusicology.

In the production of theory, ethnomusicologists today work primarily at two levels of generalization. Most ethnomusicologists who explicitly create theories of musical structure do so at the level of the musical tradition. While scholarship arguing for these kinds of theories may—and commonly does—incorporate close analysis of works or performances, it may not always do so. Laura Leante's study of gesture and meaning in *rāg Sri* in contemporary Hindustani classical music (2009) is one such study, as is Kwok-wai Ng's study of the history of transmission of Japanese *togaku* (2011). Leante moves beyond common methodologies for thinking about pitch, incorporating an inventive consideration of physical gesture in unpacking the ways performers think about the interval between *Re* and *Pa* (the third and fifth scale degrees). Yet ultimately, while her study may speak to broader questions of somatization of musical experience in general, its primary goals are developed with and most clearly applicable to the thorny theoretical questions about the nature of mode in Hindustani music (Leanne 2009:203).[7]

Similarly, Ng's study of togaku transmission could be used as evidence of an issue that can be found in many traditions, but he has conclusions that primarily speak to longstanding theoretical questions in Japanese music history. Ng looks at the ways oral mnemonic devices and written music notation have been used in passing down togaku from teacher to student. The main thrust of Ng's argument takes a careful analysis of small melodic figures as a way of theorizing about the nature of musical structure in a particular tradition—the kinds of patterning found in Japanese togaku music—and about the intentions and practices that underlie those structures in that tradition (2011:35).[8]

It appears that in large measure ethnomusicologists have worked with this kind of tradition-oriented music theory disproportionately in a small number of areas. It is not surprising that those studying classical musics from across North Africa, the Middle East, the Indian Subcontinent, and Southeast and East Asia would be drawn to music theoretical questions. It is not so much that the music itself disproportionately invites such study as that the local music cultures within which ethnomusicologists study these kinds of music are themselves involved in explicit, literate theoretical study, and many have histories of such study stretching back centuries and more.[9] Scholars working in other areas have also developed theories to explain aspects of musical structure, though often not in direct dialogue with a history of theoretical literature. Hugo Zemp's ethnotheoretical work with 'Are'Are bamboo pipe traditions in the Solomon Islands are a good example of such work (1978, 1979).

Africanist scholarship, much of it undertaken, not coincidentally, by British and European scholars, has been particularly productive in terms of at least locale-specific theoretical and analytical work. Simha Arom's research with Central African polyphony (1991), Gerhard Kubik's work on polyphonic traditions across the continent (1994), and the extensive bibliographies of Gilbert Rouget, Andrew Tracey, J. H. Kwabena Nketia, and others attest to the extent of such an approach in African music. Stephen Blum's article "European Musical Terminology and the Music of Africa" nicely outlines the history of theory and analysis in this literature—particularly in the work of comparative musicology—highlighting periodic ambivalence toward and problematic aspects of it (1991). As Kofi Agawu wrote in response to the essays on African music in *Music Theory Online*, African rhythm has generated analytical responses from generations of (mostly) Europeans and Anglo-Americans: "first came the early, naïve explorers who found African music at once complex and incomprehensible; then came the first generation of analysts and theorists who tried to write it down in order to unveil its metrical and rhythmic structures, and who did so using questionable concepts (like polymeter and cross rhythm); then came another group of analysts determined to rid the field of the conceptual contamination introduced by earlier analysts; now come . . . others who think the corrective efforts of recent theorizing have gone too far, and that some of African music's complexity ought to be restored" (2010:7).

Relatively few ethnomusicologists since the "interpretive turn" have tried to develop theories of music that are truly generalizable at a level higher than the musical tradition. Such theories—theories that explain specific musical elements, processes, or structures either in more than one culture or in principle without regard to culture or musical tradition—do, however, seem to be increasingly of interest to at least some ethnomusicologists. Michael Tenzer's work, which includes extensive theoretical consideration of structural patterning of melody, rhythm, and form in Balinese *gamelan gong kebyar* (2000), has also, more recently, included an attempt to develop general theories that account for structural elements of music in ways that are broadly applicable cross-culturally. Beginning with the collection *Analytical Studies in World Music* (2006), and continuing to an article in the inaugural issue of the *AAWM* journal (2011b) and another in this journal (2011a), Tenzer has looked at "periodicity," the systems of recurrence that bring structure to most music, as "music's ultimate organizer on many levels" (2006:22). As is common for general theories, periodicity allows for analyses that move between levels, from cycles that occupy seconds and minutes (as in, for instance, cyclical groove patterns and song forms in jazz) through periods that last for hours (such as the cycling of *pathet* types in a *wayang kulit* performance) to, theoretically, longer period structures lasting months, years, a lifetime, or more, in which music is used by a person, a family, a community, and a society in the process of sonically structuring life.

Tenzer's argument that "periodicity is really a universal, inseparable from a conception of music" is unlike general theories in specific musical systems, such as Heinrich Schenker's positing of the *ursatz* as the universal structure of tonal music, inasmuch as he posits universality only at the very highest level (Tenzer 2006:23; Snarrenberg 1997:24–25). Nonetheless, following Francois-Bernard Mâche, whose *Musique au singulier* (Music in the Singular) seeks "supracultural connections" between musics (Mâche 2001, quoted in Tenzer 2006:33), Tenzer is seeking a "world music theory" (Tenzer 2006:22). This is fleshed out most clearly in "Generalized Representations of Musical Time and Periodic Structures." In that article, drawing on the fact that "although different philosophies or metaphysics or ritual practices of time are legion, it is quite another thing to say that individuals (let alone cultures) have fundamentally different experiences of time," Tenzer offers a framework for a classificatory model of any music based on "the obviously foundational parameter of temporal structure rather than on culture, function, origin, psychology, cognition, meaning, or any other interpretive, subjective parameter" (2011:369–70).

Andrew Alter follows up on the themes found in Tenzer's work, among others, in a study of time in the performance of the *Mahabharata* in two quite distinct contexts: epic performance of the *Pandavalila* in Garwhal, North India, and genres of puppetry in Java and Bali (2011). He proposes that understanding these musics requires both fully grasping their social backgrounds, which confound any easy connection between Hindu culture and "cyclicity," and at the same time grasping certain shared musical problems that come from the fact that both involve performances that are quite long. He argues, "there is a difference between the experience of lengthy performances . . . and those that are short, while the ways in which audience members more generally are transformed by such lengthy performances are related to the ways musicians mark and manipulate audience members' perception of time" (ibid.:75). The particular devices employed to give audiences a sense of temporal segmentation and pacing are distinct, but the over-arching transformations—from slow and relaxed to fast and intense—are not only found in these two traditions, but may well be part of the creation of long musical experiences in jazz and new music, among other genres (ibid.:76).

Thomas Turino's work has sought ways of integrating music theory and social theory fairly consistently since his dissertation, completed in 1987. I draw particular notice to his most recent book, *Music as Social Life: The Politics of Participation*, precisely because it is the work that, on the surface, seems most likely to leave behind music-theoretical perspectives; and yet, the integration of an understanding of musical structure is central to the book's thesis. Turino's ultimate goal is to understand "the ways music is socially meaningful," and while that could be taken to mean "the social meanings music carries" (and indeed much ethnomusicology since the "interpretive turn" has developed sophisticated explanations of such meanings), Turino makes exploring the "what" of music's social meaning necessarily dependent on exploring the "how" (2008:1).

If there is a rising trend for general or universal music theories beyond Tenzer, Mâche, Alter, and Turino, it reflects a growing dissatisfaction in certain quarters with the notion of discrete "cultures," the prevailing mode of thinking in most of the second half of the twentieth century in anthropology and ethno-musicology, but one that has been challenged for some time (see, for instance, Abu Lughod 1991). Ironically, general theories of music that draw on recent studies in cognition or on other neurophysiological literature may bring us full circle to music-anthropological notions that privilege our shared biology as humans, while being informed by studies of cultural difference that have made up the bulk of ethnomusicology in the past forty years (see Becker 2004; Bakan et al. 2008; Bakan 2009).

Between these two levels of theory, the tradition-specific and the universal, a fair number of ethnomuiscologists have offered what I would call trans-musical theories, theories that account for regularities across related groups of musics without necessarily arguing for their full universality. Ingrid Monson's think-ing in "Riffs, Repetition, and Theories of Globalization" is representative of this type of theory. Perhaps not surprisingly, repetition—the basis of periodicity—is Monson's wedge for a discussion of structural connections between various musics of the African diaspora. She took a systematic approach to this aspect of African diasporic music, based in an appreciation of "simultaneous periodicities" that operate at multiple levels and create grooves that facilitate the movements of music around the globe (1999:36, 52–53). "Riffs, Repetition, and Theories of Globalization" differs from Tenzer's theory in that Monson's ultimate goal is not based in the idea of shared mental structures—the shared ways of thinking about music to which Tenzer's periodicity ultimately points; moreover, while periodicity only has the potential in Tenzer's work to explain phenomena beyond the level of the individual performance or work, Monson's argument is specifically intended as a way to move from music theory to social theory and back again. As she says, her argument rests on the idea that "whatever interpretive ideas are used for broaching the problem of globalization in music must be able to move successfully among several levels of analysis (from the individual to the global) and . . . detailed knowledge of musical processes is crucial in situating music within larger ideological and political contexts" (ibid.:33).

Music Theorization, Transcription, and Science before the "Interpretive Turn"

Perhaps the reason this extensive, and frankly intensive, work of producing music theory and using it in analytical studies in recent ethnomusicology faces metatheoretical ambivalence is that it is overshadowed in the discipline's memory by prior examples of music theory that purported to be some kind of scientific method and universal truth. Going back to comparative musicology and systematic musicology at the end of the nineteenth and beginning of the twentieth century, our discipline and its predecessors have often been characterized by attempts to understand the apparent complexity of the world's music in terms of simpler structural regularity (Nettl 2005:62).

Often, this earlier theoretical work focused on understanding phenomena related to pitch, including melody, but beginning with more abstract notions of the gamut and scales used by musical systems of the world. Alexander Ellis's work, as mentioned previously, was instrumental in establishing the cent as a basic measuring tool for understanding musical pitch (1885). Ultimately a mechanical measure—a way of objectifying the number of vibrations per second of any pitched sound wave—his theory uncovered a major implication that remains a central principle of ethnomusicology, which is that people determine pitch systems largely arbitrarily from within essentially infinite potential variation. Rather than deriving from the overtone series, and thus being arguably "natural" and by implication better than others, the Western system of pitch was but one among many equally valid solutions to the problem of how to divide up pitch space. While Marc Perlman and Carol L. Krumhansl note that "Acoustic phenomena, auditory physiology, and cognitive processes may impose constraints on the class of possible musical scales," scales nevertheless vary widely in both the internal division of the octave into smaller intervals and the range of variance in tuning found in a particular system (Perlman and Krumhansl 1996:26).

Shortly after the establishment of "ethnomusicology" proper, through the coinage of the term and establishment of the society, Mieczyslaw Kolinski—also working with pitch, in the domains of both scale and melody—proffered a number of theoretical terms through which to engage in cross-cultural musical comparison. Relatively few of his terms seem to have been widely adopted, but they may be worth noting here, nonetheless.[10] In a metatheoretical defense of music theory, Kolinsky offered a system of "tints" to understand the cross-culturally common phenomenon of octave duplication and the infinite variation of pitch "shades" within the space of an octave (1967:10–11; 1978:231–32). His synaesthetic analogy between pitch gradation and the color wheel suggested a system through which to understand similarities and differences between different musics based on patterns of "tint affinity," or intervallic relation. This could, perhaps, be applied within a given musical system to understand the unities and variations of pitch choice in melodic construction, but it does not appear to have been.

Kolinski himself did use a simpler aspect of melodic construction to argue for intercultural comparison, looking at Euro-American, Native American, and African/African American music to determine relative levels of similarity and difference (1982). His focus on pitch reiteration and positing of the "reiteration quotient" as a framework for comparative analysis produced plausible results, showing that, at least among his fairly large sample of recorded songs, in this one feature the three large culture areas (Europe and Euro-America, Native America, and Africa and African America) produced music that could be seen as more similar within the culture area and more different between the three. The study's findings generally fit with common understandings of musical style and cultural difference today, but ultimately Kolinski did not account for the inherent significance of reiteration quotients as a generator of musical meaning, except inasmuch as they produced interesting results in the particular case at hand.[11]

In her 1974 article "Analysis: Herding Sacred Cows?," Marcia Herndon summarized a number of theories and approaches to musical analysis that had been proposed by then, arguing that the diversity of thought in this area without attempts to synthesize their results or distinguish them on the basis of validity had become a problem. She offers a further theory (intended as a synthesis) to supplant the diversity of models in use at the time. This system, not unlike Monson's and Tenzer's, moves from the theory that "we must all have a basic conviction that music is patterned" (1974:245). Herndon's desire for a metalanguage—primarily made of symbols, "without semantic loading, which developed naturally out of progressive discoveries of recurring cognitive categories in specific musical systems" (ibid.:250)—bears a measure of utopianism, and is hard to square with a poststructuralist understanding of the ways power informs disciplinary knowledge in academia. That said, it is a starting point that more recent theories can point to, even while incorporating a critique of the partiality and subjectivity of music theories and analysis.

In all of these works, music analysis and theory were linked to musical transcription, and at times it is unclear whether arguments about the nature of music drove arguments about transcription or vice versa. The need to objectively render a notated version of the music under study was partly heuristic: transcriptions were often the only way many scholars could "hear" an article's musical examples. In the era of digital music this has become less and less of a problem, first as CDs became commonly incorporated into books, and now through the Internet—as most commercially produced music is available (with consideration of intellectual property issues), any recording can, in theory, be posted to a stand-alone website, to any of various multi-media sites such as YouTube or Vimeo, or to social media sites such as Facebook or Google+.[12] Nevertheless, transcription was, and is, a common step in coming to a fixed text for analysis. Already in 1964, it was clear from a "symposium on transcription and analysis" held at the society's annual meeting and published in *Ethnomusicology* that transcription was by no means an objective undertaking, and that in fact transcriptions bear within them the result of a transcriber's analytical understanding (England et al. 1964). Moreover, inasmuch as musical transcription, like analysis, is an important way of interacting with music, we ought not to ignore its crucial role in many ethnomusicological studies as we celebrate the power of new technology to facilitate our studies.

Metatheory of Ethnomusicology: Social Theory, Music Theory, and the "Interdiscipline"

Ethnomusicology has been unusually productive of metatheory, at least in relation to its sister musicologies (Nettl 2005:4; Reyes 2009:1). Whether as a function of a sense of "subalternaty" in relation to historical musicology or marginality in relation to anthropology, there is a substantial history of disciplinary self-definition, in terms of both theory and method, to draw on in a study such as this. As many readers of this journal will know, the role of musical close analysis goes back at least to the origins of ethnomusicology as a distinct discipline. Already in the third issue of *Ethnomusicology*, the journal could publish a pair of panel discussions titled "Whither Ethnomusicology?" (McAllester 1959) in which Bruno Nettl, Mantle Hood, Kolinski, Nadia Chilkovsky, George List, David McAllester, Charles Seeger, J. H. Nketia, and others appeared divided on musical analysis. McAllester put in a "special plea" for anthropological study, saying, "It is nice to know that a song is a lullaby from Bukabuka . . . but to satisfy me we have to know what the people of Bukabuka think of this lullaby and about their music in general." He went on even more provocatively to assert, "Music is essentially a matter of values rather than a matter of notes" (1959:103). Richard Waterman, in reply, offered, "There are anthropological problems not related to values. History may be traced through analysis" (ibid.:105).

Shortly thereafter, and building on what was at times implicitly and at others explicitly being argued over in the "Whither Ethnomusicology" panel discussions—and no doubt also in less formal settings—Alan Merriam influentially defined the field as necessarily, inherently, yet problematically interdisciplinary in his 1964 book *The Anthropology of Music*. On the book's first page Merriam says, "[Ethnomusicology] has always been compounded of two distinct parts, the musicological and the ethnological, and perhaps its major problem is the blending of the two in a unique fashion which emphasizes neither but takes into account both" (1964:3). Famously, Merriam offers—where Jaap Kunst, Mantle Hood, and Gilbert Chase had proposed lengthier definitions—the simple, memorable sentence, "ethnomusicology is to be defined as 'the study of music in culture'" (ibid.:6). Again, quite famously, Merriam expounded this definition in his tripartite model, in which music in (or later "as") culture could be studied through three aspects: "conceptualization about music, behavior in relation to music, and music sound itself" (ibid.:32). It is perhaps odd, then, that the rest of *The Anthropology of Music*, with sections dedicated to "Concepts and Behavior" and "Problems and Results," shows a striking absence of the third aspect, "music sound itself."[13]

Merriam was trained as an anthropologist—although he studied with Richard Waterman, and was a musician himself, his degrees and appointments were all in anthropology—and can perhaps be forgiven for having focused his research attentions on the conceptual and behavioral aspects of his tripartite model, to the relative exclusion of musical sound in most cases.[14] Nevertheless, both Hood and Kolinski saw this as a significant failing of *The Anthropology of Music,* and they offered correctives. Kolinski's argument with Merriam is perhaps more directly stated than Hood's, but *The Ethnomusicologist* takes such a very different frame of reference for the field that it is worth noting here:

> One point is clear: the *subject* of study in the field of ethnomusicology is music. Essentially different but interdependent *approaches* to the subject might well include related studies in history, ethnography, folklore, literature, dance, religion, theater, archeology, etymology, iconography, and other fields concerned with cultural expressions. In addition to purely musical information, various *objectives* toward which the study leads might encompass a better understanding of two or more societies or individuals or groups within a society as to behavior; psychology; perception; system of values; artistic, aesthetic and philosophical standards; and so forth ... Plausible approaches to, objectives in, and applications of such study are virtually unlimited. But the primary *subject* of study in ethnomusicology is *music*. (1971:3–4; emphases in the original)

Reasonable arguments can be—and have been—made about what it would mean to say that the primary subject of study in ethnomusicology is music, but the implication here, particularly given the working out of Hood's argument in the rest of the book, is that the primary subject is music as a sonic phenomenon.

I suggest that it is true that Merriam's work is ambivalent, theoretically placing sound, behavior, and conceptualization in both equal and necessarily mutually determining relationships, while in its playing out diminishing the role of sound and at least implying that it is in some ways independent of the other two categories. The article "'The Ethnographic Experience: Drum-Making Among the Bala (Basongye)'" is an extreme example of a sort. At the start Merriam mentions that *matumba* drums come in three types, which are "differentiated on the basis of size and musical function," but that his purpose is not "to discuss drums and drumming as such" (1969:75). And, indeed, in twenty-seven pages there are at most three off-hand references to the drum's sound. Nevertheless, the tripartite theory clearly articulates what I argue for here and what I believe many of us do, in fact, in practice, which is to view music as a phenomenon that integrates sound, behavior, and ideas in myriad ways, and that can be best understood through an accounting for their mutually determining relationships. It is not enough, as I see it, to do ethnomusicology this way; rather, we should retain a sense of the importance of music theory and analysis in our metatheory of the field.

Most recent metatheoretical writing in ethnomusicology typically takes the notion that we practice an "interdiscipline" combining anthropology and musicology in various ways as a starting point.[15] Rice, writing in a 1987 article aimed at "remodeling" Merriam's model, described a sense of pessimism pervasive in the field about whether "We have achieved . . . a union between anthropological and musicological approaches," but offered a new, integrative model based on studying "formative processes in music," whether those were "melody, harmony and rhythm" or "the relationship between music and politics, economics, social structure, music events, and language" (1987:472–73). Helen Myers, writing in 1992, suggested that the divisions between scholars' intent on music or anthropology had largely unified, "despite a diversification of topics" (1992:12). Nettl offers perhaps the broadest definition of the field in his book *The Study of Ethnomusicology* (2005), but ultimately comes back to the music/anthropology dichotomy, which he sees as a conflict in the discipline's history, now more or less settled:

> For some time . . . [ethnomusicologists] tended to divide themselves into two groups, frequently at odds, one concentrating on the music "itself," the other on the cultural context . . . After about 1980, the two groups tended to merge, but even in earlier times, I do not know of any ethnomusicologists who did not, in their total commitments, have a major interest in music as an aspect of human culture. (2005:8)

Yet in spite of prefatory remarks in this vein, these and similar works mostly take one or the other area—the social or the musical—and address it at length, with by far the majority writing more prominently on the social than on the musical. Myers and Nettl, both of whose books are intended to provide some measure of comprehensiveness do, indeed, include aspects of music theory and anthropological concerns, but in each case considerations of musical sound become somewhat buried or separated from the main body of the work. Myers includes major, very important articles by Stephen Blum on the "Analysis of Musical Style," and on transcription and notation by Ter Ellingson, but questions of music theory and analysis, and their role in answering anthropological questions are largely missing from other chapters in the volume. Nettl, for whom questions of musical structure are necessarily implicated in questions of social structure and vice versa, also largely focuses on the anthropological vein in *The Study of Ethnomusicology*, after part 1.

The limited role of explicit language about music theory and analysis, if not the absence of a discussion of music, is particularly notable in Timothy Rice's two most recent metatheoretical contributions, "Ethnomusicological Theory" (2010b) and "Time, Place, and Metaphor in Musical Experience and Ethnography" (2003). As noted previously, music theory occupies a dramatically fore-shortened role in the 2010 "Ethnomusicological Theory," and I suggest that in fact this is presaged in "Time, Place and Metaphor." Rice's main argument—that Ethnomusicology, in coming to grips with the problem of a weakening belief in bounded cultures, should move to a "subject-centered ethnography" in which every person would occupy a three-dimensional space made up of "time, location, and metaphor"—does not necessarily require a reduced place for music theory, much less analysis (2003:158). Rice does have a place in his model for discussions of music in a technical sense, but in such a limited (and ideologically determined) way that it is easy to imagine an ethnomusicology that used the model dedicating relatively little time and energy to thinking about music in this way. Music theory and analysis in Rice's model becomes the smallest-scale metaphor in which music lives, "Music-as-art" (ibid.:161). The shape of Rice's model is such that in theory we might all expect to move through an understanding of "music-as-art," in which he includes "Psychoacoustics, music theory, style history, and aesthetics" (ibid.:166). While the model is not necessarily intended to be read or used teleologically, it is hard to escape the implication that the lower/smaller ends of the scale (those closer to zero in the Cartesian space of Rice's graph) might be lower in importance, as well, or beginnings rather than end points. Beyond this, the choice of terminology for this metaphor is not a happy one. As Rice notes, "Ethnomusicologists have been at pains to move beyond the shadow of the music-as-art metaphor and into the light other metaphors . . ." (ibid.:166). While he raises this point in order to object to it, it might be better to use "music-as-sound-in-the-most-immediate-sense" in thinking about Rice's model. As in his other articles, in practice Rice clearly engages with musical sound deeply on this level; my concern here is that he marginalizes it metadiscursively.

J. Lawrence Witzleben, writing in the same issue of the *Yearbook for Traditional Music* as Rice, offers a metatheoretical discussion of bi-musicality, or "Learning and Making Music as Ethnomusicological Practice and Theory" (2010). This article's metatheoretical orientation is not specifically toward either music theory or social theory, but rather toward research methodology, but even so, it leads to some useful conclusions about the importance of music theory and analysis in our disciplinary practice. His concern with "the ways in which engagement with performance has shaped—and continues to shape—the ideas and theoretical perspectives of ethnomusicologists" is interesting, and inasmuch as it derives in large measure from Mantle Hood's work, might reasonably be expected to provide an explanation of the musical results of bi-musicality for those of us in the field who do learn music as a part of fieldwork. His point, that many of us do not write explicitly about the impact of performing on our studies—except, perhaps in specialized volumes such as *Shadows in the Field* (Barz and Cooley 2008) and *Performing Ethnomusicology* (Solís 2004)—is quite valuable, and his interrogation clearly points to the ways in which playing and singing music in our studies leads to deeper knowledge of that music. I wholeheartedly agree with Witzleben that playing music gives us access to what Charles Seeger called "music time-space," and does so in ways that are different from and I believe deeper than listening without learning to play. This is not the only music-theoretical aspect that learning to play music gives us access to—I think it is fundamentally important in accessing much more straightforward musical phenomena, such as feeling the regularities and irregularities that make up different periodicities, or feeling the particular tensions that come from singing one note or another and singing in one timbre or another—but entering music time-space is one thing that is not only facilitated by playing but that may be impossible without it. I agree with Witzleben when he says that, "music space-time is quite different from a unidimensional focus on music sound alone—an emphasis that is so often used to stigmatize so-called 'musicological' approaches to ethnomusicology. Rather, it is a recognition of a musical universe where profound things happen to and in us" (ibid.:153). Yet while this is true, I believe the focus on musical sound itself is important if we are not only to enjoy the experience of entering into music time-space (or experiencing "flow," or entering "firstness," or "taking it to the next level"), but also to develop shared understandings of how those things work for our scholarship and teaching.

It might be argued that each of the writers referenced above takes it as given that the purposes of the theories they expound in our discipline are intimately tied up with the investigation of musical sound, and that a fuller discussion of music theory and analysis would be an unnecessary digression given the particular aims of their projects. This, however, is belied by the relatively small percentage of writing with significant music theory and analysis in recent issues of the major journals in our field. I object to allowing the stigmatization or downplaying of so-called "musicological" approaches to ethnomusicology to stand, not because I think such approaches are sufficient in themselves, any more than is the application of social theory in itself, but precisely because I believe they are an indispensible component of the integrated study of music in human life that we are collectively working toward.[16]

Conclusion: In North America and the Southwestern Pacific, on the Value of Music Theory in an Integrated "Interdiscipline"

I do not wish to suggest that every ethnomusicological study must employ theoretically informed musical analysis or produce music theory of either localized or general types. I do, however, think that as a discipline we have produced a number of valuable insights that have come out of a focus on music as structured sound, and that we are best off if we not only continue to do so, but also retain a metatheoretical perspective on the importance of so doing. I am not interested here in developing a unified theory more specific than or beyond the most general—that, following Feld, and others, "sound structure is social structure," noting not only that sound is socially structured, but also that social life is sonically structured (Feld 1984; A. Seeger 1987). Rather, in conclusion I would like to briefly present two cases from my current research areas, cases that I think not only show ways in which analytical consideration of music is necessary in fleshing out what it might mean to think of music and society as mutually constitutive, but also suggest places where we can think of theory and analysis relating to musical sound not as an externally produced body of knowledge that we draw into ethnomusicology, but rather as endemic to our discipline, per se.

First, as an Americanist, with a particular interest in the racialization of popular music in the twentieth century, I have become interested in early blues, both in relation to the ways it has been represented following the blues revival, in our discipline and others, and as a music whose origins have been a subject of intense debate (Charters 1981; Davis 1995; Kubik 1999; Radano 2003:247–55). Both of these topics offer the opportunity to think in terms of the music/society relationship, but the question of beginnings is particularly fraught. I understand the emergence of blues—along with jazz, ragtime, gospel, and so-called "hillbilly" music—as part of a massive period of musical change. I draw inspiration from Manuel Peña's work on *conjunto* and *jaiton* music in the Southwest, seeing early blues as a "socioesthetic impulse" which relied on conscious transformations of musical sound structures by artists (1985:34). To truly understand the profound newness of blues in the late nineteenth and early twentieth centuries, studies must synthesize an understanding of the changes brought about by mass migration, by the development of fordist principles in the music industry, and by changes in musical sound as distinct yet interactive domains. Central to this, and drawing on musical analysis specifically developed in ethnomusicology, is the process of coming to terms not only with changes in aspects of pitch and rhythm theoretically, but also and perhaps more importantly with changes in timbre, some of which were precipitated by the introduction of sound recording, and some by changing ideas about music itself.

In quite a different way, my work over the past six years in Australia and Papua New Guinea poses a significant challenge in the application of music theory to produce interesting, meaningful results. For me, the process of developing this research has been slow, producing as yet relatively little completed material, in part because of ethical considerations and the need to develop extensive relationships in the field, but also because of the music itself, which, while appearing relatively simple from the bird's-eye view, is enormously complicated from a closer perspective. My work in this area has focused on the role of Indigenous arts institutions—primarily tertiary schools, but also arts management agencies—as agents that help negotiate the development of Indigenous modernities in the region. While a sociology of art perspective would be likely to see the social structures at work—capitalism, reciprocity, nationalism, civic and political modernity—as the primary unit of analysis, an ethnomusicological orientation allows for a study that treats the music being produced in these institutions as a significant force in their activities and not merely epiphenomenal superstructure. In the case of the music program at the University of Goroka, in the Eastern Highlands of Papua New Guinea, a music theoretical framework is helpful in understanding the ways students work with a broad and varied collection of songs from their home communities in combination with pan-Pacific and broadly Western song genres as source material in studies of music theory, composition, and arranging.

In the end, I would not wish to suggest that every study in ethnomusicology needs or would even benefit from music theory and analysis. Our studies of the music industry, of ritual, of music history, of musical communities, and so on may often be complete without close analysis of specific works or performances, and may not point to either local or general theories of music. Yet close analysis and the production of theory remain significant, in part because they are some of the most important ways we have of coming to know music deeply. Akin to performing, this activity draws our attention to the many significant details that inform music as a part of social worlds. Moreover, many of our most valuable contributions to creating a discipline and to the larger worlds of music study and the humanities at large have come from the investigation of musical sound and musical process as part of integrative, synthetic studies. On the one hand, I hope that there is a value in celebrating that work as much as the ways in which our study of music uses and contributes to social theory; on the other, I would offer such a celebration also as a tool to encourage more attention to musical analysis and music theory in ethnomusicology, and to viewing that work not only as an ethical problem or as a matter of drawing theory from outside our discipline, but rather as an opportunity to build on an integral, endemic aspect of ethnomusicology itself.

Notes

1. I would like to acknowledge Thomas Turino, J. Lawrence Witzleben, and the anonymous readers for the journal, each of whom gave compelling, substantive suggestions for revision.

2. Rice is careful to note that what is commonly called "social theory" in ethnomusicology often has roots in many disciplines, only some of them social sciences. We certainly draw on theory from anthropology, sociology, and political science; but we are just as likely to draw on theory from literary criticism or philosophy (2010b:101). Incidentally, Rice's "Ethnomusicological Theory" article is related to, but in fact notably different from, his other major metatheoretical article published in 2010, "Disciplining Ethnomusicology," which was subjected to extensive critical response in the pages of *Ethnomusicology* (2010a). Consequently, my argument with "Ethnomusicological Theory" moves along different lines than do those of Rice's respondants in that issue of *Ethnomusicology*.

3. I am committed to the idea, proposed by Charles Seeger many years ago, that "musicology" is, properly, the superordinate category for the field of academic study of music, and ought not be used to describe one subordinate category—historical musicology—but rather to subsume (at least) historical musicology, ethnomusicology, and music theory (Seeger 1968; 1970; 1971).

4. For an example of metatheoretical writing that respects the ongoing presence of musical theorizing in ethnomusicology, see Martin Stokes's section on "Contemporary Theoretical Issues" (Part IV) in Pegg et al. n.d.

5. The problem of distinguishing these domains in theory is at least as thorny as that of accounting for their connections in practice.

6. In an email exchange, Rob Schultz indicated that there had been some discussion of establishing an AAWM society, but that there was precisely the concern that such a society could produce the kind of disciplinary splintering forecast here (email, 20 June 2011, 8:55 am).

7. Rāg theory is a long tradition and currently quite active. For more, see, among others, Jairazbhoy (1995), Bor (1999), Brown (2003/2004), Capwell (2002), and Clayton (2005).

8. As with rag, *togaku* is a music with a long, but also recent and vital, tradition of theoretical writing, much of it in Japanese. See, among others, Endo (2002, 2003), Ng (2007), and Terauchi (1996).

9. For a review and bibliography of music theory in the history of the Middle East, see Section 1, "Theory, Composition, and Performance," and Section 6, "Historical Roots," in v. 6 of the *Garland Encyclopedia of World Music* (Danielson et al 2002:31–144, 349–424). For a review and bibliography of music theory in the history of the Indian subcontinent, see the essays on "Theoretical Treatises" and "Scholarship since 1300" in v. 5 of the *Garland Encyclopedia of World Music* (Rowell 2000; Simms 2000).

10. One notable exception: Simha Arom found Kolinski's terms "commetric" and "contrametric" quite useful in his study *African Polyphony and Polyrhythm* (1991).

11. Ironically, Kolinski criticized Merriam for precisely this failing elsewhere, saying, "The eminent significance of statistical methods for a comparative investigation of musical traits is obvious; but an essential precondition is a structurally meaningful analysis capable of providing a sound basis for statistical evaluation" (Powers and Kolinski 1970:77).

12. Catherine Ingram reports having videos taken of Kam singing during field work in Western China posted to the Chinese website YouKu by the singers themselves (http://v.youku.com/v_show/id_XODM3NDg0NzY=.html) (personal communication).

13. One reasonable explanation for this gap in *The Anthropology of Music* would be that there was a great deal of theoretical and methodological literature on music theory elsewhere, but very little on the other domains upon which he focuses.

14. Though not in all cases. In fact, his *Ethnomusicology of the Flathead Indians* (1967) is divided into two sections, the second (and larger) of the two entirely dedicated to description and analysis of songs. Recognizing the salience of this division, when *Ethnomusicology* commissioned a review of the book it was divided among two scholars. In a total of thirty-two pages, William Powers reviewed Part I and Kolinski Part II (Powers and Kolinski 1970). Kolinski's main criticism, that Merriam fails to live up to his ideal of analyzing music as "an integrated system of concepts, behaviors, and sounds," is reasonable (ibid.:77). Nettl recalls that toward the end of his life Merriam came, privately, to the conclusion that an integrated analysis of the two domains in any given instance was impossible (personal communication).

15. Marcia Herndon's point—that ethnomusicologists seldom have formal training in both musicology and anthropology, and occasionally in neither—while still probably true, is less significant than it was in the 1970s. With most academic ethnomusicologists now receiving graduate degrees in ethnomusicology from departments in which ethnomusicology is a formalized area of study, it makes sense to me to think of ours as an "interdiscipline" (which is to say, a discipline in itself that has roots in two distinct, older disciplines), rather than an interdisciplinary field.

16. One anonymous reader for this journal suggested that the reason for a relative emphasis on social-theoretical writing and de-emphasis on music-theoretical writing in our discipline could be that the social is often more "writable" (in his/her words). This may be true—the "linguocentric predicament," as Seeger called it, is less of an issue with other domains of social life, inasmuch as they are often already linguistically mediated. And yet, this fails to account for a) the genuine difficulty involved in writing social theory, b) the extent to which music theory has been written over the years, and c) the rise, in at least some quarters, of a renewed emphasis on music theorization. I am more inclined to think that the reason lies in the value and translatability our social theorizing has in other parts of academia, and the equivalent lack of value and translatability our music theorizing has been accorded, at least in the last quarter century.

References

Abu Lughod, Lila. 1991. "Writing Against Culture." In *Recapturing Anthropology*, edited by Richard G. Fox, 137–62. Santa Fe, NM: School of American Research Press.

Alter, Andrew. 2011. "Controlling Time in Epic Performances: An Examination of Mahabharata Performance in the Central Himalayas and Indonesia." *Ethnomusicology Forum* 20(1):57–78

Arnold, Alison, ed. 2000. *Garland Encyclopedia of World Music. Volume 5: South Asia: The Indian Subcontinent*. New York: Garland.

Bakan, Michael. 2009. "Measuring Happines in the Twenty-First Century: Ethnomusicology, Evidence Based Research, and the New Science of Autism." *Ethnomuiscology* 53(3):510–18.

Bakan, Michael, et al. 2008. "Saying Something Else: Improvisation and Music Play Facilitation in a Medical Ethnomusicology Program for Children on the Autism Spectrum." *College Music Symposium* 48:1–30.

Barz, Gregory F., and Timothy J. Cooley, eds. 2008. *Shadows in the Field: New Perspectives for Fieldwork in Ethnomusicology,* 2nd ed. New York: Oxford University Press.

Bates, Eliot. 2010. "Mixing for *Parlak* and Bowing for a *Büyük Ses*: The Aesthetics of Arranged Traditional Music in Turkey." *Ethnomusicology* 54(1):81–105.

Becker, Judith. 2004. *Deep Listeners: Music, Emotion, and Trancing*. Bloomington, IN: Indiana University Press.

Bor, Joep, et al. 1999. *The Raga Guide: A Survey of 74 Hindustani Ragas*. Rotterdam: Nimbus Records, Rotterdam Conservatory of Music.

Brett, Philip, Elizabeth Wood, and Gary Thomas. [1994] 2006. *Queering the Pitch: The New Gay and Lesbian Musicology*. London: Routledge.

Brown, Katherine Butler. 2003/2004. "The *Ṭhāṭ* System of Seventeenth-Century North Indian *Rāgas*: A Preliminary Report on the Treatises of Kāmilk͟hānī." *Asian Music* 35(1):1–13.

Buchanan, Donna A., and Stuart Folse. 2006. "How to Spin a Good Horo: Melody, Mode, and Musicianship in the Composition of Bulgarian Dance Tunes." In *Analytical Studies in World Music*, edited by Michael Tenzer, 58–91. New York: Oxford University Press.

Capwell, Charles. 2002. "A Rāgmālā for the Empress." *Ethnomusicology* 46(2):197–225.

Charters, Samuel. 1981. *Roots of the Blues: An African Search*. New York: Da Capo.

Chase, Gilbert. 1958. "A Dialectical Approach to Music History." *Ethnomusicology* 2(1):1–9.

Clayton, Martin. 2005. "Communication in Indian Raga Performance." In *Musical Communication*, edited by Dorothy Miell, David Hargreaves, and Raymond MacDonald. Oxford: Oxford University Press.

Davis, Francis. 1995. *History of the Blues*. New York: Hyperion.

Danielson, Virginia, Scott Marcus, and Dwight Reynolds, eds. 2002. *Garland Encyclopedia of World Music. Volume 6: The Middle East*. New York: Garland.

Ellis, Alexander J. 1885. "On The Musical Scales of Various Nations." *Journal of the Society of Arts* 33:485–527.

Endo, Toru. 2003. "Heianchō Tōgaku no Chōshi Kōzō no Kenkyū" [A study of the structures of *tōgaku* modes used in the Heian period]. Ph.D. diss., Tokyo National University of Fine Arts and Music.

———. 2002. "Gakubiwa no Hidarite no Gihō to Chōshi no Kanren—Sango Yōroku no Bunseki niyoru" [The relationship between the left-hand techniques and the modes of the four-stringed lute: an analysis of *Sango Yōroku*]. *Tōkyō Gakugei Daigaku Kiyō Daini Bumon Jinbunkagaku* 53:203–12.

England, Nicholas, et al. 1964. "Symposium on Transcription and Analysis: A Hukwe Song With Musical Bow." *Ethnomusicology* 8(3):223–77.

Feld, Steven. 1984. "Sound Structure as Social Structure." *Ethnomusicology* 28(3):383–409.

Guilbault, Jocelyne. 2005. "Audible Entanglements: Nation and Diasporas in Trinidad's Calypso Music Scene." *Small Axe* 17:40–63.

Handy, W. C. 1926. *Blues: An Anthology*. New York: A & C Boni.

———. 1941. *Father of the Blues: An Autobiography*. New York: Da Capo Press.

Herndon, Marcia. 1974. "Analysis: The Herding of Sacred Cows?" *Ethnomusicology* 18(2):219–62.

Hood, Mantle. 1971. *The Ethnomusicologist*. New York: McGraw-Hill.

Jairazbhoy, Nazir. 1995. *The Rāgs of North Indian Music: Their Structure and Evolution*. Bombay: Popular Prakashan.

Katz, Mark. 2010. *Capturing Sound: How Technology has Changed Music*, rev. ed. Berkeley: University of California Press.

Krims, Adam. 1998. "Disciplining Deconstruction (For Music Analysis). *19th-Century Music* 21(3):297–324.

Kolinski, Mieczslaw. 1967. "Recent Trends in Ethnomusicology." *Ethnomusicology* 11(1):1–24.

———. 1978. "The Structure of Music: Diversification vs. Constraint." *Ethnomusicology* 22(2):229–44.

———. 1982. "Reiteration Quotients: A Cross-Cultural Comparison." *Ethnomusicology* 26(1):85–90.

Kubik, Gerhard. 1999. *Africa and the Blues*. Jackson: University of Mississippi Press.

Leante, Laura. 2009. "The Lotus and the King: Imagery, Gesture, and Meaning in a Hindustani Rag." *Ethnomusicology Forum* 18(2):185–206.

McClary, Susan. [1991] 2002. *Feminine Endings: Music, Gender and Sexuality*. Minneapolis: University of Minnesota Press.

McDonald, David. 2010. "Geographies of the Body: Violence and Manhood in Palestine." *Ethnomusicology Forum* 19(2):191–214.

Mâche, François-Bernard. 2001. *Musique au Singulier*. Paris: Éditions Odile Jacob

Marett, Alan. 2005. *Songs, Dreamings and Ghosts: The Wangga of North Australia*. Middletown, CT: Wesleyan University Press.

———. 2010. "Vanishing Songs: How Musical Extinctions Threaten the Planet." *Ethnomusicology Forum* 19(2):249–62.

McLean, Mervyn. 2006. *Pioneers of Ethnomusicology*. Coral Springs, FL: Llumina Press.

McAllester, David, ed. 1959. "Whither Ethnomusicology?" *Ethnomusicology* 3(2):99–105. (Journal editor's summary, based on notes by Roxanne McCollester, of two panel discussions chaired by Mantle Hood and Leonard Meyer in the 1958 Society for Ethnomusicology annual meeting.)

Merriam, Alan P. 1964. *The Anthropology of Music*. Evanston, IL: Northwestern University Press.

———. 1967. *Ethnomusicology of the Flathead Indians*. New York: Aldine Publishing Co.

———. 1969. "The Ethnographic Experience: Drum-Making Among the Bala (Basongye)." *Ethnomusicology* 13(1):74–100.

Myers, Helen, ed. 1992. *Ethnomusicology: An Introduction*. New York: Norton/Grove.

Miller, Karl H. 2010. *Segregating Sound: Inventing Folk and Pop Music in the Age of Jim Crow*. Durham, NC: Duke University Press.

Moehn, Frederick. 2009. "A Carioca Blade Runner, or How Percussionist Marcos Suzano Turned the Brazilian Tambourine into a Drum Kit, and Other Matters of (Politically) Correct Music Making." *Ethnomusicology* 53(2):277–307.

Monson, Ingrid. 1999. "Riffs, Repetition, and Theories of Globalization." *Ethnomusicology* 43(1):31–65.

Nettl, Bruno. 2005. *The Study of Ethnomusicology: Thirty-One Issues and Concepts*. Urbana: University of Illinois Press.

Ng, Kwok-Wai. 2007. "The Modes of *Tōgaku* from Tang-period China to Modern Japan: Focusing on the *Ôshikichô, Banshikichô* and *Hyôjô* Modal Categories." Ph.D. dissertation, The University of Sydney.

———. 2011. "Orality and Literacy in the Transmission of Japanese Togaku: Its Past and Present." *Ethnomusicology Forum* 20(1):33–56.

Palmer, Robert. 1982. *Deep Blues: A Musical and Cultural History from the Mississippi Delta to Chicago's South Side to the World*. New York: Penguin Books.

Pegg, Carole et al. "Ethnomusicology." In *Grove Music Online*. Oxford Music Online, http://www.oxfordmusiconline.com/subscriber/article/grove/music/52178pg4 (accessed 14 January 2012).

Peña, Manuel. 1985. "From Ranchero to Jaiton: Ethnicity and Class in Texas-Mexican Music (Two Styles in the Form of a Pair)." *Ethnomusicology* 29(1):29–55.

Perlman, Marc. 1998. "The Social Meaning of Modal Practices: Status, Gender, History, and Pathet in Central Javanese Music." *Ethnomusicology* 42(1):45–80.

Perlman, Marc, and Carol L. Krumhansl. 1996. "An Experimental Study of Internal Interval Standards in Javanese and Western Music." *Music Perception: An Interdisciplinary Journal* 14(2):95–116.

Powers, William K., and Mieczslaw Kolinski. 1970. "Review: Merriam, Alan P. *Ethnomusicology of the Flathead Indians*." *Ethnomusicology* 14(1):67–99.

Povinelli, Elizabeth. 2002. *The Cunning of Recognition: Indigenous Alterities and the Making of Australian Multiculturalism*. Ann Arbor: University of Michigan Press.

Radano, Ronald. 2003. *Lying Up a Nation: Race and Black Music*. Chicago: University of Chicago Press.

Reyes, Adelaida. 2009. "What Do Ethnomusicologists Do? An Old Question for a New Century." *Ethnomusicology* 53(1):1–17.

Rice Timothy. 1987. "Toward the Remodeling of Ethnomusicology." *Ethnomusicology* 31(3):469–88.

———. 2003. "Time, Place, and Metaphor in Musical Experience and Ethnography." *Ethnomusicology* 47(2):151–79.

———. "Disciplining Ethnomusicology: A Call for a New Approach." *Ethnomusicology* 54(2):318–25. (Followed by responses from Kofi Agawu, Ellen Koskoff, Suzel Ana Reily, T. M. Scruggs, Mark Slobin, Martin Stokes, and Jane Sugarman.)

———. 2010b. "Ethnomusicological Theory." *Yearbook for Traditional Music* 42:100–34.

Rowell, Lewis. 2000. "Theoretical Treatises." In *The Garland Encyclopedia of World Music. Volume 5: The Indian Subcontinent*, edited by Alison Arnold, 17–41. New York: Routledge.

Seeger, Anthony. 1987. *Why Suyá Sing: A Musical Anthropology of an Amazonian People*. Cambridge: Cambridge University Press.

Seeger, Charles. 1968. "Factorial Analysis of the Song as an Approach to the Formation of a Unitary Field Theory." *Journal of the International Folk Music Council* 20:33–39.

———. 1970. "Toward a Unitary Field Theory for Musicology." *Selected Reports in Ethnomusicology* 1(3):171–210.

———. 1971. "Reflections upon a Given Topic: Music in Universal Perspective." *Ethnomusicology* 15(3):385–98.

Shuster, Lawrence, and Rob Schultz. 2011. "Editor's Note." *Analytical Approaches to World Music* 1(1). http://www.aawmjournal.com/articles/2011a/editors_note.htm (accessed 21 August 2011).

Simms, Robert. 2000. "Scholarship since 1300." In *The Garland Encyclopedia of World Music. Volume 5: The Indian Subcontinent*, edited by Alison Arnold, 42–46. New York: Routledge.

Snarrenberg, Robert. 1997. *Schenker's Interpretive Practice*. Cambridge: Cambridge University Press.

Solís, Ted, ed. 2004. *Performing Ethnomusicology: Teaching and Representation in World Musics*. Berkeley: University of California Press.

Strehlow, Theodore G. H. 1972. *Songs of Central Australia*. Sydney: Angus and Robertson.

Stuckey, Sterling. 1988. *Slave Culture: Nationalist Theory and the Foundations of Black America*. New York: Oxford University Press.

Subotnik, Rose Rosengard. 1991. *Developing Variations: Style and Ideology in Western Music*. Minneapolis: University of Minnesota Press.

Tenzer, Michael. 2000. *Gamelan Gong Kebyar: The Art of Twentieth-Century Balinese Music*. Chicago: University of Chicago Press.

———. 2011a. "Generalized Representations of Musical Time and Periodic Structures." *Ethnomusicology* 55(3):369–86.

———. 2011b. "Temporal Transformations in Cross-Cultural Perspective: Augmentation in Baroque, Carnatic, and Balinese Music." *Analytical Approaches to World Music* 1(1):159–75.

Tenzer, Michael, ed. 2006. *Analytical Studies in World Music*. New York: Oxford University Press.

Terauchi, Naoko. 1996. *Gagaku no Rizumu Kōzō—Heian Jidai Sue niokeru Tōgakukyoku nitsuite* [The rhythmic structures of gagaku: focusing on the tōgaku pieces performed in the late Heian period]. Tokyo: Daiichi Shob.

Tomlinson, Gary. 1993. *Music in Renaissance Magic: Towards a Historiography of Others*. Chicago: University of Chicago Press.

Turino, Thomas. 2008. *Music as Social Life: The Politics of Participation*. Chicago: University of Chicago Press.

Waksman, Steve. 1999. *Instruments of Desire: The Electric Guitar and the Shaping of Musical Experience*. Cambridge, MA: Harvard University Press.

Witzleben, J. Lawrence. 2010. "Performing in the Shadows: Learning and Making Music as Ethnomusicological Practice and Theory." *Yearbook for Traditional Music* 42:135–66.

Wild, Stephen. 1987. "Recreating the Jukurrpa: Adaptation and Innovation of Songs and Ceremonies in Warlpiri Society." In *Songs of Aboriginal Australia*, edited by Stephen A. Wild et al., 97–120. Sydney: University of Sydney Press.

Zak, Albin. 2001. *The Poetics of Rock: Cutting Tracks, Making Records*. Berkeley: University of California Press.

Zemp, Hugo. 1978. "'Are'Are Classification of Musical Types and Instruments." *Ethnomusicology* 22(1):37–67.

———. 1979. "Aspects of 'Are'Are Musical Theory." *Ethnomusicology* 23(1)5–48.

The University of Illinois Press
is a founding member of the
Association of American University Presses.

_____

Composed in 10.25/12.25 Minion Pro
by Kirsten Dennison
at the University of Illinois Press

University of Illinois Press
1325 South Oak Street
Champaign, IL 61820-6903
www.press.uillinois.edu